RE-VISIONING CHANGE

RE-VISIONING
CHANGE
CASE STUDIES OF CURRICULUM IN SCHOOL SYSTEMS IN THE COMMONWEALTH CARIBBEAN

ZELLYNNE JENNINGS

The University of the West Indies Press
Jamaica • Barbados • Trinidad and Tobago

The University of the West Indies Press
7A Gibraltar Hall Road, Mona
Kingston 7, Jamaica
www.uwipress.com

A catalogue record of this book is available from the National Library
of Jamaica.

ISBN: 978-976-640-912-8 (print)
978-976-640-913-5 (ePub)

The University of the West Indies Press has no responsibility for the
persistence or accuracy of URLs for external or third-party internet
websites referred to in this publication and does not guarantee
that any content on such websites is, or will remain, accurate or
appropriate.

Printed in the United States of America

Dedicated to
Justin, Gabriella, Michelle
and to the loving memory of my mother, Ida "May" Bennett

Contents

Tables

Figures

Acknowledgements

Some of the case studies presented in this book draw on the research of my undergradute and graduate students whose work I supervised during the years I taught at the University of the West Indies in Kingston, Jamaica, and at the Turkeyen campus of the University of Guyana. They taught me a great deal, for which I am truly grateful.

I am also grateful to my colleagues who took time out to review chapters of this book during the process of writing. They are Dr Frank Reeves, former vice principal of the Bilston College of Further Education in the United Kingdom and executive officer at Race Equality West Midlands; Dr Sabeera Abdul-Majid, lecturer at the School of Education, UWI, St Augustine campus; and Dr Carol Hordatt-Gentles, lecturer at the School of Education, UWI, Kingston, Jamaica. Dr Rose Davies, senior lecturer, School of Education, UWI, Mona, Kingston, Jamaica, also provided comments which helped me to produce a much-improved chapter 8. My deepest sympathies for her untimely passing before the publication of this book.

My sincere appreciation to the peer reviewers appointed by the University of the West Indies Press. Their insightful comments and critical appraisal prompted me to make improvements which resulted in a much better work.

My heartfelt thanks to all of you.

Abbreviations and Acronyms

ASEP	Alternative Secondary Education Programme
ASTEP	Alternative Secondary Transitional Education Programme
BP	Basic Proficiency
BSPS	Basic School to Primary School
CC	Commonwealth Caribbean
CARICOM	Caribbean Community
CARIFTA	Caribbean Free Trade Association
CETT	Caribbean Centre for Excellence in Teacher Training
CRSAT	Caribbean Reading Standards Achievement Test
CSEC	Caribbean Secondary Education Certificate
CXC	Caribbean Examinations Council
EC	Early Childhood
ETV	Educational Television
G4LT	Grade 4 Literacy Test
GCE	General Certificate of Education
GOJ	Government of Jamaica
GP	General Proficiency
HTTP	Hinterland Teacher Training Programme
ICT	Information and Communication Technology
IDB	Inter-American Development Bank
IDRC	The International Development Research Centre
IMPACT	Instructional Management by Parents, Community and Teachers
JBTE	Joint Board of Teacher Education
LAPs	Learning Activity Packs
NCERD	National Centre for Educational Resource Development
PEIP	Primary Education Improvement Programme
PESP	Primary Education Support Project
PLAS	Primary Language Arts Scheme
PRIMER	Project for the Improved Management of Educational Resources
PSM	Primary School Manager
RD&D	Research Development and Diffusion

REDO	Regional education officer
REXO	Regional executive officer
R&T	Resource and Technology
ROSE	Reform of Secondary Education
REAP	Rural Education and Agriculture Programme
RPC	Revised Primary Curriculum
SCDP	Secondary Curriculum Development Project
SIM	Self-Instructional Materials
UNDP	United Nations Development Program
UNESCO	United Nations Educational Scientific and Cultural Organization
UNICEF	United Nations International Children's Emergency Fund
UWI	The University of the West Indies
WIF	West Indies Federation

Introduction

Education in a Crisis of Change: Reflections

Education is not static. It is forever going through a process of change. The description as "process" suggests that change is "an overlapping series of dynamically complex phenomena" (Fullan 1994, 21). Some of these can be anticipated, but others are unpredictable. The enormity of this statement struck me as I was reflecting on the first version of this book and working on the revisions. Something unanticipated and unpredicted engulfed the world: the Covid-19 pandemic described by the United Nations (2020, 4) as presenting "the greatest test the world has faced since the Second World War". All at once life changed. Countries sealed their borders. Air travel was halted, and cities were put on lockdown. Economies plummeted. Curfew hours were instituted, and schools were closed. Life was under siege.

I was particularly struck by three things. First, that a virus that originated thousands of miles away in a distant continent could so quickly affect a group of countries that in the psyche of the First World were but grains of sand on a sun-soaked beach! The interconnectedness of the world! Globalization, after all, has been described as "a social process whereby the constraints of space and time on economic, political and cultural arrangements weaken gradually" (Little 1996, 427), giving this sense of interconnection. Globalization, however, has also resulted in widening the gap between rich and poor countries and between the rich and poor within countries. "The world is more unequal today than at any point since World War 11", wrote UNDP (2013, 1).

This leads to my second point. After protocols were put in place to deal with the health hazard, it was remarkable how attention then turned to the economy. The mantra was "if Covid-19 doesn't kill you, hunger will". Research in the Caribbean carried out in April 2020 found that "for households earning less than the minimum wage, a striking 34.3 percent of respondents declared that they had gone hungry in the previous week, and just over half stated that they consumed less healthy food. These issues even persist, at substantially lower levels, in the higher-income categories" (Mooney and Rosenblatt 2020, 13). In Jamaica, affluent businessmen spent huge sums of money to argue in the media for the airports to be opened, and the engine of the economy wound up again.

And so, they were. The tourists came back to enjoy the sand and sea and the virus reared its ugly head even more.

The third thing. After much ado about health issues and the economy, something came to us almost as an afterthought: the schools had been closed! What had been happening to the children? They were supposed to be learning online, but Hanuchek and Woesmann (2020) cite international studies that showed that the learning progress of students had suffered a strong decline during the crisis, especially in schools in low-income areas. In the Commonwealth Caribbean (CC), however, the concern was more about the parents who had to stay home with their children and could not go to work. It was by no means clear how possible or effective working from home was. Again, more thought was on the economy than on the children. The integral connection between the two was made clear by Hanuchek and Woesmann (2020, 1), who wrote, "The worldwide school closures in early 2020 led to losses in learning that will not easily be made up for even if schools quickly return to their prior performance levels. These losses will have lasting economic impacts both on the affected students and on each nation." The children at the greatest disadvantage are those from poor homes where families are unable to afford the technology needed for the children to access learning online. These writers argue that the current students can expect 3 per cent lower career earnings in their lifetime if the schools on reopening can return to their 2019 performance levels. As far as nations were concerned "the impact could optimistically be 1.5 per cent lower GDP throughout the remainder of the century – and proportionately even lower if education systems are slow to return to prior levels of performance" (Hanuchek and Woesmann 2020, 6). "This is going to be the hardest fall we've had maybe in the modern history of education", wrote Greenberg (2020).

It is not just the academic aspect of the children's education that we should be concerned about at this time of crisis. Children's physical, social and emotional development is in jeopardy. School closures mean that physical education classes cannot take place. Social distancing protocols prevent children from playing together as before and learning the social and emotional skills which are so important in their everyday lives as well as their eventual careers. Children who need it do not have access to guidance and counselling services and breakfast and lunch programmes offered by the schools. This is a particular disadvantage for those who live under crowded home conditions where they may be subject to abuse, food shortages and cruelty. There is also the fact that "children's reliance on online platforms for distance learning has also increased their risk of exposure to inappropriate content and online predators" (United Nations 2020, 3).

We must also think about the parents. The success of out-of-school learning depends on the strength of their instructional skills, but they have been thrust into a role for which most have not been prepared. They need to know mathematics and English and be familiar with the school's curriculum so that they can give their children the help they need. They need to be able to troubleshoot the technical glitches of online access to learning. They need to offer guidance to the children, supervise their work, keep them occupied while at the same time do their normal everyday activities. Some of this is not new to parents as they were encouraged to participate in their children's education long before the crisis. Covid-19, however, has thrust them into the limelight through online learning out of school – a task with which parents from low-income homes can barely cope. If globalization widened the gap between the rich and poor, the pandemic threatens to deepen the divide even further.

This Book's Purpose

What is the relevance of all of this to the book? It was striking how the pandemic threw the world into confusion. There was no past knowledge for reference on how to treat it because there was nothing quite like it before, not even the Spanish flu of 1918. Even the wearing of face masks became a contentious issue because of a lack of research to support one choice rather than the other. We came to recognize the value in being able to draw on evidence from the past to inform present action.

This book presents several case studies of attempts to introduce change into school systems in the CC which can inform action that needs to be taken to address many of the issues that the countries face as they try to restore normality in the education system post the pandemic. Hanuchek and Woessmann (2020) argue that to address the differences in learning loss of students from high- and low-income backgrounds, individualized instruction is the best strategy to adopt. There is much that can be learned from the case studies that deal with a similar problem during the early 1980s. Because rural children often had to help their parents to take goods to the market, they were frequently absent from school and thus incurred learning loss. The solution devised was the use of self-instructional materials that the students could work on in their own time under the guidance of the teacher. There is much to be learned from the Grade 10–11 Programme and Project PRIMER[1] on the use of individualized instruction in the Caribbean context.

Hanuchek and Woessmann (2020) also emphasize the need for attention to education at the early childhood level, especially at this time of crisis, since it is the foundation on which learning at other levels rest. Particular attention, they say, should be given to the disadvantaged students. The case study of the transition from basic school to primary school (see chapter 8) highlights the issues that must be dealt with in schools in impoverished rural areas. One of the issues is encouraging parents' involvement in the education of their children. The findings of this study support those reported in Hoover-Dempsey et al. (2005), which suggested that positive school staff attitudes towards students' families and communities are particularly important to parental empowerment and involvement.

Several of the case studies also address the issues of equity and social justice. There are examples of innovations designed to reduce the gap between the rich and poor in school systems and cater to children with learning difficulties. The first chapter elaborates on the goals of the innovations discussed in this book and draws attention to those that used both traditional and modern technology to address problems in the school system. While there is no example from the past that deals with system-wide use of modern technology in schooling from home, the case studies show that much of what is being experienced now – inadequate supplies of laptops or computers, weak technology infrastructure, teachers ill prepared for the task – are repeats of our past experience in using modern technology in our school systems. In a sense it is like going on a journey "back to the past".

The essence of this book can be summed up thus: "When practitioners are better able to understand the past, chances are that they will be able to impart greater sensitivity to their plans for change and as a result improve the probability for success in their programmes. This is a perspective needed in most developing nations today, and it is a position anchored in the view that the past prefigures the present."[2]

Through an analysis and discussion of case studies of curriculum change in school systems in the CC, the author unearths and analyses the problems experienced with a view to deriving from these some broader insights into the dynamics of implementing change in Caribbean schools. Ultimately this book is about improving student learning because if policymakers and practitioners become more sensitive to their plans for change, this is more likely to lead to programme success which is normally measured in terms of student achievement. The book should also be useful in the training programmes for teachers, principals and other education stakeholders who need to understand the processes of change as experienced in CC education systems. Hopefully, the book will appeal to a wider range of readers who will find something of interest in it. It is also hoped that the book will prove a stimulus to further research on curriculum change in the wider Caribbean.

1.

Context, Change and the Curriculum

Background to the Case Studies

"The change process", as Fullan (1994, 19) maintains, "is uncontrollably complex, and in many instances 'unknowable'". "Change" and "innovation" are terms which have been used interchangeably. Miles (1964, 27), for example, defines innovation as "a deliberate, novel, specific change which is thought to be more efficacious in accomplishing the goals of a system". Hall and Hord (2006, 8) contend that "when most people think or talk about change, they focus on what will be changed – in other words, the innovation (which) can be either products, such as computers, curriculum texts, or assessment techniques, or processes such as constructivist teaching". Innovation, as interpreted in this book, draws on the definition given by Rogers (2003, 12) as "an idea, practice or object that is perceived as new by an individual or unit of adoption". It does not matter if the innovation is "objectively" new, adds Rogers, as long as it seems new to those adopting it. Constructivist teaching, for example, may long have been in use in Europe, but to teachers in CC countries, mandated to implement it for the first time, it is new. This book focuses on curriculum innovations.

"Curriculum" is replete with conceptual biases resulting in many different definitions which are explored in Eisner and Vallance (1974). Curriculum is interpreted here as what goes on in classrooms: the actions and interactions between teacher and learners as a result of the decisions made about such elements of the curriculum as the choice of objectives, selection of content, teaching/learning strategies and assessment of learning. These actions and interactions are transformed by the context in which they take place so that the same curriculum implemented in different schools in different parts of the country takes on a unique life of its own. No doubt the notion of context as a transforming agent was in the minds of the new educational planners in the post-independence era of the former British colonies when, as part of the process of nation building, "nationalizing and regionalizing the curricula at all levels of the education system became a major focus of reform. . . . Curriculum reform became an important item on the education agenda" (Miller 1999, 222).

Purpose

"Change is a journey, not a blueprint", writes Fullan (1994, 21). The purpose of this chapter is to explore the journey that was mapped out by educational planners in CC countries who wanted to put their countries on a new path post-independence from Britain. This will be done by looking at the goals of the innovations that make up the case studies of curriculum change in this book. In so doing the reader should get a fairly good overview of what this book is about. We begin, however, with the contextual background of the Commonwealth Caribbean, with highlights on their economies, educational systems and culture. The innovations span the EC, primary, secondary and tertiary levels of the education system. They are listed in three tables with the goals in the following categories: philosophical/pedagogic; cultural, social equity/emotional; and economic. The sources for these goals are identified. In the chapters that focus on particular innovations, the reader will note that in most cases the author either conducted the research on which the case studies are based or was involved in them as leader of an evaluation team or supervisor of a master's or doctoral thesis relevant to the studies.

Particular attention is drawn to the goals of innovations that focus on technology with a view to illuminating our intentions in using technology in the past. How can these experiences from the past inform our use of technology in education during the crisis brought on by the Covid-19 pandemic? The question is raised in this chapter. Hopefully in a later chapter in the book, there will be an answer.

The CC Context

The CC comprises seventeen countries which have a common history of colonial dependency as enslaved plantation economies in the British Empire. Most of these countries gained their independence in the 1960s and 1970s; but some, like Belize, became independent in the 1980s. Twelve of these countries are now sovereign states while six territories still remain dependent under the United Kingdom.[1]

CC countries vary in size both in terms of land and population. Jamaica and the twin island republic, Trinidad and Tobago are the most populous with populations that exceed two million, nine hundred thousand and one million, three hundred and ninety thousand, respectively. With countries like the Turks and Caicos Islands, Anguilla and the British Virgin Islands having populations under thirty-nine thousand CC countries have been designated "small states". Land size varies from Montserrat (102 square kilometres) and Anguilla (91 square kilometres) to the largest, Guyana, which has 214,969 square kilometres. Guyana, though with the largest land mass, has a population of less than seven hundred and ninety-one thousand. With the growing concern for sustainable development, the "small states" designation has been replaced by "small island developing states" in recognition of the similarities they face with sustainable development issues, "including remoteness, susceptibility to natural disaster, and external shock vulnerability" (Crossley and Sprague 2012, 26). There is great diversity between the small island developing states, particularly in income and levels of development as measured by the Human Development Index.

Economies

From agriculturally based economies exporting sugar and rum, most CC countries have transformed into middle-income economies as in the case of Barbados whose economy is built largely on tourism, light manufacturing, insurance services and offshore banking. Barbados was designated "developed country" status in 2010 (UNDP 2010). It is ranked fifty-sixth out of one hundred and eighty-nine countries in the Human Development Index (with a score of 0.813). This is above other countries in the region such as Jamaica which is ranked ninety-sixth. Human Development Index indicators are supported by a strong social protection system, which is centred on social insurance, social safety net programmes and public health and education services. Jamaica hopes to achieve developed country status by 2030. In 2011 the Organization for Economic Cooperation and Development removed Trinidad and Tobago from its list of developing countries. Trinidad and Tobago have an industrial economy with large reserves of oil and natural gas as compared with Jamaica whose economy is dependent on remittances, tourism and bauxite production. Between 2013 and 2019, however, Jamaica's economic reform effort has been quite successful resulting in a reduction of the public debt to Gross Domestic Product (GDP) ratio from 146 per cent to 94 per cent (Christie and Mooney 2020). Statistics for 2018 show that Trinidad and Tobago's per capita income was US$16,930.88 compared with that of Barbados (US$18,365.99) and Jamaica (US$5,393.38).[2] These figures disguise real economic difficulties experienced by some CC countries. For example, Barbados has experienced chronic fiscal deficit over 4 per cent of its GDP and −0.8 per cent growth in 2018[3]. Jamaica has had to resort to the help of the International Monetary Fund on more than one occasion and Trinidad and Tobago has experienced a downturn in its petroleum industry which contributed to its GDP growth rate falling as low as −6.08 per cent in 2016[4]. The only CC country whose economic prospects are healthy is Guyana on account of the volume of its expected oil production. Despite unstable economies, for the most part, CC countries generally invest quite heavily in education. Miller and Munroe (2014) report that in 2010/2011, Jamaica spent 13.4 per cent of its national budget on education. According to Welch (2014) Barbados allocates between 18 and 20 per cent of its national budget to education and its policy for many years of free education from primary through to tertiary developed a highly educated population.

Education Systems

The education systems of the CC countries are influenced by superpowers in close proximity geographically as well as further afield. Many educational projects would not get off the ground without financial aid from the United States, but in its structure, persistent attitudes and values, the influence of their former colonial master, the British, is clearly evident. The foundations of inequity are laid even at the primary level where there are both public and private schools. In Jamaica, the rich and wealthy of the middle/upper class send their children to private preparatory schools where the human, physical and material resources provided are better than in the public primary schools, which are attended largely by children from lower-income households. Six years of primary schooling culminates in an exit examination taken at age eleven plus which is different in each country. In Jamaica, the Grade Six Achievement Test was replaced in 2019 by the Primary Exit Profile; in Barbados and Guyana it is the Secondary School Entrance Examination. The Common Entrance examination in St Vincent and the Grenadines was replaced in 2013 by the Caribbean Primary Exit Assessment (CPEA). St Kitts and Nevis abolished the eleven plus examination in 1970 and all children at age twelve were automatically promoted and sent to high school. Students attend the nearest comprehensive high school in the area in which they live – a practice which discourages the emergence of prestigious and non-prestigious schools. In other countries the exit examination determines the select few who gain entry to the prestigious general secondary or high schools which have an academic emphasis geared to university entry. Children who are deemed unsuccessful in the exit examination go to schools which offer a more technical, vocational-type programme geared for the world of work. Examples of these are the community high schools in Guyana and the new secondary schools which are now called upgraded high schools in Jamaica.

Culture and Cultural Goals

The populations of CC countries are predominantly of African origin, but East Indians predominate in Guyana and Trinidad and Tobago. Belize has a mix of Creoles (Belizeans of African origin), Mestizos (of Hispanic-Indian origin) Black Caribs (descendants of Africans and Carib Indians), descendants of the

Mayans, East Indians and Chinese. Guyana, which is located on the South American mainland, has a population which includes Portuguese, Chinese, Europeans and Amerindians.[5] These are the indigenous people and make up about 6 per cent of the population "but account for seventeen per cent of the poor because they live in the geographically isolated and inaccessible rural interior" (The Government of Guyana 2002, 13). There are nine Amerindian tribes, each with its own language, related to the three-language families: Carib, Arawak and Warrau. While English is the official language of CC countries each country has its own Creole vernacular including French-based Creole in St Lucia, Dominica, Grenada and Trinidad (Craig 2006).

Given this diversity of population, it is not surprising that a desire to tailor their education systems to become more relevant to their culture gathered momentum after the CC countries gained their independence from Britain beginning in the 1960s. They sought to move away from the Eurocentric content of their education and examination systems in a drive to become more culturally relevant and upgrade and expand teacher training. In 1968 at a meeting of the CC ministers of education in Jamaica, the recommendation was made for the CARICOM secretariat to commence the preparatory work for the establishment of the Caribbean Examinations Council (CXC). Shortly after the formation of the CXC in 1972, work began on the selection of subject panels to develop the syllabi for the first five Caribbean Secondary Education Certificate (CSEC) subjects which were examined in 1979. Offering examinations in subjects the contents of which were culturally relevant was a main goal of the CSEC. The examination replaced the Cambridge General Certificate of Education (GCE) Ordinary level examination. While the latter examination provided for the testing of 20 per cent of the ability range of students exiting secondary school, CSEC tested 40 per cent of the ability range.

Language as an essential part of culture was another significant issue in CC countries post-independence because while English was the official language, some linguists believed that more importance should be accorded the Creole language as a means of the people enhancing "their self-concept and their sense of individual, social and national identity" (Devonish and Carpenter 2007, 33). Consequently, a number of innovations in education centred on how best to teach literacy and English in Creole-speaking contexts. Thus, the language experience and awareness approach was advocated for the Literacy 1-2-3 programme in Jamaica (see table 1.1). Giving children practice in the use of the English language by methods appropriate for second-dialect situations was an objective of the NCERD Skills Reinforcement Guides in Guyana. The use of the Jamaican Creole was integrated into the Foundation textbooks developed for the ROSE curriculum, as an objective of the Foundation textbooks was: "The

Table 1.1. Goals of Case Studies at the Early Childhood and Primary Levels

Innovation/Year/School type	Country	Goals (category)	Sources
From Basic School to Primary School (BSPS) (2002–05) (basic/primary)	Jamaica (rural)	Develop readiness skills for transition to primary school; use integrated approach to teaching appropriate for age level. Use of group work in resource-rich learning environment.* Train parents to become involved in children's education; appreciate role of play in child's education.** Improve skills in listening, concentration, organization of children at risk. Improve opportunities for children from disadvantaged backgrounds.#	Ashby et al. (2004) Jennings (2005)*
Literacy 1-2-3 (2006 to present) (primary)	Jamaica	To support the "language arts window" in the Revised Primary Curriculum.* To use the integrated approach to teaching.* Use culturally developed and relevant support materials to teach literacy. To show the connection between oral and written language through use of the language experience and awareness approach.**	Ministry of Education Youth and Culture (2005)
Caribbean Centre of Excellence for Teacher Training (CETT) grades 1-3 (2002–06)	Belize, Guyana, Jamaica, St Lucia, St Vincent and the Grenadines	To develop common standards for literacy to measure and monitor achievement.* To improve the teaching of reading in grades 1–3 so that all children can read by the end of grade 3.* To support schools serving disadvantaged populations.**	Warrican, Spencer-Ernandez and Miller (2013)

Programme	Country	Goals	References
Rural Education and Agriculture Programme (REAP) (1975–85) (all age)	Belize	To integrate the Learning Activity Packs (LAPs) into the teaching of the academic subjects.* To foster value of the dignity of work on the land and being able to produce for oneself and family.* Prepare children in rural Belize for a rewarding life in the countryside.## To enable them to participate in the development of the agricultural basis of the economy for the benefit of themselves and the nation.##	Edmond (1985) Massey (1982) Jennings (1988)
NCERD Skills Reinforcement Guides (SRG) (1989–91) (primary)	Guyana	To give children practice in the use of the English language by methods appropriate for second-dialect situations.* To link the teaching of reading to children learning English.* To reinforce the learning of English and literacy and mathematics in all other subjects.*	Craig (2006/07)
Project for Reshaping and Improving the Management of Educational Resources (PRIMER) (1979–83) (all age)	Jamaica	To help pupils secure higher levels of academic achievement in literacy and numeracy and to acquire basic study skills.* To foster independence in learning and encourage sharing and interaction between older and younger pupils.* To train teachers to become instructional supervisors.* To raise pupils' level of self-confidence, improve their ability for self-assessment and help them develop attitudes of independence and interdependence.# To improve educational opportunities for children from economically and socially deprived regions.# (To reduce teacher costs through change of their role).##	Ministry of Education, Jamaica (1979) Minott (1988) Jennings (1993)

Key for type of goal: * Philosophical/pedagogic; ** Cultural; # Social Equity/Emotional; ## Economic materials must motivate the students by focusing on the mother tongue and using texts that accurately portray the characteristics of the spoken word in everyday context" (Cousins 1995, 15).

This development was so controversial that an advisory committee was set up to look into the issue. According to Cousins (1995, 15), "the committee formally stated that the use of the creole as a learning strategy might be considered a bold step but **was one that should be taken**" (Cousins' bold).

Another cultural issue that certain CC countries sought to address post-independence was the attitude of the people towards the land. This is captured by Manley (1982, 49):

> We tried to reintroduce an agricultural element into the school system by a regular programme of attaching farming areas to schools in rural Jamaica. We insisted upon increasing emphasis on work/study methods in teaching, so as to develop an understanding of the working environment. Finally, we wished to develop a more positive and natural view of work itself in a society whose experience still tended to a negative perception of work as something unpleasant that is imposed by an alien authority.[6]

Manley's democratic socialist government only had time to experiment with one school that adopted the work/study model – the Jose Marti New Secondary School which was a gift from the people of Cuba. This school was then an all-boarding institution in which the entire school (teachers and students) were involved in a programme that combined academic study with vocational activities. During the school day which extended from 5.30 a.m. to 10.00 p.m. teachers and students worked in shifts to tend to the piggery, dairy, poultry and agronomy units. The sale of the products from these units to the surrounding communities enabled the school to become self-sufficient (Earle 1977).

The defeat of Manley's democratic socialist government in the general election of 1980 led to the axing of all things that connected Jamaica to Cuba. The life of the so-called Cuban school was cut short and labour on the land continues to be perceived in Jamaica as "dirty" and demeaning. The Rural Education and Agriculture Programme (REAP) in Belize, however, provides a striking contrast. An objective of REAP was to foster the value of the dignity of work on the land and to produce for oneself and family. Belize had the advantage that its people never acquired the stigma attached to labour on the land found in other CC countries (Edmond 1985).

Social Equity and Quality Goals

Educational changes are triggered by changes in political ideology, social changes, technological advances, turbulences in a country's economy and combinations thereof. In more recent times we have seen educational changes brought about by the global health crisis, Covid-19, which has also impacted the economies of many countries. Post-independence the change in education that most CC countries placed emphasis on was access to education particularly for the underprivileged in society. For example, in 1966 in Jamaica, four years after its independence, the Minister of Education Edwin Allen introduced a sweeping plan for education reforms which was entitled, "New Deal for Education in Independent Jamaica". Fifty new secondary schools were built to augment the existing forty-seven schools at the secondary level and forty primary schools were also constructed with funding from the World Bank. Post-independence in Trinidad and Tobago, the Fifteen Year Plan (1968–83) which was also funded by the World Bank focused on system expansion at both the primary and secondary levels (De Lisle 2012). Access is an important prerequisite for the achievement of goals such as equity and quality. According to the director-general of United Nations Educational Scientific and Cultural Organization, quality "must pass the test of equity" (UNESCO 2004, Foreword). Hickling-Hudson (2002, 572), arguing for quality and equity to be integrally linked in definition, states, "No longer would it be posed as dichotomously different, with quality on the one hand and equity/equality on the other". According to the Ministry of Education, Jamaica (2012, 11), "Equity in the education system is linked to both access and quality". It is not by accident that Sustainable Development Goal 4[7] ("ensure inclusive and equitable quality education and promote lifelong learning opportunities for all") has a number of targets that focus on equal access (for example, "equal access to quality pre-primary education").

Social equity goals are emphasized at all levels of the education system. Improving opportunities for children from disadvantaged backgrounds was a goal of the Basic School to Primary School (BSPS) project in Jamaica (table 1.1). The Caribbean Centre for Excellence in Teacher Training (CETT) which initially served five CC countries sought to support schools serving disadvantaged populations (see table 1.1). The Reform of Secondary Education (ROSE) in Jamaica sought to achieve greater equity in the secondary system up to grade 9 (table 1.2) and the primary target for training in the B. Ed Secondary Distance Programme in Jamaica (see table 1.3) were teachers from newly upgraded secondary schools which catered largely to children from low-income homes.

That social equity should be an important goal for innovations introduced into their education systems is understandable given that the CC is part of a globalized world with a culture that is unique and its societies (and in turn its education systems) are today beset with problems which to a degree are rooted in its colonial past as well as the social divisions that exist in these societies. An explanation for why goals of access, equity and quality have proven difficult to attain is offered by King (1998, 46), who says that "the roots of inequalities in access, equity, quality . . . lie deeply buried in (our) colonial past". King explains that during the colonial era secondary and elementary education in Jamaica were administered by separate bodies and this had the effect of driving a wedge between the middle and upper class and the lower-social class.

Other Social Goals

Apart from pursuing social equity goals, some innovations targeted personal and social goals. Innovations that targeted children from economically and socially deprived areas tended to have goals that centred on raising pupils' self-confidence (e.g. PRIMER see table 1.1). ASTEP (see table 1.2) which targeted children who had failed the Grade Four Literacy Test on four consecutive occasions consisted mainly of boys. Building the students' self-esteem and sense of self-efficacy was an important objective in a course of study on "Personal Empowerment" which formed part of the curriculum. Innovations like the BSPS, Literacy 1-2-3 (see table 1.1) and Resource and Technology (R&T) (see table 1.3) which tried to get teachers to adopt an integrated approach to teaching ultimately had social objectives in mind such as building a spirit of cooperation and teamwork, even though these were not explicitly stated. R&T, for example, involved the use of a teaching-learning approach based on themes that served to draw on the commonalities of the five elements that made up the subject to integrate or make them into a cohesive whole. To achieve such integration, teachers of the five elements needed to plan together. This is a change from working in isolation when the subjects were taught separately. Students working in groups was an important teaching strategy in R&T. Basil Bernstein, in his seminal work on the classification and framing of educational knowledge, argued that how knowledge is organized and taught symbolizes power structure and principles of control and "the less rigid social structure of the integrated code makes it a potential code for egalitarian education" (Bernstein 1971, 67). Working in groups placed responsibility for their own learning more in the hands of the students themselves thereby replacing the teacher as "knowledge-giver".

Quality Goals

Long before Sustainable Development Goal 4 post-2015, CC countries were concerned with the quality of education. The World Bank study on the Caribbean region in 1993 saw quality as *outcome* and inferred "quality" from the pass rates of children taking the primary exit examination, or the CSEC. In

Table 1.2. Goals of Case Studies at the Secondary Level

Innovation/Year	Country	Goals (Category)	Sources
Caribbean Secondary Education Certificate (CSEC) (1979 to present)	Antigua Barbados Belize British Virgin Is. Cayman Is. Dominica, Grenada Jamaica, Guyana, Montserrat, St Kitts/ Nevis/Anguilla, St Lucia, St Vincent, Trinidad and Tobago, Turks and Caicos Is.	To offer examinations to a wider ability range than tested by the GCE "O" level.* To enable teacher participation in syllabus development.* To enable teacher involvement in school-based assessment.* To offer examinations in subjects more relevant to the needs of the region.** To incur cost saving by being able to offer the secondary school exit examination in the region.##	Caribbean Examinations Council (1991)
Reform of Secondary Education 1 (1993–98)	Jamaica	To provide access to quality education.* To improve the quality of education.* To respect the use of the vernacular.** To achieve greater equity in the secondary system grades 7–9.# To enable Jamaican students to become productive citizens.## To infuse career issues in the curriculum.##	Ministry of Education and Culture, Jamaica (1993)
Sixth Form Geography Project (1979–81)	Jamaica	To encourage geography teachers to produce original teaching units related to topics in the Cambridge "A" level syllabus with an emphasis on enquiry activities.* To ensure that the materials developed are Jamaican oriented.**	Morrissey (1981)
Alternative Secondary Transition Education Programme (ASTEP) (2010–12)	Jamaica	Through a curriculum underpinned by constructivism, to strengthen the literacy skills of students who, after multiple sitting, failed to achieve mastery of the Grade 4 LiteracyTest.* To integrate technology across the curriculum.* To ensure that the curriculum is relevant to the students' needs and interests.** To build the students' sense of self-efficacy through personal empowerment.#	Ministry of Education, Jamaica (2010) Jennings-Craig (2011)

Key for type of goal: *Philosophical/pedagogic; **Cultural; #Social equity/emotional; ##Economic

Table 1.3. Goals of Case Studies in the Use of Technology in Teaching and Learning

Innovation/ Year/Education level	Country	Goals (category)	Sources
EduTech 2000 (1999–2008) (primary/ secondary)	Barbados	To ensure that all students leaving the school system in the twenty-first century have adequate skills in, good knowledge of and favourable attitudes towards the use of information technology.* To encourage all teachers in the system to integrate technology into the teaching/ learning process to achieve a child-centred approach to teaching.* To develop favourable attitudes towards the use of technology.** To encourage cooperation among students through project-based learning.# To instil responsibility for one's own learning.#	Ministry of Education, Youth Affairs and Culture, Barbados (1998) Pirog and Kioko (2010)
The Grade 10–11 Programme (1971–78) (secondary)	Jamaica	To introduce technical/vocational skills and work experience into the curriculum of new secondary schools.* To inculcate a spirit of self-reliance and independence in study through the use of SIM.* To nurture the value of all types of work including agricultural labour.** To enable the development of students' personal and social skills through the "Life Skills" curriculum.# To equalize opportunities in the working world for children from low-income homes.# To stem unemployment among schools leavers in new secondary schools.##	Abbott (1980) Jennings-Wray (1984)
Educational Television (ETV) (1964 to present) (secondary)	Jamaica	To improve the quality of education in schools by presenting TV programmes in support of new curricula.* To provide programme guides/workbooks, tapes, etc. to assist in training teacher in audiovisual instructional techniques.* To provide opportunities for all children to be exposed to the best teachers.#	Ministry of Education, Jamaica (1980) Jennings-Wray and Wellington (1985)

Table 1.3. (Continued)

Innovation/ Year/Education level	Country	Goals (category)	Sources
E-Learning Project (2006–10) (secondary)	Jamaica	To provide digital instructional materials for teachers and students in 11 subject areas. * To improve the quality of education in 150 secondary schools.* To provide equipment and software to schools to enhance teaching and learning using modern technology.* To train teachers to use interactive software to teach "hard to grasp" areas.* To contribute to changing cultural practices in teaching and learning using technology.** To acquire values and attitudes that will be considered by employers.#	Ministry of Commerce, Science and Technology (MCST) (2005) Butler (2012)
E-Connect and Learn Programme (e-Cal) (2010–15) (secondary)	Trinidad and Tobago	To improve the quality of instruction and support the infusion of ICT in teaching and learning and the development of twenty-first-century skills.* To enhance learning environment for students and bring about pedagogical shift in teaching methodology.* To raise student achievement.* To foster a collaborative culture in schools.** To reduce inequity in access to computers and information between students from wealthy and poor families.# To facilitate the development of collaborative teaching and learning.#	Ministry of Education, Trinidad, and Tobago (2010)
Resource and Technology (R&T) (1993 to present) (secondary)	Jamaica	To provide opportunities for the application of scientific and mathematical principles so students understand how they influence technology.* To introduce practical experiences through student-centred teaching/learning methods.* To provide experiences to bring out students' creative abilities.** To instil a sense of confidence and pride in their abilities through problem-solving and decision-making processes.# To produce productive citizens.##	Reform of Secondary Education Secretariat (1995) Jennings (2012)

(Continued)

Table 1.3. (Continued)

Innovation/ Year/Education level	Country	Goals (category)	Sources
Guyana In-service Distance Education (GUIDE) (1995–99) (post-secondary)	Guyana	To use distance teaching methodology to improve the quality of teaching.* To help teachers master the content of mathematics, science and English.* To offer basic training in education.* To enhance the learning experiences of children in the hinterland with limited educational opportunities.** To focus on untrained teachers who were teaching grades 7–9 in primary schools with tops (PWT)+, community high schools and junior secondary schools.#	Hamilton (1999)
B. Ed Secondary Distance Programme (2001–11) (tertiary)	Jamaica	To upgrade 3,000 diploma trained teachers in secondary schools to the bachelor's degree level.* To strengthen the content knowledge of teachers at the upper secondary level.* To improve the performance of students in the targeted CSEC subjects.*** To change cultural practices in teaching and learning using technology.** To target primarily for training the teachers in the newly upgraded secondary schools.# To contribute to reducing the social divide in society.# To ensure that teachers trained at the government's expense give back to the country through a period of bonding.*	Ministry of Education, Youth and Culture (2001)

Key for type of goal: *Philosophical/pedagogic; **Cultural; #Social equity/emotional; ##Economic
PWT+ are schools that cater to children from grades 1 to 9. Most of these are in rural areas and the children come from low-income homes.

***Biology, chemistry, physics, computer science, English/literature, geography, history, mathematics, Spanish and French.

Latin America and the Caribbean, quality is seen in the cognitive achievement of students as is evident in the statement by Bruns and Luque (2014, 3): "It is quality – in terms of increased student learning – that produces the economic benefits from investing in education." Quality seen as being in the *process* of learning is evident in objectives relating to nurturing the learner's creativity, problem-solving and creative thinking, use of the local language in schools, having one's identity reflected in the content of the curriculum, and an approach to teaching that is learner centred (UNESCO 2014). In the 1960s, use of educational television (ETV) in Jamaica was designed to improve the quality of education in schools (table 1.3). The ROSE programme in Jamaica sought to improve access to quality education and to improve the quality of education (see table 1.2). One of the goals of the e-Connect and Learn programme in Trinidad and Tobago was to improve the quality of instruction and support the infusion of Information and Communication Technology (ICT) in teaching and learning in schools. It also sought to develop twenty-first-century skills such as creative thinking and problem-solving. The concern with quality is also reflected in the goals of case studies such as the BSPS and Literacy 1-2-3 that wanted to change the method of teaching from a didactic approach that delivers bits of disconnected information to one that adopts an integrated approach (see table 1.1). An explicitly stated outcome of EduTech 2000 in Barbados (see table 1.3) was "a shift in teaching methodology throughout the education system from didactic to child-centred" (Ministry of Education Youth Affairs and Culture) (1998, 144).

Economic Goals

The magnitude and abruptness of a political shift can dictate the extent of educational reform (Cummings 2010). Jamaica in the 1970s provides a good example of this. The democratic socialist government of the time sought to introduce extensive changes in all aspects of life including the economy and education. According to Prime Minister Michael Manley, "we wanted to create an economy that would be more independent of foreign control. . . . We wanted to work for an egalitarian society" (Manley 1982, 39). There is a tendency to see the solution to any problem in the society as resting in the school and in most instances involving some change in the curriculum. Invariably, curriculum change is just *one part* of the solution, but it is understandable that such significance should be given to the curriculum, because the curriculum is what gives life to whatever we conceive education to be. Thus, Manley's government was determined to "shift the emphasis away from the academic/classical emphasis bequeathed by colonialism to a system better geared to the needs of a developing economy. This meant a greater emphasis on technical and trade training which we sought to achieve by an experimental expansion of the secondary system" (Manley 1982, 49). The Grade 10–11 Programme, to which Manley refers, is one of the case studies examined in this book (see table 1.3). The major goal of this programme was to provide equality of educational opportunity for students from low-income homes who had difficulty finding jobs on leaving school. Providing them with two additional years of schooling in which they acquired technical/vocational skills was considered the solution to equalizing their chances for employment with those of their peers from more affluent homes who attended prestigious high schools.

REAP's economic goal was clearly stated: to prepare children in rural Belize for a rewarding life in the countryside and to enable them to participate in the development of the agricultural basis of the economy for the benefit of themselves and the nation. Other innovations had economic goals, but these are not explicitly stated as objectives. For example, cost saving was one of the arguments that justified the introduction of CSEC. The cost of the examination would be shared among participating countries, and this would amount to each paying less to the Cambridge examining board. The students would also be the beneficiaries of cost saving. ROSE's goal was to enable the students to become productive citizens. Infusing career education into all the subjects of the curriculum was envisaged as a way to better prepare them for their role in the economy.

The goal statements of PRIMER do not include any economic goals but the reduction of education cost was a major motivation for undertaking the project. PRIMER is the only case study that represents educational borrowing from the Third World. The International Development Research Centre (IDRC) had invested in project IMPACT (Instructional Management by Parents, Community and Teachers) in a group of Southeast Asian countries. One of those countries was the Philippines where initially IMPACT "appeared to be educationally effective and to have the potential for cutting costs nearly in half" (Cummings 1986, 22). According to the director of the IDRC, "It has long been considered crucial by IDRC to examine whether the promise and potential of the IMPACT experiment could stand up in the quite different setting of Latin America, the West Indies or Africa."[8] Under the auspices of the IDRC, a visit to the Philippines by a team of Jamaican educators led by the minister of education made it clear to the funding agency that "the cost element and low student achievement" were the significant problems that Jamaica needed to address. Furthermore "the quality of education in Jamaica at the primary level . . . is still not providing the quality of education which will make for effective learning at the secondary level".[9] The objectives of PRIMER as approved by the IDRC included:

> To continue to develop and test an effective and economical delivery system which will reduce costs. . . . Learning will be largely by programmed teaching in grades 1-3 and individualized and self-paced in grades 4-6. . . . Community resources will be mobilized and . . . will serve as volunteers in providing specialized instruction. . . . The professionally trained teachers will be the Instructional Supervisor . . . who will be responsible for many more pupils than the conventional teacher, thereby reducing the cost of the delivery system.[10]

Interestingly, Cummings (1986, 58) notes that while the experimental project was intended to "develop and test an effective and economical delivery system which will reduce costs, the specific cost-saving elements were not spelled out" in the proposal from Jamaica. Clearly the intentions of the fund recipient were not aligned with the terms of the experimental research project that the funding agency had approved.

Technology and Innovation

The innovations that focus on technology are listed together in table 1.3. What is apparent from this table is that traditional technology has been used in schools since the 1960s. ETV, for example, was used in Jamaica since 1964 to help upgrade the quality of education in schools. This included providing teachers with workbooks and programme guides needed for training in audiovisual instructional techniques. In fact, because of the speed with which the Grade 10–11 Programme had to be developed, teachers were trained by viewing "model classes" on ETV (Jennings-Wray 1984). SIM were used in this programme as part of the drive to instil independence in learning thus relying less on the teacher. Self-reliance was an integral part of the ideology of democratic socialism. Traditional technology was also used in Guyana's GUIDE programme to improve the quality of education by strengthening the content knowledge of untrained teachers in core areas of the lower-secondary curriculum. The teachers selected for training lived in the rural and hinterland areas of Guyana and so the programme was a way of addressing the poor educational provision for the Amerindian people. Interestingly, strengthening trained teachers' content knowledge was also a main goal of the B. Ed Secondary Distance Programme in Jamaica. Here the emphasis was on the content of CSEC subjects and modern technology was used.

R&T in Jamaica's ROSE programme provides an unusual example of the use of traditional technology to develop twenty-first-century skills. A key feature of R&T is the *design process* which involved the students working in groups through five stages: identifying a problem that affects their lives, developing ideas for solving the problem using resources in the natural environment, planning activities to solve the problem, making the product (e.g. a waste recycling bin, a garment, designing a system) which solves the problem and then evaluating the success of the solution to the problem. Problem-solving, creativity, critical thinking are examples of the twenty-first-century skills that the students were expected to develop through this programme.

From the 1990s Trinidad and Tobago wanted to capitalize on the potential power of technology to enhance student learning, improve student achievement with a view to increasing the twin island's productivity. A main aim of the Secondary Education Modernization Programme which commenced in 1999 was technology infusion in the curriculum (DeLisle 2012). In Barbados "a decision was made in the 1980s to provide schools with the capacity to expose children to information technology" (Ministry of Education, Youth Affairs and Culture 1998, 138). From that time primary schools were using computers for classroom instruction in mathematics and language arts and the secondary schools were using computers for classroom instruction, preparation of instructional materials and student records management. From the mid-1990s, "all secondary schools are equipped with computers and free unlimited access to the Internet" (Ministry of Education, Youth Affairs and Culture 1998, 139). The government of Barbados identified knowledge-based and skill-intensive industries as its area of interest for which it was essential to keep abreast of the emerging technologies "since access to these technologies will position a small developing country to take full advantage of the information and developments which are so crucial in a competitive world" (Ministry of Education, Youth Affairs and Culture 1998, 135). For this reason, over two decades ago Barbados embarked on a massive education sector enhancement programme (EduTech 2000) with the aim to computerize all public primary and secondary schools in the country. This included providing the hardware, software and the necessary networking infrastructure. The expected outcome of all of this was "to equip the nation's youth with the skills, tools and thought processes necessary for active participation in an increasingly dynamic information and technological age by expanding their access to the universe of information available" (Ministry of Education, Youth Affairs and Culture 1998, 142). The Ministry of Education Youth and Culture (1998, 142) envisaged that to achieve the goals of EduTech 2000, the education system would have to undergo "radical change which will place the student at the centre of the teaching/learning process".

What is remarkable about EduTech 2000 is that it was inclusive in that it involved all schools – primary and secondary. Both the e-Learning project in Jamaica and e-Cal in Trinidad and Tobago involved only the public secondary schools. In all of these countries the infusion of technology into the curriculum was seen as the way to change the traditional method of teaching from the didactic teacher-centred approach to one that was student centred. Like the government in Barbados, the Jamaican government also saw the need for the country to become a competitive knowledge-based society, but according to the Ministry of Commerce Science and Technology (MCST) "the low level of education is a major hurdle to the creation of a knowledge-based society" (MCST 2005, 1). The low level of education was to be addressed by an "extensive remedial programme based on volunteerism" (MCST 2005, 4). Specifically, this involved high-performing students and qualified persons from the public to volunteer to assist children with reading difficulties and other problems in the upgraded high schools. The MCST also saw the use of technology as transforming values and attitudes. It is not specific on which values and attitudes the programme would seek to develop but advises that the grades awarded should be entered on students records for future employers to consider.

The only example of online teaching combined with face-to-face delivery in table 1.3 is the B. Ed Secondary Distance programme. There is much to learn from the implementation and outcome of this programme, but it deals with adults. Covid-19 has thrust CC countries into the uncharted territory of using combinations of online and face-to-face teaching with primary and secondary school children who are being schooled at home. There is no past experience in this that we can learn from. We just have to "muddle along". The effect of this is evident from newspaper reports and social media. Homemakers and parents who work from home have found themselves having to multitask – carrying out their regular duties at the same time as acting almost like a substitute teacher, ensuring that the child is focused on academic work and not secretly hooked into a computer game or on social media. One parent summed up the situation in this way:

> There's no way they can get a fulsome education from online schooling – it's just too impersonal. They're just going through the motions; we're basically breeding robots. My concern as a parent is mostly from a mental health standpoint. My child is miserable, because she is an all-rounder, and the focus is just on academics. They have online guidance counselling sessions, but I worry that the months with no peer socialization and no extra-curricular activities will hurt her.[11]

This underscores an important aspect of introducing changes in education. We tend to focus so much on the innovation or change itself (in this case the school-at-home approach using online teaching) that we do not anticipate the unintended consequences of the change (for example, the social/emotional impact on the child). We have already noted the learning loss suffered by children as a result of school's closure due to Covid-19 (Hanushek and Woessmann 2020). Another unintended consequence is the widening of the gap between the rich and the poor in society. We noted earlier that a goal of e-Cal in Trinidad and Tobago was to reduce inequity in access to computers between children from poor and wealthy families. However, this only applied at the secondary level. In Jamaica, because online teaching was instituted without the necessary preparation, children from high-income homes were able to have access to laptops and computers for accessing online learning. However, parents of children from low-income homes could not afford to purchase the necessary hardware. In certain households several siblings have to vie for the single mobile phone in the home in order to access learning online. Since the Ministry of Education was unable to provide each child with a laptop, children from disadvantaged homes risked suffering greater learning loss.

Summary

Table 1.4 summarizes the main focus in the elements of the curriculum innovations examined in this book. The innovations span the CC, even though weighted on the larger countries. They also span all levels of the education system. While all had philosophical/pedagogic goals, a number had social equity goals: for example, ROSE and e-Cal. Only in the REAP programme in Belize and the Grade 10–11 Programme in Jamaica were economic goals made explicit, although reduction in education costs was an important goal of PRIMER when Jamaican educators initially approached the funding agency. The achievement of cultural goals underpinned innovations that focused on the teaching of literacy with the thrust being on respect for the native language. Only two innovations focused on assessment: CETT which produced literacy standards for the lower primary level and the CSEC which offers a secondary exit examination for sixteen participating CC countries. Eight of the innovations focus on either traditional or modern technology. Educational television has been used in Jamaica since the 1960s to help upgrade the quality of education. Self-instructional materials were used in the Grade 10–11 Programme in Jamaica to develop self-reliance and independence. Most of the innovations in modern technology focused at the secondary level with a view to enabling teachers to integrate ICT into their teaching. EduTech 2000 was the only innovation that spanned both the primary and secondary levels. It was seen as enabling citizens "to access the evolving technologies and therefore position Barbados to take its rightful place in the emerging global economy of the twenty-first century" (Ministry of Education, Youth Affairs and Culture) (1998, 144).

Table 1.4. Summary of Main Focus of Curriculum Innovations

School Level/Type	Innovation	Country	Goals/Objectives	Content	Method/Organization	Assessment
Primary	REAP (1975–85)	Belize	Economic	Whole curriculum	Integration	–
	NCERD (SRG) (1989–91)	Guyana	Pedagogic/cultural	Literacy	Reinforcement of literacy across curriculum	–
	CETT (2002–06)	5 CC countries	Pedagogic	Literacy/teacher Ed.	–	Literacy standards
	Literacy 1-2-3 (2002 to present)	Jamaica	Cultural	Literacy	Integration	–
Early Childhood	BSPS (2002–05)	Jamaica	Social Equity	Whole curriculum	Integration	–
All Age	PRIMER (1979–83)	Jamaica	Social/(Economic)	Literacy/numeracy	Self-instruction	
Primary/secondary	EduTech 2000 (1999–2008)	Barbados	Philosophical/social	Whole curriculum	Infusion ICT/student centred	–
Secondary	ETV (1964 to present)	Jamaica	Philosophical	Whole curriculum	Teacher centred	–
	Grade 10–11 (1971–78)	Jamaica	Social equity/economic	Tech-Voc	Self-instruction/teacher centred	–
	CSEC 1979 to present	16 CC countries	Cultural	Academic/Tech/Voc	Teacher centred	Regional examination

(Continued)

Table 1.4. (Continued)

School Level/Type	Innovation	Country	Goals/Objectives	Content	Method/Organization	Assessment
	Sixth Form Geography Project (1979–81)	Jamaica	Cultural	Geography	Enquiry approach	–
	ROSE 1 (1993–98)	Jamaica	Social equity/cultural	Whole curriculum	Student centred	–
	R&T (1993 to present)	Jamaica	Philosophical/economic	Tech/Voc/21st-century skills	Student centred	–
	e-Learning Project (2006–10)	Jamaica	Pedagogic	Whole curriculum	Infusion of ICT	–
	e-Cal (2010–15)	Trinidad and Tobago	Pedagogic/social equity	Whole curriculum	Infusion of ICT	–
	ASTEP (2010–12)	Jamaica	Social/emotional	Literacy	Student centred	–
Post-secondary	GUIDE (1995–99)	Guyana	Social equity	English, mathematics, science, education	Distance	–
Tertiary	B. Ed secondary (2001–11)	Jamaica	Social equity	Secondary curriculum	Distance	–

Conclusion

We will remember the 2019–20 school year as one in which the precipitous decision was made to change system-wide to online teaching using a schooling-at-home approach as a result of Covid-19 pandemic. In an effort to keep children learning, the goals of this change were not clearly worked out and consequences which were not intended soon emerged. What is evident from this chapter is that the goals for introducing change are worked out in advance. Curriculum innovations pursue a wide range of goals. Some of these goals are explicit but others not. For example, those who want teachers to adopt an integrated approach to teaching seek to correct a weakness in the academic subject-based curriculum that teachers deliver as bits of disconnected knowledge. On the face of it integration then seeks to organize knowledge more coherently so that meaning is more readily engendered when students can see relationships between areas which were once disparate. Integration, however, means more than this because it takes place on several levels: at the level of content (how knowledge is organized); at the level of the teacher (requiring teachers to work together to plan for integration as in the case of R&T); and at the level of the students who are usually organized in groups and given more responsibility for their own learning. This in turn implies a change in relationship with the teacher who is no longer the "fount of knowledge". "Teaching is a lonely profession", says Sarason (1971, 44). When teachers move from working in isolation to having to work in teams and when the normal relationship between teacher and students is altered, this represents a change in the power structure in schools. If this is envisaged by policymakers and educational planners, it is not a goal that is made explicit but as we will learn from our study of curriculum changes, it nevertheless impacts on the attitude of the teacher towards innovations.

"Change is a journey" (Fullan 1994, 21). Let us begin ours. From the literature (e.g. Rogers and Shoemaker (1971), Fullan and Stiegelbauer 1991, Fullan 1994) we can identify stages of an innovation. Put simply, the innovation/change process begins with the *initiation* of the new idea before its *design* and *development* and then *implementation* before becoming *institutionalized* and, hopefully, *sustained*. This implies a linear process, but it is far from being so because of the complexities involved at each stage. The innovation has to be evaluated to determine if its goals have been achieved but the analysis of the innovations will show the importance of evaluation being built into the entire innovation/change process. The *consequence* of change is a relatively neglected area in education, but the need for more attention to be given to this will become evident particularly in the examination of PRIMER. But let us start at the beginning – with how we introduce change into our education systems. This is the focus of the next chapter.

2.

How Do We Introduce Change into Our School Systems?

Contrasting Models of Change

Purpose

The purpose of this chapter is to illustrate how largely centralized education systems such as ours in the CC introduce change into their school systems. The concern is not so much to identify "best practice", because, as Crossley and Sprague (2012, 35) have pointed out, "what might be 'best practice' in one context may not be appropriate elsewhere". To explore how we introduce change, two contrasting models/approaches – the Research Development and Diffusion (RD&D) and the Problem-Solving – will be examined. Curriculum change can refer to changes in the elements of a curriculum such as the philosophy; aims and objectives of a curriculum; changes in the content, methods, organization, assessment and evaluation of learning; or combinations thereof. A change in how learning is assessed, for example, can affect what content is selected for teaching and how it is taught. The examples of curriculum change used in this chapter are the CSEC, the ROSE, NCERD Skills Reinforcement Guides (RD&D) and the Sixth Form Geography Project (Problem-Solving). All of these involve the introduction of ideas which were perceived as new at the time of their initiation. Consequently, in this and subsequent chapters they are also referred to as "innovations". Which approach proved to be the most successful in bringing about change? The answer to this question will begin to emerge in this chapter but will become more explicit in the next chapter where the implementation of the models will be discussed. The graphical presentation and description of the models in practice is preceded by an explanation of terms used and a description of phases or stages in the change process followed by a description of the innovations themselves. The chapter ends with highlights of key themes that emerge from the innovation/change models.

Innovation and Change

There is a close link between innovation, reform and change. Miles (1964) defines innovation as a deliberate, novel, specific change, and to Clark and

Guba (1965, 7) innovation is "the process of change". To Fullan (1994, 4), teachers are engaged "in the business of continuous innovation and change". In this chapter, innovation is "an idea, practice, or object that is perceived as new to an individual or another unit of adoption"; thus, the idea does not have to be objectively new (Rogers 2003, 137), but new to the users in their specific context. Change is the desired result which comes from putting the new idea(s) into practice. Change involves innovation. The same can be said of reform which is defined in the dictionary as "change made in order to remove imperfections". Reform does not imply a complete overhaul of a system, but rather an attempt to change such aspects of it that are considered undesirable. The ROSE programme in Jamaica, for example, did not attempt to change the entire secondary system. It focused on the lower secondary level in certain schools. The examples of curriculum change discussed in this chapter all relate to schools' curricula and involved innovations which were designed to bring about change in curricula or assessment of achievement.

Stages in the Change Process

Rogers (2003) describes the change process as commencing with the initiation of an innovation. This process, according to Rogers, consists of all the decisions, activities and the impacts that these have "from recognition of a need or a problem, through research, development . . . through diffusion and adoption of the innovation by users to its consequences" (Rogers 2003, 137). Diffusion is "the spontaneous and unplanned spread of new ideas" (Rogers 2003, 6) while dissemination applies to the use of planned strategies for putting the curriculum into practice (Fullan and Stiegelbauer 1991). "Dissemination" is the more appropriate term to use in the CC where education systems are largely centralized and engaged in planned change. The nature of the phases or stages described by Rogers is not linear but interactive. Indeed, one could describe them as interconnected because in the process of developing a new curriculum, for example, it is implemented and disseminated in pilot schools, thereby involving three overlapping stages (development, implementation and dissemination). Because what happens at one stage of the process affects subsequent stages, the process is infused with an element of the unpredictable. If at the development stage, principals of schools and teachers are not involved in a way that leads to their understanding of the rationale, purpose and methods of the change and what they need to do to bring about the change, effective implementation is unlikely to take place. In fact, it has been argued that if teachers are the ones who have to adopt and implement the ideas in the new curriculum, then they should be involved in all the stages of the curriculum change process (House

1979). Such involvement has proven successful as in the case of teachers who participated in the Haifa University curriculum project (Ben-Peretz 1980). Will the same apply in the Caribbean context? This is an important question to ask given that culture has been shown to be an important variable in the attempts to bring about change (Kay 1975, Warwick et al. 1991). Kay, for example, contends that the spontaneity, individualism and pupil-initiated questioning associated with the progressive Western primary curriculum could not take root in the Kenyan society which cherishes values of collectivism and reverence for elders.

The Models of Change

Models of change make assumptions about teachers' willingness and competence to participate in the curriculum change process. Examples of such models are the "Power-coercive" strategy of Chin and Benne (1969), the Research Development and Dissemination/Diffusion (RD&D) model of Havelock (1971), the Centre-Periphery and Proliferation of Centres models (Schon 1971) and Rogers and Shoemaker's (1971) authority-innovation decision-making model. Rogers and Shoemaker contend that there are two groups of decision-makers: namely the superordinate group (e.g. Ministries of Education, donor agency consultants) who initiate and direct the development and dissemination of the innovation and the subordinate group (e.g. teachers and principals) who implement the decisions made by the superordinate group.

Embedded in the RD&D is the notion of the change process involving a rational sequence of activities in which an innovation is initiated, then developed, produced and disseminated to its users who are assumed to be passive consumers willing to accept the innovation. Essentially this is how teachers were perceived in the 1960s and 1970s when the products of curriculum development were made "teacher proof" in that they were expected to be used without any adaptation. This is known as the "fidelity" perspective towards implementation (Fullan and Pomfret 1977). In the centre-periphery (or top-down) model, a central agency such as the Curriculum Development Unit in the Ministry of Education or the Project Team develops the curriculum and, after trial in pilot schools, the curriculum is disseminated to teachers in the wider school system (the periphery). Bennis, Benne and Chin (1969) associate this model with "power-coercive" strategies, as evident in the Ministry of Education's exercise of power over the teachers and principals in the public schools. The problem with these strategies, argues Per Dalin (1983, 136), "is the lack of coherence between intention and reality. The strategies indicate procedures for the *formulation and adoption* of innovation, but we are left with problems concerning the *implementation* of these policies." This is supported by Carter and Hacker (1988) who found that the use of the centre-periphery strategy to introduce a new social studies curriculum in secondary schools in Western Australia resulted in changes which were antithetical to the intentions of the curriculum developers. Carter and Hacker suggest that the lack of in-service training of the teachers contributed to the result. The Proliferation of Centres model distinguishes between primary and secondary centres with the primary concentrating on training the trainers. They deploy, monitor and manage resources and support the secondary centres which focus on the dissemination of the curriculum.

There are two characteristics common to all the preceding models. First, they are associated with approaches to curriculum change which have their origins outside of the particular schools in which the curriculum is to be implemented. Secondly, the user is perceived as a passive receiver or consumer. In the problem-solving model, the user is an active participant. The change process here begins when the users articulate a problem within their own situation. The users then search for a solution to the problem from available alternatives with the help of a change agent who collaborates with them without giving directives. The solution selected is likely to have direct relevance and appropriateness for the specific context in which it is to be implemented. Implementation, therefore, is more likely to be successful.

Curriculum Innovations

The four examples of curriculum innovations/changes are summarized in table 2.1.

The CSEC

The CXC is a regional examining body established in 1972 by agreement between thirteen CC countries, with a further two added in 1973. CXC has the following objectives: to introduce examinations to replace the General Certificate in Education (GCE) Ordinary (O) level offerings; to develop syllabi in subject areas relevant to the needs of the region; and to set examinations which test a wider range of abilities than tested traditionally by the GCE "O" level. CSEC originally had three schemes classified as General Proficiency, Basic Proficiency and Technical Proficiency. They tested the abilities of 40 per cent of grade 11 students. This constituted a wider ability range since the GCE "O" levels only tested 20 per cent of the students. In 1965 the UK examination boards introduced the Certificate of Secondary Education (CSE) for students in British colonies and former colonies. The CSE targeted the 40 per cent of students below the 20 per cent that the GCE "O" level catered for, with the result

Table 2.1. Examples of Models of Curriculum Change in Caribbean School Systems

Example of Curriculum Change (Timeline)	Country/ Education Level	Main Goals	Model	Sources of Data
CSEC (1975 to present)	14 Caribbean territories *(secondary)	Introduce exams to replace GCE "O" level; develop syllabi relevant to the region; set exams to test wide ability range	RD&D/ proliferation of centres	Griffith (1981), Griffith (2015), Jennings-Wray (1985)
Sixth Form Geography (1979–81)	Jamaica (traditional high schools)	Stimulate teachers to develop "A"-level geography materials relevant to the Jamaican context	Problem-solving	Morrissey (1981), Jennings-Wray (1984)
NCERD Skills Reinforcement Curriculum Guides (1988–92)	Guyana (primary grades 1–5)	Reinforce language structure and mathematics concepts across the curriculum; use of activity/higher-level cognitive skills development	RD&D/centre-periphery/ proliferation of centres	Craig (2006/07)
ROSE 1 / R&T (1993–98)	Jamaica (non-traditional secondary schools)	To improve quality, efficiency and equity in disadvantaged schools in grades 7–9. To develop a common curriculum which is activity-oriented, and student-centred with emphasis on problem-solving; to prepare graduates with work-ready skills or for further study. To develop the capacity of the MOE to manage and evaluate the impact of ROSE	RD&D/centre-periphery	Ministry of Education, Jamaica (1993), Davis (1994, 1995), Jennings (2012)

*Antigua, Barbados, Belize, British Virgil Islands, Dominica, Grenada, Jamaica, Guyana, Montserrat, St Lucia, St Vincent and the Grenadines, Trinidad and Tobago, Turks and Caicos Islands (Cayman Islands withdrew 1977), St Kitts/Nevis/Anguilla

that "by implication, the bottom 40 per cent of the population was regarded as 'unexaminable'" (Griffith 2015, p13).

The General Proficiency (GP) is designed to provide a foundation for further studies in the specific subject areas beyond grade 11: and the Basic Proficiency (BP) level aimed largely at those students who were not likely to study a subject beyond the fourth year of secondary school. The Technical Proficiency level is designed for those students who require "a greater practical orientation and preparation for further technical studies . . . than offered in a subject in the same area at General Proficiency" (Griffith 2015, 15). The GP is awarded in five grades ranging from grade 1, where the candidate has a comprehensive working knowledge of the syllabus, grade 11 where the candidate has a working knowledge of most aspects of the syllabus, to grade 5, where the candidate has not produced sufficient evidence on which a judgement can be made. Only passing at grades 1 and 11 GP level are considered equivalent to a GCE "O"-level pass.

The Sixth Form Geography Project

This innovation represents a rare attempt to introduce innovation at the Sixth Form level (grades 12 and 13). It was modelled off the British Geography 16–19 project, a curriculum development project that was funded by the British Schools Council. The Sixth Form Geography Project was initiated by Morrissey (1981), a lecturer of geography at the University of the West Indies (UWI) who, through his interaction with teachers of the GCE Advanced (A) Level Geography in Jamaica's traditional high schools, became aware of their expressed need for curriculum materials in the subject that were relevant to the Jamaican context. He sought to stimulate the teachers to develop original teaching units related to topics in the "A"-level syllabus with a Jamaican orientation. The expectation was that this would diminish the teachers' reliance on foreign textbooks. The teachers were encouraged to use an enquiry approach in order to change the traditional patterns of teacher–student interaction in the classroom which were teacher centred.

The Skills Reinforcement Curriculum Guides

With the assistance of United Nations Educational Scientific and Cultural Organization in 1986–87 the government of Guyana through its Ministry of Education created the National Centre for Educational Resource Development (NCERD) by bringing together six previously existing separate agencies under a centralized management. These were the Curriculum Development Centre which developed curriculum materials for the primary and lower secondary levels; the Schools Broadcasts Unit which used radio to teach selected subjects at the same levels; the Mathematics and Science Unit which had responsibility for developing teaching materials and schemes of work for teaching these subjects at the secondary level; the Test Development Unit which produced all of the tests and examinations used in the Guyanese school system; the Learning Resource Centre which provided in-service training in teaching methods; and the Materials Production Unit which provided printing and reproduction services for all other agencies of the Ministry of Education. The aims of NCERD therefore included improving teaching methodologies in schools, providing resource materials for schools through modalities of materials production and dissemination, workshops and so on and providing continuous in-service training for teachers and principals of schools (Craig 2006/07).

This chapter is concerned with a specific aspect of NCERD's work, namely the development of the Skills Reinforcement Guides. This involved the development of curriculum guides in language arts, mathematics, science, social studies and health education for grades 1, 2 and 3. The objectives of these guides were to give children an English-based Creole-language background systematic practice in the use of the English language "by methods appropriate for second-dialect situations" (Craig 20067, 12); to reinforce the learning of English and literacy by setting it as an objective in all other subjects in the school curriculum; to link number concepts to the systematic learning of English and literacy; and to reinforce the latter in the teaching of mathematics (Craig 2006/07).

ROSE programme with Special Reference to R&T

R&T is an innovation introduced in the ROSE programme in Jamaica in 1993. Prior to the inception of ROSE, technical–vocational subjects offered in secondary schools in Jamaica were agriculture, art and craft, business education, home economics and industrial arts. Delivered separately, students were able to neither establish meaningful relationships between the subjects nor gain a basic understanding of the concept and application of technology in everyday life. R&T was developed from the discrete areas previously offered and organized into five elements: namely, agriculture and the environment, home and family management, product design and development, resource management (including information technology) and visual arts. R&T used themes to draw on the commonalities of the five elements to integrate them into a cohesive whole. To achieve this integration, teachers of the five elements needed to plan together and principals of schools were expected to facilitate such planning during school hours (Jennings 2012). The *design process* is described by the Ministry of Education and Culture, Jamaica (1993, 7), as "being at the heart of all five elements". This involved the students going through stages that involved identification of needs or problems, designing proposals for solving the problem or addressing the need, planning the work to be completed in a set time, then making a product or designing a system to solve the problem or meet the need identified and finally evaluating the success of the solution to the problem.

A Comparison of Change Strategies

There are many versions of the RD&D, but in this chapter we will use the version of Clark and Guba (1965). The first stage of the Clark-Guba paradigm is research which serves two main purposes: first, to ascertain the state of knowledge in the area of concern and, secondly, to determine how this knowledge can be applied to the product being developed. According to Clark and Guba, a solution to an operating problem is then invented and built by a central team during the development stage. They define invention as "the formulation of a new solution to an operating problem" (Clark and Guba 1965, 11). This is introduced to practitioners in the diffusion stage and then fully incorporated into the school system in the adoption stage.

Table 2.2 shows a comparison of Clark and Guba's RD&D with the change strategies involved in the CSEC and the first phase of the ROSE programme in Jamaica with particular reference to the subject, Resource and Technology (R&T). What is immediately obvious is the length of time taken in both cases in analysing the educational situation and deliberating on the various problems. It took some twenty-six years before the CXC was formed and ten years before ROSE was officially launched. In the case of ROSE, deliberations began with the UNESCO (1983) Report on the Development of Secondary Education in Jamaica. This, among other things, highlighted the low performance of the primary education system and the vast disparity in the quality of educational offering at the secondary level. This was followed by several studies commissioned by the Ministry of Education and Culture, including studies on all age schools which cater to children in grades 7–9. The quality of educational offering in these schools was shown to be at the lowest level. There were also studies on mathematics, literacy, school administration and curriculum practices at the lower secondary level (Ministry of Education and Culture 1993). The inclusion of resource and technology in the ROSE curriculum was informed by a study on Science and Technology Education in Jamaican Schools conducted by Sheila Haggis in 1984 (Davis 1995).

While ROSE clearly was informed by research, this is not so obvious in the case of CSEC. The CXC credits Eric Williams, the former prime minister of Trinidad and Tobago, with initiating, in 1946, the idea of replacing British external examinations by locally developed ones, especially as the University College of the West Indies (a college of the University of London) was soon to be opened in Jamaica. These ideas were expressed in the book *Education in the British West Indies*, which gives a detailed analysis of the problems facing the British West Indian education systems in the 1940s. While this would have entailed a good deal of research, it is not the same as the commissioned research that informed ROSE. The Sixth Form Geography Project was informed by research undertaken by Morrissey (1981) on the Geography 16–19 project in England. The approach to teaching literacy across the curriculum in the Skills Reinforcement Guides was informed by research conducted by Dennis Craig on teaching English in Creole-speaking contexts (see Allsopp and Jennings 2014). Dennis Craig, himself a Guyanese, was appointed the first director of NCERD.

Search for Solutions: Deliberations

Neither in the case of the Sixth Form Geography Project or of the Skills Reinforcement Guides was much time spent in the search for solution to the problem. Morrissey (1981) in fact selected the solution for the "A"-level geography teachers who needed more culturally relevant materials for use with their students. He knew of the success of the Geography 16–19 project in England and communicated this to the teachers. Craig (2006/07) documents the kinds of arguments that he used at staff meetings to persuade his staff of the justification for focusing on strengthening literacy and numeracy skills at the primary level as the foundation of a much more sound and robust secondary education.

The experience of ROSE 1 (R&T) and CSEC provides an interesting contrast to the other two attempts at curriculum change under study. The search for solution to the problem of inequality and inefficiency at the lower secondary level in Jamaica took some seven years before ROSE 1 was initiated. In the case of CSEC this search took the form of deliberations which continued over two decades. The search gathered momentum in 1958 under the West Indies Federation (WIF), a political body introduced to unite the separate territories under one regional government which, through collective management and a pooling of resources, sought to strengthen the West Indian countries as an economic and political force. It was within the framework of WIF that the regional governments envisaged the new examining body being established. WIF fell victim to the pride in national independence cherished by each of the West Indian countries and in particular Jamaica, which had the largest population. With the demise of WIF in 1962, discussions on the examining body ceased until the setting up of the Caribbean Free Trade Association in

Table 2.2. A Comparison of the Phases in the RD&D with Major Phases in the Change Process for CXC/CSEC and ROSE 1 (R&T)

Phases in CXC/CSEC Change Process	Year	Phases in RD&D (Clark and Guba)	Year	Phases in the Change Process for ROSE (Resource & Technology)
SITUATION ANALYSIS		DEVELOPMENT		SITUATION ANALYSIS
• Initiation (Eric Williams 1951)	1946		1983	• Study by UNESCO 1983
DELIBERATION		Research		DELIBERATION
• Decision to innovate (WIF)	1958		1985/93	• Preparatory projects by UNDP (1985–88) and World Bank (1989–93)
• Collapse of WIF	1962			
• Idea revitalized (CARIFTA)	1965		1987/91	• 9 studies commissioned See MOE&C (1993)
COLLECTIVE AUTHORITY DECISION		Invention		AUTHORITY DECISION
• CXC established	1972		1990	• ROSE 1 initiated
DEVELOPMENT		Design		DEVELOPMENT/Implementation
• First subject panels appointed/development of 5-subject syllabi	1974/75		1990	• 5 subjects developed
			1991	• Pilot testing of 5 subjects in 4 all age schools
• Training of examiners by Cambridge University Local Exams syndicate	1975		1992	• Pilot testing in 7 additional schools
• Publication of 5-subject syllabi	1977		1994	• 60 schools offering R&T
DISSEMINATION		DIFFUSION/		DISSEMINATION
• Public relations team tours participating countries/ CXC Fact Sheet published	1978	Dissemination Demonstration	1991	• In-service training of teachers begins and is ongoing
• CXC/USAID SCDP initiated	1979		1993	• Training of principals and board chairpersons/ meetings with parents/community
				• Official launch of ROSE

(Continued)

Table 2.2. (Continued)

Phases in CXC/CSEC Change Process	Year	Phases in RD&D (Clark and Guba)	Year	Phases in the Change Process for ROSE (Resource & Technology)
ADOPTION/IMPLEMENTATION		ADOPTION		ADOPTION /IMPLEMENTATION
Dissemination				Dissemination/Development
• First CSEC offered in 5 subjects	1979	Trial	1994	• First issue of ROSEGRAM
• 8 new subjects added	1980			• 28 schools adopted ROSE
• Publication of CXC News/CXC Questions & Answers	1981	Installation	1994	• Training of education officers
				• Conference on ROSE
• Production of 10th anniversary booklet & film/use of TV/radio	1982		1994	• Guidance & Counselling curriculum developed
• Review of syllabi began	1983		1995	• Pilot testing of the Arts
• Total of 28 subjects offered	1985			• Training of curriculum developers/assessors
			1996	• First Junior High School Certificate exam
			1997	• ROSE incorporated in Teachers College Curricula
				• 128 schools in ROSE
INSTITUTIONALIZATION	1987	INSTITUTION-ALIZATION	1998	INSTITUTIONALIZATION
• CXC institutionalized				• Institutionalization of ROSE

UNESCO: United Nations Educational Scientific and Cultural Organization
CARIFTA: Caribbean Free Trade Association
MOE&C: Ministry of Education and Culture
UNDP: United Nations Development Program

1965, which eventually led to the establishment of the Caribbean Community and Common Market. The latter had a regional education desk within its secretariat. At a meeting of the Commonwealth Caribbean Ministers of Education held in Jamaica in 1968, it was recommended that the secretariat be responsible for the preparatory work for the formation of the CXC which eventually materialized in 1972.

The Decision-Making Process

Where the CSEC, ROSE (R&T) and NCERD Skills Reinforcement Guides differ from Clark and Guba's RD&D is with respect to the nature of the decision-making process, which is not identified in Clark and Guba's model. Rogers and Shoemaker (1971, 269–70) distinguish between three types of innovation decisions. There are optional decisions made by individuals of their own free will, "authority decisions, which are forced upon an individual by someone in a superordinate power position" and "collective decisions, made by the individuals in a social system by consensus". Authority decisions typify most attempts at educational change in the CC. The Ministry of Education representing the government (the centre) has the superordinate power to issue mandates relating to the proposed change to be carried out by principals and teachers in schools (the periphery). This is commonly described as the "centre-periphery" model. CSEC is most appropriately categorized as a "collective authority decision" made by participating governments. The decision to establish the CXC required the approval of the CC countries. The latter was represented by elected governments and not by referenda from the people of these countries. Rogers and Shoemaker observe that collective decision-making is slow (as evident in table 2.2) but its advantage is increased stability, once effected, for a decision made by a group can be changed (discontinued) only by that group. Thus, individual countries may withdraw from the CSEC (see note 1) but CSEC remains intact. ROSE 1 (R&T) is an example of authority decision in that the government of Jamaica (GOJ) decided on the introduction of ROSE 1 and appointed a national coordinator, supported by a secretariat to carry out its will. The NCERD Skills Reinforcement Guides (SRGs) is also an example of authority decision, but the director had to persuade the staff of the need and relevance of the SRGs.

The Sixth Form Geography Project is an example of optional decision-making because while Morrissey initiated the project, he saw himself as the change agent, willing to guide and offer advice as needed, but not to force anything on the teachers. The teachers organized themselves into six consortia which were located in various parishes throughout Jamaica. Each consortium elected its own leader to spearhead the process of developing the teaching units. The consortia were left on their own to work as they wished.

Development

The RD&D model implies a very rational process which requires technical and professional expertise, adequate finance and sufficient time to operationalize. To date funding has not been a serious problem for CSEC. The CXC derives its revenue from major sources such as contributions from participating governments, registration fees paid by candidates, examination (subject) fees and grants from international agencies. The policy of CXC is to allot at least two years to the development of a subject syllabus. Table 2.2 shows that the first subject panels were appointed in the 1974–75 academic year to review existing syllabi and develop new ones in the areas slated for examination in 1979 (English, geography, history, integrated science and mathematics). A syllabus must be examined for three consecutive years before any major modifications are made or a new syllabus introduced. In a sense for those three years the syllabus is "on trial"; however, CXC introduced some subject syllabi as "pilot projects". For example, integrated science was piloted for five years in thirty schools in seven participating countries (Guyana, Barbados, Jamaica, Trinidad and Tobago, St Lucia, St Vincent and the British Virgin Islands). Feedback from this project led to substantial revisions as well as policy changes. For example, problems encountered particularly with the competence of the teachers (who at the time were trained in the separate sciences) to teach an integrated curriculum resulted in syllabi for the separate sciences being developed. These were examined for the first time in 1985. Integrated science is only taken by students in two countries (Jamaica and Guyana).

What the example of integrated science (CSEC) shows is that the pilot testing of curricula appears much earlier in the change process than represented by Clark and Guba. Thus, there is an overlapping of the trial and development phases. This is also borne out in the curriculum change process used in ROSE 1 (see table 2.2). What is also worthy of note is that the development of curricula took place on a phased basis in both CSEC and ROSE 1. Thus, while five-subject syllabi had been developed for CSEC by 1977, another twenty-three had been developed by 1985. Likewise while five subjects (including R&T) had been developed in ROSE 1 by 1990, curricula for the eleven subjects that comprised the common core curriculum had been developed by the time the World Bank funds ceased in 1998.

At the time when ROSE 1 was introduced, Jamaica had a Core Curriculum Unit in the Ministry of Education which had responsibility for the development of curricula for the primary and lower secondary levels. ROSE 1 curricula, however, were developed by consultants with specializations in the particular area. Johnson (1995) reports that contracts were signed with consultants to develop curricula in drama, art, Spanish and religious education in 1994. Three of these consultants were lecturers at the UWI. The "A"-level teachers of geography themselves were responsible for developing and trying out the teaching units they developed in the Sixth Form Geography Project. The change agent offered editorial services for the teaching units (Morrissey 1981). The subject specialists employed in the Curriculum Development Unit at NCERD which incorporated the Mathematics and Science Unit were responsible for the development of the Skills Reinforcement Guides over a period of six months (Craig 2006/07).

Dissemination

The dissemination strategy used by CXC corresponds to what Schon (1971) describes as a "proliferation of centres" strategy. The development of curricula and the determination of examination policy and procedure are managed centrally by the primary centre – the School Examination Committee – whereas the dissemination of materials to schools in individual countries is carried out by secondary centres which take the form of National Committees (with the exception of Jamaica where this is handled by an overseas examination office). CXC has also used various means of not only spreading knowledge about the examinations but also addressing concerns held by its users. Rogers (2003) suggests that interpersonal channels involving face-to-face exchange between persons are best used to form or change strongly held attitudes. In 1978 a public relations team toured the participating countries to promote the CSEC in an effort to dispel fears about the parity of the examination with foreign examining boards and its acceptability internationally as an entry qualification to further study. Local public relations teams were subsequently formed in some of the participating countries to serve similar purposes. These efforts were supported by radio and television programmes, a documentary film produced for the CXC's tenth anniversary, information leaflets such as "CXC News" and in more recent times the journal *The Caribbean Examiner*.

The ROSE secretariat used similar dissemination strategies. It produced the publication ROSEGRAM and a ROSE PRESS Fact Sheet to spread information and updates on the progress of the reform. A ROSE conference was also held (Greene 1994). The Professional Development Unit of the Ministry of Education also held meetings with parents to explain the reform and address their concerns. In the Sixth Form Geography Project communication among the teachers was made possible through a conference and two workshops held over the two-year period, as well as through a newsletter which was sent out regularly to the teachers to keep them updated about the objectives and progress of the project. The newsletter also provided information on "A"-level results and on geography teaching in general. The teachers were encouraged to send their views on the project to the newsletter. NCERD could not use any of the dissemination strategies described due to lack of resources. The Materials Production Unit was too occupied with outside work to offer any assistance in disseminating information on the Skills Reinforcement Guides.

Training

The training of needed technical and professional expertise was given serious attention by CXC. In 1975, for example, the first examiners were trained by the Cambridge University Local Examinations syndicate and in the following year other examiners were trained by the Educational Testing Service in the United States. The training of teachers in the various techniques of assessment related to the CSEC was a major objective of the Secondary Curriculum Development Project (SCDP) which was funded by the United States Agency for International Development (USAID). The SCDP's training programme was organized in workshops held at the regional, sub-regional and country levels. Regional workshops were held in Barbados and Jamaica and attended by teacher representatives from the participating countries who were experienced in the teaching of the particular subject. Essentially a "cascade approach" to training was utilized because these teachers were then expected to demonstrate the new techniques learned to teachers in their respective countries. The workshops organized by the SCDP served as a catalyst for the organization of local workshops by groups of schools or subject associations (Griffith 1981). In the first two years of the project a total of eighty-two workshops were held and the SCDP evaluator described them as having had a strong impact on teachers in the region (Massanari 1981).[1]

Training for ROSE was undertaken by the Professional Development Unit of the Ministry of Education and the Joint Board of Teacher Education (JBTE).[2] The training done by the Professional Development Unit took the form of workshops for teachers and principals conducted over two weeks during the summer in which they were given an overview of the reform and then given "as much information as possible about each subject" (Greene 1996, 6). Two-week residential workshops were also organized for the education officers responsible for supervising the schools implementing ROSE (Brown and Jones 1994). The JBTE ensured that the ROSE curriculum was built into the curriculum of the Teacher Training Colleges and that lecturers were adequately prepared to train the teachers who would deliver the new curriculum.

Due to scarcity of personnel and general lack of resources NCERD was only able to hold one training workshop per year lasting four or five days in each of the ten administrative regions of Guyana. One has to bear in mind the size of Guyana (83,000 square miles) and the enormous cost incurred to reach the hinterland by air or river. The number of participants at each workshop also had to be limited to one representative from each school: the head teacher or a senior teacher "who, on return to the school, had sufficient authority to conduct in-school training sessions with other teachers" (Craig 2006/07, 15). The representative was given one copy of each Skills Reinforcement Guide to take back to the school.

The workshops organized for the Sixth Form Geography Project focused on skills in the teaching of geography and did not provide the training in curriculum development that the teachers needed.

Summary and Overview of the Change Models

While the phases of Clark and Guba's RD&D appear linear, the analysis of the change efforts in this chapter shows that this is by no means the case. Two of them, in fact, were introduced on a phased basis. In the case of CSEC the process for development of the five-subject syllabi began in 1975 and the process was repeated for eight new subjects in 1979 and repeated again and again; by 1985 twenty-eight subjects were offered for examination. The process has continued because currently thirty-three subjects are offered – twenty-eight at General Proficiency and five at the Technical Proficiency.

ROSE began with the development and pilot testing of five subjects in 1990/1991. R&T was one of the five. Five years later the process was repeated with Guidance and Counselling and the Arts, and was repeated several other times until the eleven subjects that comprised the common curriculum were developed. Thus, the phases of development, dissemination, adoption and implementation overlapped.

There is a particular element in the change model for CSEC and ROSE which is not emphasized in the RD&D or the authority-innovation decision-making model of Rogers and Shoemaker (1971), namely, *deliberation*. This is an element of Walker's (1971) Naturalistic Model of curriculum development. Deliberation is a process involving debate, discussion, thinking, using arguments to justify taking a particular decision, weighing alternatives, considering the consequences of a particular choice and so on. In the fourteen years which elapsed between the decision to develop its own examination system (1958) and the establishment of CXC (1972) (see table 2.2), the governments of the CC engaged in deliberation of this nature. Walker (1971) refers to the importance of data in informing the processes of deliberation. The GOJ, through its Ministry of Education, had a wealth of data from research studies to deliberate on in the seven years before ROSE came on stream. One would expect deliberation to be central to the problem-solving model, but it was not evident in the Sixth Form Geography Project. While the strategy of reinforcing literacy skills across the curriculum was informed by a wealth of research conducted by the director of NCERD himself (see Allsopp and Jennings 2014), there was an absence of research on the existing situation in schools, particularly in the remote rural and hinterland areas of Guyana. The limitations of research, however, did not exclude deliberations on the existing educational situation. Craig (2006/07, 10), for example, describes the impact of political and economic forces on education in Guyana and explains the limitations of resources that engulfed NCERD's Skills Reinforcement Guides as being rooted in "a failed socialist-society experiment, and suffering from the resultant brain drain".

ROSE is an example of "authority-innovation decision" defined by Rogers and Shoemaker (1971, 301) as those decisions "forced upon an individual by someone in a superordinate power position". In the case of CC countries with centralized education systems, it would be Ministries of Education that issue mandates to schools. CXC came about as a result of a collective decision because it required the greatest number of the CC countries to participate. Rogers and Shoemaker (1971, 271) acknowledge the "relative slowness of collective decisions". At the level of the individual participating countries, the adoption of CSEC was an authority-innovation decision which took much less time. NCERD's Skills Reinforcement Guides is also an authority-innovation decision given that NCERD is a unit in the Ministry of Education with a mandate to implement the appropriate goals of the Ministry.

The problem-solving model of the Sixth Form Geography Project provides a contrast to the other three "top-down" models. The "A"-level geography teachers were active participants in that they had voiced a need for materials relevant to the Jamaican context to Morrissey in his capacity of a university lecturer who had been training these teachers for many years. However, it was not the teachers themselves who searched for a solution to their problem. Rather it was the change agent (Morrissey) who did the research and came up with a proposal to solve the problem. Apart from offering an example of what he proposed, Morrissey left the teachers to use their own initiative and collaborate with each other to solve their problem. If the teachers succeeded in developing good "A"-level geography materials, these could be disseminated to all secondary schools that taught the subject.

Conclusion

"Top-Down" Models Vary

What is clear from this chapter is that there is much variation in "top-down" models/approaches to change, often referred to as "power-coercive" and "centre-periphery". CSEC was a collective authority-innovation decision model. According to Rogers and Shoemaker (1971), authority decisions are forced upon those in a subordinate position by those in a superordinate position. Individual CC countries were not forced to participate in CSEC. Rather in the process of deliberation, they were persuaded of the advantages of CSEC over the GCE "O" level (relative advantage), of the idea being consistent with the drive to be independent of the former colonial power (compatibility) and of its ease of use (non-complexity), given that assessment would be done in the region. If the superordinates can persuade the subordinates of the relative advantage, compatibility and non-complexity of the innovation, among others, the subordinates are more likely to adopt the innovation (Rogers and Shoemaker 1971). In the same vein, "force" is hardly the term to use in the case of ROSE because the Ministry of Education required the schools to meet certain conditions before they could participate in ROSE. This gave the schools the element of choice. Most of the prestigious high schools simply chose not to participate. Furthermore, the conditions that the schools had to satisfy put pressure on already disadvantaged schools to provide resources they needed for the programme. Many of the schools that did participate were unable to provide resources that were sufficiently adequate.

NCERD's case was not a straightforward "top-down" model because mandates from the Ministry of Education to schools needed the blessing of the regional executive officer (REXO) who controlled resources in the region. The REXO's priority on education was not guaranteed. To the regional education officers, the REXOs were a more immediate "superordinate" to be reckoned with than the Ministry of Education, because for many the distance they had to travel to reach Georgetown where the Ministry is located was more than a flight between two islands in the Caribbean.

The Danger of Lack of Cognizance of the Cultural Context

The Sixth Form Geography Project did not prove to be a good example of the problem-solving approach which "attempts to base itself firmly on the practitioner's needs, but it does not take the view that these can be met without substantial support from the centre" (Becher and Maclure 1978, p74). While the "A"-level geography teachers had the support of a change agent, they did not have the support from the centre (i.e. Ministry of Education). They expected support in the form of some incentive for taking on what they perceived as additional work or at least some release time to work on the project. The Ministry of Education offered none. Perhaps Morrissey could have been a stronger advocate in this regard, as House (1979) argues that advocacy is essential for securing resources and providing social rewards. However, putting the teachers at the centre of curriculum change was an innovative feature of the Sixth Form Geography Project at a time when the practice was to develop curricula that were "teacher proof". This, however, was done with insufficient thought to the cultural context. The geography teachers' lack of confidence in their skills in curriculum development, the absence of incentives, heavy timetables and the pressure of their own domestic commitments combined to result in the project producing only a brief outline of a unit for comment from one of the consortia (Morrissey 1981). The bottom line is that the teachers did not see themselves as curriculum developers. It is hardly surprising, therefore, that the attempt of the Sixth Form Geography Project to transfer wholesale from a developed to a developing country, a curriculum change model which assumed the capability of teachers to develop their own curricular materials, should encounter difficulties in a context where the policy has been traditionally to view teachers as implementers.

Change Takes Time

We live in an era of rapidly advancing technology where everything is expected to move and happen "fast": fast food, transactions online "with a click" and change also is expected to happen fast. The examples of curriculum change examined in this chapter have shown the opposite to be the case because of the time taken for the various phases involved. It took some ten years of *deliberation* on how the secondary system in Jamaica should be reformed before ROSE took shape and it was some twenty-six years after the initiation of the idea that the CXC came into being and planning for the CSEC could begin. Deliberations are informed by *research* which takes time. ROSE, for example, was informed by nine studies commissioned by the Ministry of Education and Culture in Jamaica. Curriculum materials have to be *piloted*, a phase which involves monitoring, evaluation and use of feedback to inform revisions. The attention given to piloting of the innovations was variable. The NCERD Skills Reinforcement Guides, for example, were implemented system wide without piloting. The *training* of teachers takes time – at least it should as they are key to the implementation of the curriculum. For the NCERD Skills Reinforcement Guides the teachers were not trained, but the principals were, on the assumption that they in turn would train the teachers. The cascade *approach* used in training does not allow enough time for teachers or principals to fully grasp the strategies for implementing the innovation. But more on implementation in the next chapter.

3.

Implementing Curriculum Change at the Secondary Level

What Measure of Success?

Purpose

Having described the models used in introducing change into our schools' systems in the previous chapter, in this chapter we examine how the curriculum innovations (the CSEC, the ROSE (R&T), the Sixth Form Geography Project and the NCERD Skills Reinforcement Guides were implemented and with what outcomes. The chapter continues with an explanation of the meaning of implementation and its link to determining the success of an innovation. This is followed by a discussion of factors that affect implementation which precedes a comparison of the presence of these factors in the innovations. The chapter ends with an accounting for success/failure in the innovations discussed.

Meaning of Implementation

"Implementation is a highly complex process involving relationships between users and managers, and among various groups of users, in a process characterized by inevitable conflict and by anticipated and unanticipated problems", write Fullan and Pomfret (1977, 290). According to Fullan and Stiegelbauer (1991, 65) implementation is "the process of putting into practice an idea, program or set of activities and structures new to the people attempting or expected to change". They identify a number of factors that affect implementation which fall into four categories: (1) *characteristics of the change* such as need for the change and complexity of the change, (2) *characteristics at the local level* such as expectations and training of the principal, technical assistance for teachers, (3) *characteristics at the school level* such as the principal's actions and (4) *factors external to the school system* such as the role of government and funding agencies. Rogers (2003) further develops on the first characteristic when he underscores the importance of perception in explaining human behaviour; more specifically "the individuals' perceptions of the attributes of an innovation, not the attributes as classified objectively by experts or change agents" (Rogers 2003, 223). This points to the fact that the problem of innovation or change is not just a matter of providing information about the desired change, it is most importantly a matter of changing people's perceptions (and knowledge is perception as it is often said), attitudes and values as well as their skills. This is central to normative-reeducative strategies for bringing about change which assume that change starts with individuals and their attitudes (Bennis, Benne and Chin 1969).

The factors that affect implementation identified by Fullan and Stiegelbauer (1991) point to areas that need to be given attention if the implementation of the innovation is to be effective. These factors are characteristics of the change, local characteristics and external factors. These have been modified and expanded in table 3.1 to make it more relevant to the Caribbean context. Fullan and Stiegelbauer contend that these factors form a system of variables that interact over time to determine success or failure: the more factors that support implementation, the more likely that change in practice will occur. The more factors work against implementation, the more remote the chances of success. In other words, effective implementation of an innovation will likely lead to its success.

Measuring Success

But how is success determined? Cuban (1998) warns that judging the success or failure of an innovation is no easy task because it all depends on who is doing the judging and what criteria are being used. He identifies three criteria or standards most widely used by policymakers (effectiveness, fidelity and popularity) and two which are used by practitioners (adaptability and longevity). The *effectiveness* standard is essentially concerned with the extent to which intended goals have been achieved, as determined by students' test scores and performance at external examinations. *Popular* innovations are those that are "fashionable" and that disseminate rapidly, aided by the media. Examples are desktop computers and laptops, special education and things which "easily translate into political support for top policy makers endorsing the reform" (Cuban 1998, 457). The *fidelity* standard is determined by the extent to which the implementation of the reform remains faithful to what the policymakers originally intended. In contrast, those who are mandated to implement the innovation, primarily teachers and principals, invariably adapt it to suit their particular situation. Thus, the more *adaptable* the innovation, the more implementers find it compatible with their needs and fitting well with their situation.

Table 3.1. Factors Affecting Implementation of Innovations

	CSEC (14 CC Countries)	ROSE 1 (R&T) (Jamaica)	NCERD SRG (Guyana)	Sixth Form Geography (Jamaica)
Characteristics of the innovation				
Perceived by users as relevant to needs	#	Y	X	Y
Goals are clear to users and means of implementation made explicit	#	Y	#	X
Perceived by users as not difficult to understand and use	#	X	X	X
Materials are of good quality and fit well with teaching situation	Y	X	X	N/A
Characteristics at school level				
Change strategy involves participation by teachers and principals	Y	Y	#	#
Principals are supportive	Y	Y	Y	X
Staff appropriately trained	Y	Y	#	X
Community is involved and supportive	#	#	#	N/A
Adequate resources (human, physical, material)	Y	X	X	X
Characteristics at national level				
Support of the government	Y	Y	Y	N/A
Realistic time for materials development	Y	Y	X	Y
Provision for evaluation and monitoring of change process	#	Y	#	X
Adequate supply of staff to support innovation	#	X	X	X
External factors				
Realistic time frame for funding by donor agencies	Y	Y	N/A	N/A
Provision of international technical assistance	Y	Y	N/A	Y

Key: Y = yes/present; # Present to some extent; X = no/absent and N/A = not applicable.

Durability or longevity is the final criterion for judging an innovation's success. Cuban (1998, 167) identifies *longevity* as the single most commonly used indicator of the success of a change effort and adds that this is "not a mere year or two, or a decade, but a quarter or half century of survival".

How effectively implemented were the four innovations being studied? The next section will attempt to answer this question.

Characteristics of the Innovations

Need and Relevance

The users' perception of whether the innovation satisfies a need is more important than that of the initiator of the idea (Rogers and Shoemaker 1971). Differences arise in how the users and initiators perceive the innovation because they have competing needs. Post-independence beginning in the 1960s it was particularly important for countries in the Anglophone Caribbean to achieve intellectual independence from their former colonial masters. This argument was used by governments to justify the need for the CSEC to people in the individual territories. What was more important to the students and their parents, however, was the response of employers and foreign universities to the CSEC. Being more accustomed to the GCE qualifications, in the early years employers, local colleges and universities were reluctant to accept the CSEC, especially below grade 11 at the General Proficiency level. It took many years before foreign universities recognized the CSEC. Understandably, parents were anxious about the effect that the CSEC would have on the prospects for their children's tertiary education. More than four decades since the first sittings of CSEC, we hardly remember these early concerns about the examination.

The national coordinator of ROSE emphasized that ROSE was "specially designed to be used in *all* institutions with students in grades 7-9" (Davis 1994, 10). By 1993 ROSE was in thirty-four schools, twelve of which were new secondary schools, thirteen all age schools and nine traditional high schools (Davis 1994). The all age schools were renamed junior high schools and the new secondary schools were renamed comprehensive high schools (these schools have since become known as upgraded high schools). This reclassification was done to erode the differences between the other school types and the prestigious traditional high schools. The intake for these schools was largely from the upper and middle classes in the society while the intake into the other school types was largely from the lower-social class. Evans (1997) found a positive response to the need for the ROSE programme on the part of teachers in the junior high and comprehensive high schools. It was the first time that these schools were given curriculum guides, textbooks and other materials and they also received supervision from officers in the Ministry of Education. The traditional high schools had a negative attitude towards R&T. Table 3.2 shows that teachers in the other school types perceived R&T as essential for developing skills needed in a technological society but as not being the sole source for the development of skills in critical thinking and problem-solving (Jennings 2012). Teachers in the traditional high schools felt that they had little to gain from the introduction of ROSE and questioned the value of a common curriculum for all types of secondary schools. According to Evans (1997, 10), "they believed that their social status and prestige as a grammar school were eroded when a common curriculum made them appear to be equal to the all age and new secondary schools, attended by students of a different social class."

The teachers of "A"-level geography saw the need for materials that were relevant to the Jamaican context (Morrissey 1984), but they perceived having to work in groups to develop their own materials as incompatible with their role as teachers. Neither working in groups nor developing their own materials were things they had to do normally as part of their professional duties.

While the leadership at NCERD and the staff saw the need for the Skills Reinforcement Guides, the users gave priority to other needs. The introduction of the first workshop "was immediately greeted by a most unexpected series of negative statements and protests" (Craig 2006/07, 18) from the head teachers[1] present. They argued that it was unreasonable of the Ministry of Education to expect them to ask teachers to use new techniques to improve their teaching, given the dilapidated buildings, poorly furnished and uncomfortable conditions in the classrooms. There were no books in the schools and teachers who were poorly paid and frustrated had to contend with the lack of such basic materials as paper and chalk. Furthermore, the head teachers argued, the economic problems of members of their communities contributed to the poor attendance of their children as well as poor attitudes in school (Craig 2006/07). To the head teachers these problems needed to be fixed before any new ideas could be introduced into their schools. The head teachers, however, were persuaded to use the Skills Reinforcement Guides within the constraints of their environment since no funds were available to address their resource deficiencies.

Clarity and Complexity

Clarity and complexity are related. Complexity refers to "the difficulty and extent of change required of the individuals responsible for implementation" (Fullan and Stiegelbauer 1991, 71). Morrissey (1981) discovered that one of the reasons why the teachers in the Sixth Form Geography Project failed to produce a single unit for teaching "A"-level geography was their lack of

Table 3.2. Teachers' Perceptions of the Characteristics of R&T

Characteristics		Teachers (N = 85)		
		A	U	D
Need and relevance	R&T is essential for developing the skills needed in a technological society	82.4	9.3	8.3
	Without R&T our children will not become critical thinkers and problem-solvers	14.1	22.0	63.5
Clarity of goals and means	The distinction between the elements in R&T and what each involves is not clear	64.7	12.9	22.3
	The teachers know how to use themes to link the elements of R&T	70.6	15.3	14.1
Complexity	It is difficult to infuse career education into R&T	69.4	18.8	11.9
	Most teachers are only equipped to teach one of the elements of R&T	76.5	9.4	14.1
Quality and practicality	It is impractical for teachers to use R&T workbooks with children who can barely read	37.1	18.0	54.1
	Students need relevant and appropriate texts for R&T	96.4	2.4	1.2
Observability	Students still expect to be told what to do rather than work things out for themselves	20.0	12.9	67.1
	R&T has not provided a satisfactory base for tech-voc subjects for CSEC	27.0	24.7	48.3

Source: Extracted from Jennings (2012).
Key: A = agreed; U = undecided; D = disagree.

confidence in their skills in curriculum development. In fact, none of them had training in this area and did not know where to start. In using the NCERD Skills Reinforcement Guides, the teachers were unclear about the difference between "integration" and "reinforcement". Some felt that reinforcing language skills in mathematics classes was the same as integrating the subjects (Ganesh 1992). The head teachers who attended the workshops should have been able to explain the difference to the teachers. However, some head teachers did little else than give the teachers the guides with instructions to prepare their schemes of work from them (Craig 2006/07).

The issue of lack of clarity arose in relation to the Basic Proficiency (BP) scheme of the CSEC. The General Proficiency scheme came to be regarded as "the gold standard of secondary school achievement in the region" (Griffith 2015, 14). It targeted students who planned to do further studies in the subject while the BP catered to the needs of students who were unlikely to pursue further studies in areas related to the subject. The CXC explained that the BP made "different cognitive demands on candidates than those made by the general proficiency" (Griffith 2015, 14). However, students who sat the BP complained of its difficulty and stakeholders questioned the difference in cognitive demand between the two schemes. Furthermore, employers showed a distinct preference for students who achieved in the General Proficiency. Stakeholders clearly felt that CSEC was being examined at different levels given that after five years of secondary education, not all students could be expected to achieve at the same level. The CXC, however, "avoided making any statement about the examinations being at different levels" (Griffith 2015, 15). Craig (1998, 61) urged that the "CXC must set its house in order where the Basic Proficiency level is concerned. For many years now, educators and the business community have been complaining about the dysfunctional nature of this level." The consequence of this lack of clarity was a gradual decline in the number of students taking the BP to the point where it was discontinued.[2]

An area of difficulty in the CSEC is school-based assessment (SBA) which is regarded as the "flagship innovation by CXC in the examinations system of the Caribbean" (Griffith 2015, 42). SBA enables a part of the curriculum to be individualized and the mark given by the teacher contributes about 20 per cent to the overall marks for the examination in most CSEC subjects that have this component. Griffith argues that stakeholder concerns about SBA "is largely due to the lack of full understanding . . . about the nature of this form of assessment" (Griffith 2015, 42). For SBA to be fully effective, teachers should do a diagnostic assessment of the students' prerequisite knowledge and skills for engaging in the school-based assessment task. They should also specify students' learning outcomes, monitor and continually assess each student's performance as he or she engages in the required tasks and plan carefully to ensure that students have the materials, or supplies needed for the tasks. Teachers will only be able to do these things if they are given manageable numbers of students to supervise. The reality, however, is that teachers have large class sizes which make it difficult for them to give the individualized attention that school-based assessment requires. Organizing the students to work in groups is a strategy that teachers use to help them cope with large classes, but high-performing students are reluctant to participate in group work for fear that it will affect their grades negatively (Griffith 2015).

There is also the problem of the same grade being assigned to each member, despite disproportionate contribution of members of the group to the task. Furthermore, some teachers do too much for the students as they carry out the tasks while others offer little guidance and see themselves more as an assessor. To address these issues Griffith (2015) recommends, first, the need for class sizes to be reduced or teachers be given class assistants. Second, he suggests that Ministries of Education should provide teachers training in SBA so that they learn to clearly demarcate their role as a guide to the student and that of an assessor of the student's achievement. Despite these recommendations the problems with SBA have persisted for nearly four decades, as is evident in the case of the CSEC English syllabus. The SBA component was added to this syllabus in 2015 and the first candidates were assessed on the revised format of the English examination in May–June 2018. In an investigation into the level of preparedness of teachers of English in Jamaican secondary schools and the challenges they face, Williams-McBean (2018) found that teachers felt that they were not prepared enough for the SBA and given insufficient guidelines.

Apart from the SBA teachers in the traditional high schools in Jamaica also took issue with group work. They questioned the value of group methods, cooperative learning and the enquiry approach fostered by ROSE. Given that they were more accustomed to the didactic teacher-centred approach to teaching, the use of such methods, they felt, made the students' acquisition of content uncertain. They also thought that these methods were not compatible with their perception of themselves as subject-matter specialists. It is rather surprising that teachers in these prestigious schools which are valued for their quality education should consider that they needed to transmit knowledge to their students when teachers in the other school types were of the view that their students did not want to be told what to do but wanted to find things out for themselves (see table 3.2).

In the case of R&T, the teachers felt that the distinction between the elements of R&T was not clear. This is most likely because schools were not able to offer all of the elements due to resource constraints. While the teachers felt that they knew how to use themes to integrate the elements (see table 3.2), they had difficulty in doing so as their principals did not give them time in school to get together and do the necessary planning (Jennings 2012). The teachers also had difficulty in infusing career education into R&T. A more general concern about the ROSE curriculum was the lack of alignment with the CXC syllabuses. In fact, this is evident in the item – "R&T has not provided a satisfactory base for tech-voc subjects for CSEC" (see table 3.2). The World Bank (2001) exhorted the need for this alignment to be addressed in ROSE 11.[3]

Quality and Practicality

Doyle and Ponder (1977/78) refer to the "practicality ethic" of teachers, underscoring the fact that teachers evaluate the numerous messages they receive about modifying their performance and select those that are seen as "practical" to incorporate into their plans. Consequently, innovations that involve use of curriculum materials should not only ensure that such materials are practical in the sense that they fit well with the teacher's situation but need also to ensure the materials are of good quality and available. CXC produced syllabuses for the subject teachers which did not require them to change their accustomed practices in any significant way. If they followed the syllabuses, they were confident of being on the right track for the students to be successful in the CSEC. The CSEC is the de facto standard at the secondary level and many traditional schools in the region align the content of their grades 7–9 curricula with the content of the CXC syllabuses (Jennings 2001).

Given the limited financial resources of NCERD the curriculum guides for Skills Reinforcement were cyclostyled and did not benefit from any assistance from the Materials Production Unit as the latter, though a part of NCERD serviced the entire Ministry of Education and other public-sector agencies. The guides were not pilot tested, and the quality of the guides developed is summed up thus:

> The guides, being rapidly developed . . . and without the benefit of much central editing, were not expected to have any permanency at this stage (hence the cheapness of their production) but were expected to become corrected and perfected in the process of being used (Craig 2006/07, 14).

NCERD was only able to provide each school with one copy of each curriculum guide, on the understanding that the school would reproduce copies as necessary for the teachers. This was wishful thinking, because most schools had neither the funds nor the equipment and materials to reproduce the copies. When the NCERD team made its annual visit to the schools in the regions, in many instances it was observed that the single curriculum guides were safely locked away in the head teacher's cupboard, as new as the day they were distributed.

In the case of the Sixth Form Geography Project, Morrissey (1981) developed two units for "A"-level geography as exemplars for the teachers. These units were welcomed enthusiastically by the teachers, and they used them with their students. Based on their feedback, Morrissey was able to modify the units accordingly. The teachers, however, did not produce a single unit in their consortia. They cited domestic commitments, having to do extra work after school to supplement their income, heavy timetables, and staff shortages in their schools as reasons for them not taking on the role of curriculum developers.

It is evident from table 3.2 that there were quality issues related to the literacy levels of the workbooks used in R&T. An explanation for this lies in the multi-level nature of the ROSE programme. Four groups of students were identified, and materials were to be written at the appropriate levels which were based on differences in reading level: namely, *foundation 1* for students reading at least five grades below grade level, *foundation 2* for those reading at least two grades below grade level, *normative* for those students reading at grade level or one grade below and *enrichment* for students reading at or above grade level (Ministry of Education and Culture 1993). The Secondary Schools Textbooks Project described as "the direct publishing arm of the ROSE programme" (Rickards 1995, 3) published reading materials particularly for foundations *1 and 2* students which integrated the use of the Jamaican Creole (Cousins 1995). These books were favourably assessed by the students (Reform of Secondary Education Secretariat 1995). The R&T workbooks were not written at the appropriate level for students who were at the foundation levels. In fact, no books were provided for R&T in the Secondary School Textbook Project. However, there was a deeper problem that led to much confusion – the identification of ability with reading level. The fact that a decade into the new millennium the Ministry of Education was still grappling with this problem is evident in the fact that the Alternative Secondary Transitional Education Programme (ASTEP) was designed to address the problem of children unable to read or reading well below their grade level and accessing secondary school (see chapter 4).

Characteristics at the School Level

Participation/Principal Support

That the change strategy involved participation by teachers and principals is one of the characteristics at the school level that impact implementation identified by Fullan and Stiegelbauer (1991). They argue that "within the school, collegiality among teachers, as measured by the frequency of communication, mutual support, help, etc., was a strong indicator of implementation success" (Fullan and Stiegelbauer 1991, 131). To some extent teacher participation was facilitated by CXC through the use of subject panels. These consist of six members of the education systems of the participating countries, three of whom must be practising teachers of the subject at the level of the examination. These panels develop syllabuses, recommend methods of teaching, receive criticisms and suggestions from teachers and consider examiners' reports. Teachers are also involved in the marking of CSEC papers and in so far as the same teachers meet each year to do table marking in their subject specialization, their relationship is characterized by collegiality and mutual support. That participation is ongoing is evident in the description of the first January sitting of English Literature in 2011 as "in part, the result of an exciting process of teacher involvement in the Council's active, sensitive and professional response to the often-conflicting calls by stakeholders for change" (Stephens and Jones (2011, 54)).

Whereas NCERD focused on the head teacher–as the agent of change, the Sixth Form Geography Project centred on teachers who were expected to develop their own materials for use in their "A"-level geography classes. However, collegiality, mutual support, frequency of communication among them and so on never developed despite Morrissey's attempt to encourage the teachers to share their ideas and experiences in a newsletter on the project that he managed.

A notable feature of the ROSE programme is that the Ministry of Education did not mandate that all schools should be involved from the start, but instead planned a phased inclusion. Schools were allowed to participate if they met certain criteria. The principal of the school first had to ensure that the necessary buildings, equipment and supplies were in place; that the teachers were trained to deliver the curriculum; and the support of members of the community or private sector had been harnessed to enable the criteria to be met. It appears that principals satisfied these criteria at a faster rate than expected because the 124 schools identified to be included after 5 years had in fact been included by the beginning of the fourth year (Raymond 2006).

Training of Staff

The nurturing of collegiality, mutual support and so on among teachers is difficult to achieve on account of the model used by Ministries of Education to train for implementing change. The minister of education and culture in Jamaica acknowledged that all the training needed for the ROSE programme could not be carried out entirely by curriculum officers and so "we plan to train a large number of trainers to spread the new curriculum into the participating schools and to monitor its implementation" (Whiteman 1992, 3). This is reference to the use of the cascade model. This model is multi-tiered in that it first involves experts training trainers over a period that can range from a few days to a week or more. These trainers are recognized as exceptional teachers whose task is then to train the teachers in their own and neighbouring schools in the new ideas and practices of the innovation. This model has the advantage of producing, within a short period of time, a large number of trained teachers which aid agencies find impressive. However, the limited period of training results in trainers in many instances being ineffective because of their failure to adequately grasp the knowledge and skills from the training. What they then transmit to the teachers they train may well be distorted information (Dadds 2014). The cascade model fails to address teachers' identified learning needs (Nyarigoti 2013).

A forward-looking feature of the ROSE programme is that it attached as much importance to the training of administrators and the involvement of the community as to the training of teachers. Residential workshops were held with principals, vice principals, heads of department, grade supervisors and persons who chaired the school boards to help them understand their roles in the effective implementation of ROSE. Training workshops were also held with the education officers who had responsibility for supervising the participating schools.

NCERD trained the head teachers to be the trainers. While some trained their own teachers, others simply handed the guides to the teachers and left them to figure things out for themselves (Craig 2006/07).

The CXC was able to secure funding for four years (1979–83) from the USAID for the SCDP Project. This project involved fourteen countries and used the cascade approach to provide training to teachers in the various techniques of assessment related to the CXC syllabi and examination. Regional workshops were held in Barbados and Jamaica and conducted by specialists employed by CXC. These workshops were attended by teacher representatives from the participating countries. These representatives were then expected to demonstrate new techniques learned and disseminate other new ideas to teachers in their respective countries. Griffith (1981) reports that sixteen workshops were organized by individual countries but could only point to data which gave "very strong indication that the classroom practices of teachers who participated in CXC/USAID workshops have undergone changes" (Griffith 1981, 328). What about the hundreds of teachers who were not able to attend these workshops? Their training depended on initiatives undertaken by the local coordinators in the participating countries.

The Sixth Form Geography Project did not use the cascade model. In fact, it offered no training at all, based on the assumption that teachers of "A"-level geography must already have the necessary training to undertake the task of writing materials for teaching in their own classes.

Community Support

Fullan and Stiegelbauer (1991, 143) make the point that "too often we think of the need for change only in terms of the teacher. If there is any changing to be done, everyone is implicated and must face it in relation to his or her own role". Hall and Hord (2006, 11) argue that despite the efforts of teachers "if administrators do not engage in ongoing active support, it is more than likely that the change effort will die". Hall and Hord (2006, 23) also include "parents and community members as partners and allies" as integral to providing a caring and productive environment which is conducive to change. These ideas were clearly acknowledged by those who conceptualized the change process for the ROSE programme. Brown and Jones (1994) describe meetings held with parents and guardians and members of the communities in which the schools participating in ROSE were located to solicit their support for the reform. The communities are described as "receptive" and optimistic that the reform would give all students the same chance of receiving a good quality education. Brown and Jones (1994, 5) report that the parents were at first sceptical that the reform would improve the education of their children, "but most welcomed the changes". Principals of participating schools were very supportive as is evident in several articles in the ROSEGRAM. A typical example is that of the principal who attended most of the workshops and "took time to fully understand the methodologies of the programme, so that he was able not only to implement them, but to assist his teachers with the implementation" (Reform of Secondary Education Secretariat 1995, 3).

The CXC also recognized the importance of wider community support and used various strategies not only to spread knowledge about the CSEC but also to change deep seated attitudes held by its users. For example, a public relations team toured the participating countries in 1978 to "sell" the CSEC in an effort to dispel fears about its parity with the GCE "O" level it had replaced and its international acceptability.

NCERD's challenge in gaining the support of the community was that much greater because of the vast terrain it had to cover. Guyana is divided into ten regions, each with its own regional education officer (REDO) and a REXO, who is the political representative of the area. The usual protocol for NCERD was to commence the visit to a region with a courtesy call on the REXO. This was essential because the head teachers' concern referred to earlier about "the economic problems of members of their communities (which) contributed to the poor attendance of their children" could not be addressed without the support of the REXO. He controlled the budget allotted by the government for the region. NCERD had to win over the support of the REDOs because they controlled access to the schools. Each REDO had to prepare an annual work programme for the region for submission to the Ministry of Education. The REDOs requested the NCERD work programme in advance of the preparation of theirs, so that they could use the proposed NCERD activities as a base. Thus, according to Craig (2006/07, 24), "The NCERD annual work programme, in respect of addressing critical problems of curriculum implementation, thus assumed the role of a focusing and coordinating mechanism."

Resources

NCERD's decision to train the head teachers to implement the Skills Reinforcement Guides was influenced not only by a desire to ensure that the guides were actually used in the schools, but it was also in recognition of the fact that "administrators have to secure the necessary infrastructure changes and long-term resource supports if use of an innovation is to continue indefinitely" (Hall and Hord (2006, 11)). The support of the REXO was needed to provide some of the "long-term resource supports". The NCERD's programme was funded initially on a "shoestring budget" from the Ministry of Education's allocation from the budget to NCERD and such funds as each of the ten regions was able to contribute from their budgets. The programme was planned as a "low-cost preliminary" (Craig 2006/07, 21) that would prepare the groundwork for the Primary Education Improvement Programme (PEIP) funded by the Inter-American Development Bank (IDB) which was scheduled to begin in 1990. One of the aims of PEIP was the production of primary level textbooks in language arts, mathematics, science and social studies. PEIP did not get off the ground in 1990 and the textbooks did not appear for another six years. However, this was to NCERD's benefit because its programme received some of the funds allotted for PEIP.

The Sixth Form Geography Project was not funded. The Ministry of Education, Jamaica, encouraged Morrissey to go ahead with the project but on his own initiative. Morrissey was advised that the Ministry of Education could not provide the teachers any release from their duties to work on the project (Morrissey 1981). The ROSE programme was funded by the World Bank, but these funds only covered the development of the curriculum and teachers' guides and the ROSE secretariat. The schools were responsible for providing all necessary equipment, adequate furniture and space to accommodate the necessary facilities. They were expected to solicit cash and pledges from their communities and the private sector (Raymond 2006). Much cash and pledges did not materialize with the result that "the curriculum could not be effectively delivered in all types of school because the infrastructural work and material and equipment had not been provided" (Raymond 2006, 159). For example, the schools did not have the resources to offer all five elements of R&T. Jennings (2012) found that the greatest challenges faced by principals in implementing R&T was providing the resources, materials and equipment needed for the delivery of the subject. Finding teachers for R&T was also problematic because teachers were trained in subject specialization and not for teaching an integrated vocational subject.

As mentioned earlier, CXC has put much emphasis on the training of teachers but at the same time expects individual territories to organize training to help their teachers implement innovative ideas. The Curriculum Development Unit of the Ministry of Education in Trinidad and Tobago, for example, produced a handbook on school-based assessment in physics, using the expertise of its graduate teachers in the school system. For many years after the inception of CSEC, in some countries (e.g. Dominica and St Lucia) teachers of CSEC subjects had only GCE advanced level qualification themselves. The situation has changed over time with the setting up of the Open Campus of the UWI which has provided the Caribbean with a range of degree programmes online. CXC has also harnessed the use of technology to make available a range of resources and materials on its website to teachers and students.

Characteristics at the National Level

Government Support

The CSEC could not have been introduced had the support of most of the English-speaking Caribbean countries not been obtained, and this includes that of Jamaica which has the largest population. Ministries of Education in individual countries determined the date when the schools would cease teaching for the GCE "O" level and prepare for the CSEC instead. The teachers simply had to comply. ROSE received government support, but this was at a time when the state's role in relation to education had changed. "No longer is the Government being seen solely as a benefactor. . . . The Ministry is now strengthening its role as a facilitator, formulating, and publicizing the policy and getting the outside community (corporate and school) more involved in identifying and satisfying the needs of educational institutions" (Reform of Secondary Education Secretariat (1995, 4)). In other words, schools and the community had to assume some responsibility for the outcomes of ROSE.

Neither the Sixth Form Geography Project nor the NCERD Skills Reinforcement Guides received government support, but for different reasons. In the case of the former, the need for government support is not assumed in a periphery to centre change strategy. NCERD appears to have incurred some measure of hostility from the Ministry of Education. Craig (2006/07) notes that the cooperation developed between NCERD, the REXOs, REDOs and field officers of the Ministry of Education should have been encouraged. Instead, field officers "started to feel obliquely threatened by the Ministry's response. . . . Some officers were pointedly asked by top level administrators in the Ministry whether they worked for the Ministry of Education or for NCERD" (Craig 2006/07, 25). This kind of insistence of Central Ministry officials on the supremacy of their control is not unexpected in the personalized contexts of small states (Bray and Packer 1993).

Lead Time for Materials Development and Provision for Monitoring and Evaluation

It takes time to develop materials which are of good quality and practical. During the development process, draft materials are field-tested and evaluated, and revisions or modifications are made based on feedback from the evaluation before they are finally produced for system-wide dissemination. This process was applied in the ROSE programme. Consultants, many of whom were from the UWI, were hired to develop curricula in subject areas. Davis (1994) reported that the pilot testing of five subjects commenced in four all age schools in September 1991 and an additional seven schools joined one year later. The Programme Monitoring Unit in the Ministry of Education monitored the use of the curricula in the schools and provided feedback to the curriculum developers. Fraser (1997) reported that evaluators from the Caribbean Applied Technology Centre and other educators met to review the evaluators' findings on the ROSE curriculum. The JBTE (1994, 4) reporting on curriculum revision between July 1995 and March 1996 noted that feedback on R&T indicated that "further work is necessary as there are serious concerns about this subject".

One year was allotted to the consortia of teachers to develop "A"-level geography units for the Sixth Form Geography Project while CXC allots two years for the development of subject syllabuses. Subject Panels receive comments and criticisms of syllabuses on the basis of which amendments are made. While CXC and the Ministry of Education, Jamaica, had to rely on teachers and consultants with full-time positions elsewhere to develop syllabuses for CSEC and curricula for the ROSE programme, the developers of the Skills Reinforcement Guides were employed full time to NCERD. The members of the Curriculum Development Unit, therefore, were able to develop the materials in six months (October 1988–March 1999) (Craig 2006/07, 13). NCERD had neither the time nor the resources to field test the materials. However, a system was put in place for NCERD to receive feedback from the schools on the use of the guides. The head teacher at each school was required to complete a form that reported on any problems encountered in implementing the guides and the number of in-school training sessions held during the term (Craig 2006/07).

Staff to Support Innovation

The "A"-level geography teachers bemoaned the fact that they could not be given time off to develop their units for the Sixth Form Geography Project, because there was no replacement in their schools to take their classes in their absence (Morrissey 1981).

Lack of staff to teach certain subjects has resulted in reduced numbers of candidates in CSEC subjects such as physics, geography, French and Spanish.

From a study of teacher education in eight CC countries, Jennings (2001) found that Spanish, for example, was treated as a "third–class" subject in the schools and given reduced time on the timetable if extra time was needed for high-status subjects like the sciences. Preparation of students to do CSEC Spanish ideally should be done by teachers with a postgraduate diploma in education specializing in Spanish. In the case of Guyana, Jennings (2001) noted that over a period of more than a decade no candidate with a degree in foreign languages sought admission to the postgraduate diploma in education programme at the University of Guyana. The experience of the same programme at the UWI in Jamaica was similar.

The Ministry of Education, Jamaica, ensured that teachers were adequately trained to teach in the ROSE programme. The JBTE, which had overall responsibility for training teachers for ROSE, ensured that each teacher training college had designated ROSE teacher trainers. However, two main problems were experienced with staff to support the sustainability of ROSE. First, because the colleges focused on training in separate subjects, training for R&T proved problematic due to its integrated nature. As a result, most schools were only able to offer two or three areas as they were unable to find staff (and other resources) to teach all five areas that made up the subject. Second, all was well for ROSE while funds were available (1993–98). After 1998, the ROSE secretariat closed and the employment of all the staff associated with it, including the national coordinator of ROSE, ended. Raymond (2006), for example, noted that the University of Cambridge which gave details of students' performance on examinations by school type withdrew its services and the Programme Monitoring Unit in the Ministry of Education did no observations of the use of the ROSE curricula beyond the end of the project.

NCERD suffered a similar fate. On the expiry of his contract in 1991, the director of NCERD assumed another position and a new director took office. In 1992 the general elections brought a new government into power, and this resulted in changes in the Ministry of Education as well as the regions. New REXOs were appointed and there were also changes in the regional education offices. By 1992 most of the persons who had developed the Skills Reinforcement Guides had also left NCERD. The Skills Reinforcement idea lost advocacy as the new director of NCERD switched focus to cross-curriculum integration (Craig 2006/07).

External Factors

Provision of Adequate Funding

The Sixth Form Geography Project was not funded and NCERD's Skills Reinforcement Guides only received some funds for implementation on account of the late start of the IDB-funded PEIP (Craig 2006/07). CXC relies on the governments of the participating countries for financial support. Examination fees are an important source of funds, but CXC has been able to attract funds from donor agencies for special training or curriculum development projects. The SCDP Project, for example, was funded by the USAID. ROSE was largely funded by the World Bank and the GOJ provided some counterpart funding. The Secondary School Textbook Project was funded by DFID (World Bank 2001). The Netherlands government also provided a grant of almost three million American dollars (Griffith 1997).[4] The schools were also expected to provide any equipment furniture or materials they needed, by soliciting funds from the community and private sector as needed. The observation by Raymond (2006, 159) that "the curriculum could not be effectively delivered in all types of school because the infrastructural work and material and equipment had not been provided" suggests that the funding for the programme was inadequate.

Foreign Technical Assistance

Neither the NCERD Skills Reinforcement Guides nor the Sixth Form Geography Project benefited from foreign technical assistance, although Morrissey did make his services available to the teachers to assist them as needed. The CXC has sought the assistance of foreign expertise in the training of its staff, in testing, curriculum development, evaluation and measurement. In 1975, for example, the first examiners were trained by the Cambridge University Local Examinations syndicate, and CXC staff members and examiners were also trained by the Educational Testing Service in New Jersey.

The ROSE programme benefited considerably from foreign technical assistance in research that informed the project: for example, in the Reform of Secondary Education study conducted in 1989–90. The consultants for career education came from the United States and the R&T was conceptualized by consultants from the Isle of Wight Education Authority in the United Kingdom. The University of Cambridge Local Examinations Syndicate was contracted to assist in the development of the Junior High School Certificate (Davis 1994).

Summary

This chapter has examined the implementation of four innovations designed to bring about change at the secondary level in schools in the CC. The analysis drew on factors identified by Fullan and Stiegelbauer (1991) as affecting implementation: namely, *characteristics of the change, characteristics at the school level, the national level* and *factors external to the school system*. Of the fifteen characteristics identified, nine are present in CSEC and ten in ROSE, six and one are "present to some extent" in CSEC and ROSE, respectively, while four are absent in ROSE (see table 3.1). NCERD Skills Reinforcement Guides and the Sixth Form Geography Project have the largest number of characteristics which are not present. Worthy of note is the fact that all the innovations, even if only in some aspect, were perceived as difficult to understand and use. The characteristics which are common to both CSEC and ROSE and work in favour of successful implementation are participation of teachers and principals, appropriately trained staff, realistic time for materials development and for funding by donor agencies. There was also some provision for monitoring and evaluation, although this was a stronger element in ROSE than in CSEC. These innovations, furthermore, received much support: for example, support given by the principals, support from the community and the government and donor agencies which provided technical assistance. The Sixth Form Geography Project had no source of funding at all and NCERD's Skills Reinforcement Guides were developed and implemented in the first year on a shoestring budget. NCERD, furthermore, suffered losses in its staff which turned out to be the last nail in the coffin of the Skills Reinforcement Guides.

Conclusion

Based on the analysis presented, can either CSEC or ROSE be described as "successful" innovations? While the CSEC has continued, ROSE 1 did not move to phase 2 as proposed by the Ministry of Education (see note 3). This had much to do with the implementation of ROSE 1 which was described by the World Bank (2001, 17) as "satisfactory" with the following comment:

> However, implementation has not been smooth. Delivery of complementary inputs was not synchronized. In-service training proceeded first together with delivery of curriculum guides, but delivery of textbooks was a few years later and civil works came even later and were not completed by project completion. So trained teachers did not have textbooks and laboratories to try out their activities approach. (World Bank 2001, 17)

Furthermore, reading improvement which was critical to raising achievement at all levels was not implemented by the project. Although the impact evaluation of ROSE 1 revealed much enthusiasm and positive support for the programme and widespread use of the curriculum in schools, it was clear that in the eyes of the World Bank, the project was not *successful*. In fact, some aspects of the evaluation design, instruments and data analysis of the Evaluation Unit in the Ministry of Education which did the impact evaluation were described as "technically weak" (World Bank 2001, 17).

Based on the longevity standard (Cuban 1998), CSEC can be considered successful, even though its original three schemes of assessment did not meet the fidelity standard given that the Basic Proficiency had to be abandoned and problems continue to be experienced with the SBA. Nevertheless, CSEC has become an integral part of the life of schools in the examination-oriented education systems of the CC. Apart from reshaping the content of secondary education to meet the needs, interests and aspirations of the Caribbean people, CSEC has also achieved a high measure of success in increasing the interaction among Caribbean educators and eroding the isolationism of the CC countries.

Because it was not implemented in *all* schools as originally intended, ROSE fails to meet the fidelity standard of success. Teachers in the traditional high schools felt that they had little to gain from the introduction of ROSE and questioned the value of a common curriculum for all types of secondary schools. This underscores the point that for innovations or reforms to succeed it is just as important to work on the changing of people's perceptions, attitudes and values as it is to develop their skills. We tend to emphasize the latter and forget the former. Change starts with individuals and their attitudes, and this requires the use of normative-reeducative strategies for bringing about the change desired (Bennis, Benne and Chin 1969). For an innovation that championed the goal of equity, ROSE perhaps more widened the divide between the social classes than healed the breach. But does this depend on how "equity" is interpreted? In the pronouncements of the Ministry of Education and ROSE secretariat, the pursuit of the goal of equity involved all schools, including the traditional high schools. To the funding agency, however, ROSE sought to "introduce a major reform of the junior secondary education system (that is, Grades 7-9) with a focus on the poorest groups within these grades" (World Bank 2001, 2). This suggests focus on the all age and junior secondary schools which take in children who failed the then primary exit examination. These children are largely from the lower-social class and are among the poorer in the society. The pursuit of equity was thus seen as exposing these children to a better quality of curriculum to help them to "catch up" with their peers in the traditional high schools who were perceived as the recipients of quality education. From this perspective, there was no need for the traditional high schools to have been invited to participate from the inception of ROSE.

The Sixth Form Geography Project died a natural death. The demise of the NCERD Skills Reinforcement Guides was perhaps by design, given the hostilities in the Ministry of Education described by Craig (2006/7). In contrast, the CSEC has been institutionalized and sustained. The World Bank (2001) gave several reasons why ROSE would be sustained, including government commitment and the fact that the ROSE trainers had been absorbed into the teacher training colleges to continue the training of teachers for grades 7–9. ROSE 1 is all but forgotten today and yet its driving principles (access, equity, quality, productivity) remain important goals in Jamaica's education system. The importance of a multi-level curriculum, student-centred pedagogy, activity-based learning, the involvement of parents and communities in the work of the school, the embedding of problem-solving, creative thinking and critical thinking skills in the curriculum are all ideas from ROSE which underpin the National Standards Curriculum[5] which was brought on stream in Jamaica in the 2016–17 school year.

4.

Implementing Innovations in Literacy in Caribbean Primary Schools

In the previous chapter we examined factors that affected the implementation of four innovations in secondary schools in the CC. These include participation of teachers and principals, appropriately trained staff, provision for monitoring and evaluation and realistic time for materials development as well as for funding by donor agencies. Those innovations were initiated in the 1970s and 1980s but only one – CSEC – has survived until the present, the development of the first syllabuses having begun in 1975. Did education policymakers and planners learn from these early experiences and ensure that the factors that influenced effective implementation were embedded in later innovations? This is a question that this chapter seeks to answer by examining innovations at the primary level which focus on literacy.

Why literacy? In 1990 at the World Conference on Education for All in Jomtien, Thailand, representatives from all over the world agreed to universalize primary education and greatly reduce illiteracy by the end of the decade. This goal was not achieved but the commitment to it was reaffirmed in the 2000 World Education Forum in Dakar, Senegal. It is against this background that the innovations selected for analysis in this chapter all concern literacy.

The Importance of Literacy

Literacy is the ability to read, view, write, speak and listen in a way that allows the individual to communicate effectively. Literacy skills are most important to acquire at the earliest stage of educational development as they are predictive of performance at the later stages. Spencer-Ernandez (2011) found that there is a positive relationship between students' language arts scores in the primary exit examination in Jamaica and their performance in English language in the CSEC. It is the children with high scores in literacy who gain entry to the prestigious traditional high schools while those with low levels of literacy or are illiterate go to the upgraded or non-traditional high schools, junior secondary or all age schools. Most of these students are excluded from CSEC. "This exclusion", writes Spencer-Ernandez (2011, 157), "is directly linked to students' literacy status and goes back to their preparation in primary school."

The acquisition of effective literacy skills furthermore creates opportunities for educational success and paves the road to upward social mobility and employment that enables a comfortable life. Improving overall literacy achievement has been directly associated with a country's economic productivity. The inference from this for those who fail to acquire good literacy skills is clear and particularly so for Creole speakers. Simmons-McDonald (2014) is critical of a linguist who claimed that "creole languages . . . constitute a distinct handicap to the social mobility of the individual and may also constitute a handicap to the creole-speaker's personal intellectual development" (Whinnom 1971, 109–10). Simmons-McDonald described this view as "preposterous" and argued that one source of the notion of handicap was "educational systems that remained heavily influenced by a relationship of domination in colonial contexts in which creoles were either ignored or labelled substandard and inferior" (Simmons-McDonald 2014, 44).

Purpose

This chapter showcases three innovations designed to address the literacy problems of different groups of children in the CC, all of whom were Creole speakers and most of whom were from disadvantaged home backgrounds.

The first innovation is the ASTEP which targeted the children in Jamaican primary schools who failed multiple times the test designed to assess their competence to sit the primary exit examination which at the time of writing was the Grade Six Achievement Test (GSAT). Most of the children who failed were boys. For decades the problems faced by these children had been known but their solution was left to individual schools to address. Many of these children drifted into secondary schools unable to read. ASTEP represents the first attempt at the national level to address the learning achievement of this target group. Although the curriculum was broad based, this chapter focuses only on language arts.

The second innovation is Literacy 1-2-3 (L1-2-3) which supported the language arts programme in the RPC in Jamaica. The RPC adopted a holistic approach to integration at the lower primary level (grades 1–3) but with provision for "opening windows" that allowed for the discrete treatment of language arts and mathematics (Bailey and Brown 1997). The L1-2-3 provided support for the language arts "window". It replaced the Primary Language Arts curriculum which had been in use for over two decades. In a context where different approaches are advocated for teaching literacy in a Creole-speaking environment, L1-2-3 represented one approach. It used the children's own experiences as a starting point for reading and raising awareness of the differences between the Jamaican Creole and Standard English. The "language awareness" approach, according to Craig (2006, 39), is based on an acceptance of the fact that "students can actively promote their own acquisition of language and literacy if they are consciously aware of the formal characteristics of their own language and can learn to contrast these characteristics with those of the target language".

The third innovation is the Caribbean Centre of Excellence for Teacher Training (CETT) which targeted children in the early primary grades who came from literacy impoverished environments and who, without the needed intervention, would most likely exit the primary system functionally illiterate. The Caribbean CETT (hereafter referred to as CETT) described as "a virtual and distributed network" (Warrican, Spencer-Ernandez and Miller 2013, 7) involved five countries: Belize, Guyana, Jamaica, St Lucia, and St Vincent and the Grenadines. CETT was designed to improve teachers' reading instruction to children in first, second and third grades in marginalized communities of the five Caribbean countries, with the objective of improving literacy levels and ultimately changing the patterns of school underachievement.

All three innovations sought to address concerns which were critical in the education systems at the time. The question is: Did they succeed in achieving their objectives relating to the literacy problems faced by their target group? How do we account for any differences in achievement of outcomes in the three innovations? This chapter addresses this question by an examination of the outcomes of the innovations because of how they were implemented. For comparative purposes, these innovations will be analysed using the same framework applied to the innovations at the secondary level. In the case studies key aspects of the innovations presented are description of their goals, inputs, implementation and outcomes. This is preceded by some background information leading to the initiation of the innovations.

Background

Acquiring Literacy in a Creole-Speaking Environment

When the Caribbean countries were under colonial rule, the vocabulary of the European languages became the dominant base of the resulting Creole. This explains the presence of French Creole in St Lucia, vestiges of Dutch Creole in Guyana and extreme forms of English Creole in Jamaica, Belize and Guyana (Craig 2006). The syntax and phonology of the Jamaican Creole emerged from the contact of West African and European languages. Its vocabulary is mainly

English but has words which can be identified as African, Spanish, French, Portuguese and Dutch (Bryan 2010). Craig (2014a) in an article originally published in 1973 outlines the difficulties faced by the creole speaker learning to read and proposed various strategies to deal with these difficulties. One of the strategies required that the language of initial reading materials be controlled "in such a way that only such English word-forms and grammar as are already present in Creole speech would appear in the materials" (Craig 2014a, 86). The second strategy proposed was that "a programme of structural language practice . . . be carried out simultaneously and in close integration with the reading programme" (Craig 2014a, 87). The Primary Language Arts Scheme (PLAS) which embodied these strategies was developed by the Language Materials Workshop established in the School of Education at the UWI in Jamaica in 1973. It was adopted by Jamaica's Ministry of Education in 1980 as the national early reading primer because "it fostered respect for the child's personal language and linguistic heritage" (Ministry of Education, Jamaica, 1977, 40). PLAS remained the principal text for the next twenty-six years. In the early years of the new millennium, it was replaced by the Literacy 1-2-3 which did not have such a structured approach to teaching literacy as the PLAS, but it drew on the children's own experiences and raised awareness of the differences between Jamaican Creole and Standard Jamaican English.

The L1-2-3 was part of the RPC which itself was innovative in that it involved teachers making a paradigm shift from a "banking concept" to a constructivist approach to teaching and learning (Bailey and Brown 1997). Key features of teachers using a constructivist approach were responsiveness to children's needs, interests, feelings and opinions; engagement of children in active learning, problem-solving, relating learning to children's experiences and use of non-traditional forms of assessment such as journals and portfolios (Jennings 2011).

Gender Differences in Performance in Literacy

Girls outperform boys in literacy at the primary level and in English at the secondary level (Clarke 2007, Bailey 2000). A good illustration of gender differences in performance is evident in the results of the Grade 4 Literacy Test (G4LT) in Jamaica. The G4LT has three components: word recognition, reading comprehension and a writing task. Students are assessed according to whether they have achieved mastery (not at risk), near mastery (uncertain) or non-mastery (at risk). Table 4.1 shows that over a three-year period, a greater percentage of girls than boys achieved mastery in the G4LT. As much as 32 per cent of the boys are in the almost mastery category (2010/11) and up to 19 per cent are in the non-mastery category. That insufficient is done to stem the tide of failure is evident in the results of the primary exit examination. The national

Table 4.1. Percentage Performance of Male/Female Students on the Grade 4 Literacy Test

Level of Mastery	2009			2010			2011		
	Female	Male	Overall	Female	Male	Overall	Female	Male	Overall
Mastery	77	53	65	76	53	65	75	50	62
Almost mastery	15	28	22	20	32	26	19	32	26
Non-mastery	8	19	14	5	15	10	6	18	13

Source: Planning and Monitoring Unit, Ministry of Education in Jennings et al. (2012).

average performance in language arts between 2006 and 2011 ranged from 47 per cent (2007) to 55 per cent in 2011. While girls consistently performed above the national average, boys consistently fell below. In 2009, for example, the average male score on language arts was forty-nine, compared with the girls' sixty, with the national average being fifty-four (Jennings-Craig et al. 2012).

Several reasons have been advanced to explain gender differences in literacy. Research has highlighted the complexity of the problem which is rooted in socialization practices in the home and the wider society (Brown and Chevannes 1995), in the toys to which they are exposed (Leo-Rhynie 1995), sex role stereotyping in reading books (Bailey and Parkes 1995) and the perception of school as "feminine space" in that most of the teachers are female. Boys are allowed more freedom than girls in their upbringing with the result of acquiring a "hard macho male image" (Parry 2000, 54) which runs counter to the demands of schooling. Being required to stay home and do domestic chores, girls become instilled with a sense of discipline and responsibility which serves their educational interest. UNESCO (2012, 49) notes a "large and increasing gender gap in reading, with boys, especially from poorer backgrounds, falling behind". Peer pressure forces boys to avoid anything perceived as girlish. This includes reading which is viewed as a feminine activity and the use of Standard English is also seen as "feminine", particularly by boys from poorer backgrounds to whom using Creole and slang is associated with being masculine (Figueroa 2004). It is also important that the content of reading materials should appeal to the interest of both boys and girls (Bailey and Parkes 1995).

Following observations that having sat the primary exit examination (the GSAT[1]) some 30 per cent of the students entering secondary school were reading below the required grade level or were not able to read at all, the competency-based transition policy (Morris, Allan and Evering 2008) was introduced in Jamaica. This required that students pass the G4LT and be deemed literate before they could access the GSAT. This policy was put into effect in 2009. Most of the students in the non-mastery category in table 3.1 were boys. The ASTEP was designed for these students and those in the near-mastery category.

BOX 1: ALTERNATIVE SECONDARY TRANSITIONAL EDUCATION PROGRAMME

Goals

ASTEP sought to provide an alternative instructional path for approximately ten thousand students who failed to achieve mastery at the G4LT after four sittings and therefore would not be able to transition to secondary school at the end of grade 6. Most students performed at the grade 2 level, with some in the rural areas especially performing at grade 1 level.

A few students performed at the grade 3 level. These students were to be exposed to a "functional academics" curriculum designed to develop competencies for readiness to transition to the standard secondary curriculum after two years.

Inputs

ASTEP centres were established in primary, all age and junior high schools that had space to accommodate the students. Small centres accommodated twenty-five while the large centres had fifty students. *The curriculum* centred on (1) functional mathematics (number sense, money management, budget, measurement, consumer math), (2) functional language and communication (language expression and reading), (3) communication skills (use of technology to improve knowledge, enable communication and perform basic application using tools such as Word and Excel), (4) science for living (health and hygiene, human and social biology, earth and agricultural science), (5) social studies (Jamaican history, geography, civics and citizenship education), (6) artistic expression and music education, (7) personal empowerment (to improve students' self-worth and encourage the ability to succeed) and (8) physical education. Literacy and critical thinking were to be integrated across all of these areas and the curriculum was to be student-centred, interactive, responsive to multiple intelligences and use alternative forms of assessment. *Resources.* Curriculum guides with accompanying student resource materials were developed by experts from the UWI in each of the seven areas and each centre was provided with interactive whiteboards, laptops, DVD players and DVDs, CD players, digital cameras, markers, crayons and musical instruments. Teachers trained in special needs were to be appointed to each centre and teachers trained in music/visual and performing arts and physical education were to be made available to the centres. Training workshops were organized to train the teachers in the use of the curriculum guides.

Implementation: Challenges

ASTEP was implemented in 237 centres in the 2011–12 school year and continued into the following year. Ministry of Education officers who reviewed the curriculum guides for the first term considered that they were "written at too low a level" for the students with the result that when they transitioned, they would not be prepared for work in form 3 (grade 9). The curriculum developers were asked to upgrade the materials. The costliness of musical equipment resulted in the music curriculum guide having to be rewritten as it assumed the availability of instruments such as drums and wind instruments. Because of the unavailability of teachers in physical education, the students basically fitted into the regular physical education programme in the schools. The teachers trained at the workshops were not the ones who taught in the centres and they were not trained in special needs. Resources were not provided to each centre equally. The student materials were not made available to the centres for use.

Outcomes

After the curriculum developers upgraded the materials, it soon became evident from the Ministry of Education's monitoring of ASTEP that most of the children could not manage the materials as they were way above their level. In their evaluations of the materials, the teachers at the training workshops appealed for activities for "non-readers" and urged that the content of the curriculum guides be reduced due to the students' low level of functioning. Social problems also emerged in the schools because ASTEP comprised mainly of boys who ought to have been in secondary schools but were interacting with children at the primary level. The effect of this on their sense of self jeopardized the achievement of the goals of the personal empowerment curriculum. Tests of the achievement of the students during the two years of the programme led to the realization that only a few students had developed sufficiently to transition to a secondary school. In fact, of 4,603 students who registered in 2011, only 1,290 transitioned to the secondary level (Ministry of Education Programme Monitoring and Evaluation Unit 2012). The vast majority functioned at too low a level in literacy to transition to the standard secondary curriculum after two years. ASTEP was superseded by a new programme: the Alternative Pathways to Secondary Education (APSE). This comprises Secondary Pathway (SP1) which is general education for those who passed GSAT. SP2 has specially developed curricula for students who failed the G4LT and are reading at grade 4 level. The assumption is that after two years they could transition to SP1. A special five-year curriculum was developed for the students in SP3 who are reading along a continuum ranging from non-readers to reading at grade 3 level. The ASTEP materials were blended into SP3. These students pursue a "functional academics" curriculum over three years and transition to a technical–vocational curriculum in grades 10 and 11.

(Source: ASTEP Terms of Reference, notes of meetings and reports of ASTEP workshops held in June, October 2011, April 2012, APSE Terms of Reference)

BOX 2: LITERACY 1-2-3

Goals

L1-2-3 sought to (1) use the children's own experiences as a starting point for reading and raising awareness of the differences between the Jamaican Creole and Standard English, (2) emphasize the development of creative skills through the use of the children's own writing, (3) provide shared language and literacy experiences through the use of Big Books which enabled the teacher to read to the children and monitor their oral reading and (4) develop the children's independent reading skills through the use of Little Books, pupils' activity books, grade-specific anthologies and other school and classroom library resources. The materials were expected to form a coherent literacy programme.

Description

Literacy 1-2-3 was initiated in 2005 and the books and other materials were developed in time for piloting in the 2006–07 academic year. The content of the books captured the interest and experiences of the children and had main characters that appealed to boys and girls alike. The print size, the illustrations and "the eye-catching nature of the book cover" (Jennings-Craig 2007, 18) were other significant features. The L1-2-3 comprised Big Books, Little Books, pupils' activity workbooks for each grade, phonic charts for grade 1, teachers' guides for each grade, anthologies for grades 2 and 3, and word cards and literacy games. The books are written by local writers and illustrated by local artists. The content is based on the themes in the first three grades of the RPC which comprises an integrated curriculum. L1-2-3 supports the Language Arts Window. This is a period of sixty minutes in the integrated curriculum which is focused on developing literacy skills (reading, speaking, writing, viewing, responding to books). Teachers are required to use a particular strategy for L1-2-3 involving three phases: (1) a whole group session of approximately fifteen minutes which could take the form of a discussion, phonics instruction and a word study, (2) group work involving four groups, in two of which the teacher interacts for about fifteen minutes each. The other two groups should be involved in paired or group activities which provide opportunities for the children to interact with each other and (3) a whole class discussion in which the children take the lead in discussing what they learned in their groups or pairs and evaluate their learning. This is consistent with the child-centred approach expected to be used in implementing the RPC. Alternative forms of assessment (e.g. portfolios, journals, field trips) were encouraged in the teaching of L1-2-3, and classrooms were to have well-stocked classroom libraries for supplementary reading. The Ministry of Education is committed to replenishing supplies of the L1-2-3 in schools every two years.

Implementation

Simms (2010) found that teachers did not use the three-phased strategy as expected. Some used the materials for reading only, others for picture discussion and building sight word vocabulary. There were also teachers who selected topics from the books that matched what they were doing in integrated studies. Simms noted that in all lessons observed, there was not a single instance of the children leading the discussion at the end of the class and evaluating their work. The anthologies were not used either because the teachers could not see their relevance to the language arts topics in the RPC or as one said, "These children are very slow; they can't read them on their own, so I read them aloud" (Mascoe-Johnson 2012, 63). Teaching pedagogy remained largely teacher centred, as evidenced in teacher-initiated closed questions which elicited choral responses, seat work and use of paper and pencil tests (Simms 2010, Mascoe-Johnson 2012, Jennings-Craig et al. 2012). This may have to do with the training received because teachers were unhappy with the training as it consisted more of telling rather than actual demonstration of the strategy. Furthermore, they received conflicting messages during implementation as the requirements of the L1-2-3 planners contradicted the principal's requirements. The situation was complicated by the fact that some schools were involved in other interventions simultaneously with L1-2-3. The furniture in the classrooms made group work problematic. Jennings-Craig et al. (2012, 42) described the seating in traditional combination desks as being "a hindrance to effective grouping". Other research at the primary level noted the absence of reading corners and class libraries due to restrictions of space and lack of storage space (Mckoy 2007). The Ministry of Education did not replenish the supply of L1-2-3 in the schools within the time frame proposed.

Outcomes

Observations by Jennings-Craig et al. (2012) in a grade 3 classroom revealed that the teacher did not have any of the L1-2-3 materials because they had all been destroyed. The teacher reported having received fourteen copies each of the Big and Little Books to share among thirty-two children. The copies were flimsy and did not stand up to hard wear and tear. The findings were similar in other classrooms. The teachers were using commercial texts (e.g. Macmillan Primary Integrated Studies, the Reggae Readers) which were readily available. They were also using the PLAS as a few copies were still available. The results of the G4LT in 2009 and 2010 in which 65 per cent achieved mastery included students who used the L1-2-3. Noteworthy is the fact that in 2011 mastery in the G4LT decreased to 62 per cent (Jennings-Craig et al. 2012), indicating fluctuation in performance over the years.

Sources: Jennings (August 2007). Literacy 1-2-3: Curriculum Specialist–Literacy Intervention Programme: Report to the Ministry of Education and Youth for January–May 2007. Jennings (November 2007). Literacy 1-2-3: Piloting of the Materials 2006–07: Report of the Curriculum Specialist to the Ministry of Education and Youth. Jennings (2011).

BOX 3: THE CARIBBEAN CENTRE OF EXCELLENCE FOR TEACHER TRAINING (CETT)

Goals

CETT was charged with the task of improving literacy levels in disadvantaged schools by improving the teachers' reading instruction to children in grades 1–3. More specifically, the main goal of CETT was that after five years of instruction, approximately 90 per cent of grade 3 students in participating schools should have mastered the fundamentals of reading and 60 per cent should be reading at or above the grade 3 level. CETT sought to achieve this goal by developing diagnostic tools to provide teachers with data for use in creating relevant programmes to meet the needs of their students: providing culturally sensitive teaching and learning materials to project schools: using improvements in ICT to enhance and support the programme.

Description

CETT is one of three Centres of Excellence for Teacher Training sponsored by US president George W. Bush and funded by the USAID as part of the Summit of Americas Initiative agreed on in Montreal, Canada, in April 2001 (Warrican, Spencer-Ernandez and Miller 2013). The other two initiatives are located in Honduras and Peru. A total of sixty-seven schools from five countries (Belize, Guyana, Jamaica, St Lucia, and St Vincent and the Grenadines) participated with the largest number of these (forty-three) from Jamaica. During the first year, 13,206 students in grades 1–3 participated in the programme. In the second and third years the numbers were 11,862 and 10,335, respectively. Some children came from small rural schools with multi-grade mixed-ability classes that were separated by chalkboards. Others came from urban or inner-city schools some of which were as large as one thousand in capacity with teacher: student ratios ranging from 1:15 to 1:54. The schools had high rates of absenteeism.

CETT had five components designed to achieve its goals: (1) teacher training in effective reading methodologies and classroom management techniques, (2) culturally sensitive teaching and learning materials for reading instruction, (3) diagnostic tools to help teachers identify and address students' literacy needs, (4) applied research to ensure efficacy of the training, materials provided and so on, (5) the use of Information and Communication Technologies to support the programme and widen access. Chesterfield and Abreu-Combs (2011) add that sustainability was also a major focus in the programme. They also maintain that "CETT also emphasized the role of parents and the greater community in embracing a 'culture of literacy' to support the importance of reading in the early grades" (Chesterfield and Abreu-Combs 2011, 3).

CETT was administered by the JBTE[2] which comprised membership of key education stakeholders such as the Ministries of Education, teacher training colleges, teachers' unions and the UWI. The JBTE is in the School of Education at the UWI in Kingston, Jamaica.

Implementation

CETT was managed by a project director and project coordinator. Other key staff were specialists in diagnostic and performance measurement, teacher training, material procurement and production, and ICT. With reference to the language arts curricula of fifteen CC countries and taking account of the national standards for literacy in these countries, CETT developed common standards for literacy for primary education (kindergarten through to grade 3) in the CC. Based on these standards, the Caribbean Reading Standards Assessment Tests (CRSAT) were developed. Five levels of mastery were identified in the test: non-mastery, approaching mastery, approaching mastery 11, Mastery 1 and Mastery 11. The teachers were not only trained in reading comprehension, phonological awareness, phonics, fluency, oral expression, written expression and vocabulary; they were also trained in classroom management and student assessment.

In each participating country a reading specialist, ICT technician and administrative assistant were located in the college or university which trained primary school teachers. Each reading specialist was responsible for thirty teachers across the grades in a cluster of schools. The reading specialists visited the teachers at least every two weeks and provided support with the implementation of the new teaching strategies. Each school was provided with a primary school manager (PSM). This was a web-based management information system which principals used to manage their schools and to record the performance of the students in each class and grade level. The ICT technicians supported the schools in each cluster in implementing the PSM. They also ensured that this data was transferred at regular intervals to the central PSM located at the JBTE on the UWI campus in Jamaica.

Outcomes

Based on data obtained within the first three years of the programme, significant differences in the pre- and post-test scores of grade 1 students indicated that even in the first year of CETT there were significant improvements in the reading scores of the students in the sample. Similar results were obtained for grade 3 students. The percentage of students in the lower mastery levels decreased with years of exposure to the programme while the percentage of higher mastery levels increased over time (Warrican, Spencer-Ernandez and Miller 2013).

At the inception of the project more girls than boys were reading at a functional level and by the end of grade 3 more girls than boys were reading above grade level (Mastery 11). A higher percentage of boys was approaching Mastery 11 "suggesting that although they were reading at an acceptable level, they would need more targeted attention to help them to move to the even higher levels of Mastery 1 and Mastery 11" (Warrican, Spencer-Ernandez and Miller 2013, 35). It was noteworthy nevertheless that the performance of all students improved the longer they were exposed to the programme.

Warrican, Spencer-Ernandez and Miller (2013) found that at the end of the third year (1) nine of the schools already had 60 per cent of their students reading at the grade 3 level, (2) twenty-six schools had between 40 and 59 per cent of their students reading at this level, (3) eight schools had 90 per cent of their grade 3 students reading at a functional level, (4) twenty-seven schools had between 70 and 89 per cent of their students reading at the functional level. To the researchers, the six schools in Guyana that participated in CETT were cause for concern. Only 2 per cent of the students were reading at or above grade level at grade 1, and by grade 3, this figure had increased to only 31 per cent. Nevertheless, the researchers concluded that if the observed trends in the majority of schools continued over the remaining years of the project the likelihood was that the majority of the schools would achieve the main CETT goal of approximately 90 per cent of grade 3 students in participating schools having mastered the fundamentals of reading and 60 per cent being able to read at or above the grade 3 level.

(*Sources*: Warrican, Spencer-Ernandez and Miller 2013; Caribbean Centre of Excellence in Teacher Training, retrieved from JBTE http://www.jbte .edu.jm/cms/Projects/Caribbean CentreofExcellence.aspx; Chesterfield and Abreu-Combs 2011)

Comparison of the Implementation of the Innovations

Characteristics of the Innovation

Need and Relevance

The Ministry of Education in Jamaica needed a replacement for the PLAS when the RPC was introduced in 2000. Literacy 1-2-3 filled this gap, especially as its stories were specially written to articulate with the themes for the integrated curriculum for grades 1–3. The materials were developed by Jamaicans who were EC education professionals, writers of children's books, librarians and teachers. The Big and Little Books were bright and colourful with characters and situations that the children could identify with. CETT was perceived as relevant to needs as it addressed a needed intervention for children on a path leading to functional illiteracy. ASTEP was clearly needed for children who were at risk of not benefiting from a secondary education, but the curriculum developed was not suited to the needs of the children who were barely able or unable to read at all. A typical observation from teachers was: "The curriculum guides are straight forward and friendly. However, if some activities and assessments were more in tandem with the level of the students, it would be more productive: The guides need to cater to students who are non-starters" (Jennings-Craig 2011, 8). In effect the guides could not be used at all by some teachers.

Clarity and Complexity

This problem arose because the curriculum developers initially wrote the materials for Alternative Secondary Education Programme (ASEP) at the appropriate level. ASEP was the original name of the programme. However, when officials from the Ministry of Education who pressed for the "transitional" nature of the programme to be emphasized read the materials, they insisted that the curriculum was written at too low a level to bring the children up to the point where they could transition and fit comfortably into grade 9 in secondary schools. To satisfy the requirements of the contract, the curriculum developers raised the standard of the curriculum which had by then become ASTEP. The revised curriculum, however, was much too difficult for most of the students. Psycho-educational testing of students about to enter the first year of ASTEP showed that 93 per cent of them were functioning below the grade 3 level. Forty-three per cent of these were classified as reading at the kindergarten (pre-primary) level (Spencer-Ernandez and Edwards-Kerr (2014)). Furthermore, the fact that the students were of secondary school age, but ASTEP was delivered in mainly primary schools undermined rather than promoted the goals of the programme.

Although the teachers were provided with teachers' guides that explained the goals of the L-1-2-3 and how to implement the three-phased teaching strategy, many were unable to do so (Simms 2010, Mascoe-Johnson 2012). In one of the L1-2-3 classes observed, Jennings (2009, 101) reported that a teacher delivered a lesson without using any of the materials because she "didn't have time to read the books". The books included the teachers' guide.

Quality and Practicality

As noted in chapter 3, innovations that involve use of curriculum materials should not only ensure that such materials are practical in the sense that they fit well with the teacher's situation but need also to ensure that the materials are of good quality and available. The Big and Little Books of Literacy 1-2-3 were of good quality in that they were bright and colourful with characters and situations that the children could identify with. Typical comments from teachers on the strength of the books were "the children can relate to it", "good print size" and "illustrations stimulate ideas" (Jennings-Craig 2007, 47). The teachers also noted that "the cover is soft, and the binding is poor" (Jennings-Craig 2007, 49). The L1-2-3 books were not sturdy enough to last more than two years and in the absence of funds to replace them, the teachers resorted to using other books that were available.

Materials were not specially developed for CETT. Materials that were culturally appropriate, interesting and colourful were selected from published children's books.

Characteristics at the School Level

Participation/Principal Support

A characteristic absent in ASTEP and the L1-2-3 but present in CETT was participation by teachers and principals. CETT sought the opinion of teachers and principals in the school on what needed to be done to improve teaching of reading and student achievement in literacy in the school. The reading specialists, based on the information received, worked with teachers and principals to design action research interventions for different classes in their schools. Teachers and principals identified the teaching and learning materials they needed and high-quality materials were procured and provided by the Project Implementation Unit.

Training of Staff

Chesterfield and Abreu-Combs (2011) attributed much of the success of CETT to the training of the teachers – an observation supported by Warrican, Spencer-Ernandez and Miller (2013, 9). They note that "the training included the latest and the best evidence-based strategies of teaching reading as well as the best practices with respect to promoting the continuing professional development of teachers in the teaching of reading". CETT used continuous teacher training throughout the year with follow-up support by reading specialists who helped to ensure that the teachers had a good grasp of the means of implementation of the new strategies. Particularly important was the stress on the acquisition of procedural knowledge in the training which ensured that teachers could apply knowledge gained in creating appropriate activities for their lessons (Chesterfield and Abreu-Combs 2011). Regular regional workshops were also held to train the reading specialists in the most up-to-date teacher training strategies. Chesterfield and Abreu-Combs (2011, viii) observed that "CETT's emphasis on effective practices demonstrated that the number of practices used by teachers influenced students' outcomes". The training in fact extended over two years. Chesterfield and Abreu-Combs (2011), however, found that the second year of training was not adequately focused on improving teacher knowledge and thus had limited impact on improving student performance in literacy. They recommended a one-year training programme in countries with limited resources.

Training for ASTEP took the form of workshops which sought to explain the key features of ASTEP, to obtain feedback on the drafts of the curriculum materials and to discuss the role of the teacher in delivering the curriculum. While the teachers found the workshops informative, they expressed a preference for workshops in specific subject areas in which they could go through the guides in detail (Jennings-Craig 2011).

Training for L1-2-3 was also done in workshops using the cascade approach. Workshops covered such topics as "principles, pedagogies and philosophical assumptions of L1-2-3", "constructivism" and "the literacy 1-2-3 strategy". The teachers trained were expected to train other teachers in their own and neighbouring schools, but many felt that more training than the one or two weeks offered was needed for the materials to be implemented effectively (Mascoe-Johnson 2012). At the workshops teachers complained that when they returned to their schools, their principals and the education officers who supervised them required them to do their lesson plans using strategies contrary to what they were taught at the workshops. Furthermore, some principals transferred teachers who had been trained to teach L1-2-3 to the upper grades (Jennings-Craig 2007) and those teachers who were not among the original batch trained had to pick up what they could from those who had received initial training (Jennings-Craig et al. 2012). The fact that teachers complained about the quality of the training received (a focus on telling rather than demonstration) suggests that written guidelines are poor substitutes for mentors who can work with teachers over an extended period and demonstrate the new techniques as they try to master these in the early stages of implementation. This was the kind of support the reading specialists provided the teachers in CETT.

The L1-2-3 books were not sufficiently sturdy. The stock in schools should have been replenished every two years, but the education budget did not allow for this. Few schools were able to stock their class libraries with support reading for the L1-2-3. In the case of ASTEP, student materials written to support teaching in the subject areas of the curriculum were never made available to the students on account of financial constraints to reproduce them. There were not sufficient art, music and physical education teachers to supply the programme. "Inadequate human and instructional resources" (Ministry of Education 2012, 4) plagued this innovation.

Community Support

Hall and Hord (2006, 23) include "parents and community members as partners and allies" as integral to providing a caring and productive environment which is conducive to change. The location of the ASTEP centres was a cause for concern of the parents who expected their children to be in secondary schools. The implementation of ASTEP coincided with the transfer of children in grades 7–9 of many all age schools into nearby junior high schools. With the loss of these grades the schools now comprised primary grades only, but the space left by grades 7–9 remained. This space, in the opinion of some officers in the Ministry of Education, was ideal to serve as ASTEP centres. There were some officers in the Ministry of Education who pointed to the psychological problems that would result from locating children of secondary school age in primary schools. The students encountered much hostility in the communities in which the ASTEP centres were located. In fact, the evaluation of ASTEP reported that students had been "subject to various levels of intimidation, including bullying and verbal abuse, and felt alienated because of issues surrounding their identity, as defined by the uniform they wore and where they fitted in the primary school" (Ministry of Education 2012, 4).

Characteristics at the National Level

Government Support

Because curriculum development at the primary to lower secondary level in CC countries is centralized, no innovation can be introduced at these levels without the support of the government. Although much of the funding for the innovation may be provided by an international lending agency, the government still has to provide counterpart funding and, furthermore, has to budget for the sustainability of the innovation. Difficulty in this regard has already been noted in the case of the L1-2-3. CETT is exceptional in that it was fully funded for its seven-year duration (2002–09) by the USAID. In fact, the CETT were announced at the 2001 Summit of the Americas as a US presidential initiative to support a systematic approach to improve early grade literacy in the Latin American and Caribbean region (Chesterfield and Abreu-Combs (2011)). ASTEP was not sustained but was absorbed into the *APSE*.

Lead Time for Materials Development and Provision for Monitoring and Evaluation

Perhaps it was both the level of funding provided and the fact that the USAID provided management support that enabled CETT, of the three innovations, to put in place provision for monitoring and evaluation of the programme. CETT was able to report on progress on meeting project goals, based on performance in the CRSAT. Furthermore, the use of the PSM in schools as well as at the JBTE enabled the monitoring of the progress and performance of the children in the project.

In contrast, in ASTEP "students' progress is assessed in an ad hoc manner because of a lack of adherence to the guidelines in place for their continuous and summative assessment" (Ministry of Education 2012, 4). Neither L1-2-3 nor ASTEP was systemically monitored during implementation but the Programme Monitoring and Evaluation Unit in the Ministry of Education conducted an evaluation of ASTEP at the end of the first year (Ministry of Education 2012). L1-2-3 was included in the mid- and end-of-project evaluation of the PESP (Tecsult International Ltd 2004, CRC Sogema 2008).

Staff to Support Innovation

Of the three innovations, ASTEP was the only one that fell short in this regard. The teachers who were trained for delivering ASTEP were not the ones who actually taught the students. "Those initially trained were reported as exiting the programme because of dissatisfaction with the proposed salary" (Ministry of Education 2012, 3). The programme was therefore adversely affected by inadequate numbers of literacy and numeracy specialists and support personnel such as guidance counsellors and school psychologists. In addition, the difficulty in finding teachers trained to teach the visual and performing arts resulted in those curriculum materials not being used (Jennings 2012).

External Factors

Provision of Adequate Funding

While CETT was well supported financially, the L1-2-3 was inadequately funded. L1-2-3 was part of the Primary Education Support Project (PESP) funded by the IDB and the GOJ. A five-year project (2000–05) which was extended to 2008, PESP was implemented "during a time of fiscal and debt constraints" (Ministry of Education, Jamaica 2008, 1–1) which impeded efforts to achieve its objectives. PESP sought to improve performance through curriculum and training and "enhance equity in the provision of opportunities" (Ministry of Education, Jamaica 2008, 1–1). Funds were identified in PESP to enhance equity through "a Literacy Pilot to introduce a four-year literacy programme in 80 low-performing urban schools" (Ministry of Education 2008, 5–4). However, because local research had indicated that low achievement in literacy was widespread in Jamaican schools, the decision was taken to use the sum allocated for eighty schools to serve grades 1–3 in *all* schools throughout the island. This approximated to eight hundred schools including all age schools which cater to ages six to fourteen plus. L1-2-3 was therefore developed to serve the entire primary system. Against this background, schools running out of supplies of Big and Little Books and the Ministry of Education being unable to replenish the stock after two years becomes understandable.

ASTEP was also inadequately funded but this was a result of poor decision-making by policymakers as well as over ambitious objectives given the contexts in which ASTEP was implemented. When the developers of the ASTEP curriculum were asked by the Ministry of Education officials to upgrade the level of the materials, this led to a disruption of the schedule for the completion of the materials. As a result, "the late delivery of curricula . . . led to delays in instructional planning" (Ministry of Education 2012, 3). The music programme did not get off the ground because the musical instruments proved to be too expensive for the budget. The few schools that obtained some instruments had to incur the additional expense of building storage spaces secured by burglar bars to ward off theft.

Summary

The level of success achieved at the secondary level is directly linked to the child's achievement in literacy at the primary level. This chapter has compared and contrasted three innovative literacy interventions spread across five CC countries, namely, Literacy 1-2-3, ASTEP and the Caribbean CETT. L1-2-3 used a language awareness approach which respected the differences between the Jamaican Creole and Standard English and accommodated the use of the vernacular as appropriate in the early stages of developing literacy. Thus, it consolidated the breaking down of negative attitudes towards the Jamaican Creole initiated in the PLAS that it replaced. ASTEP was innovative in that it was the first centrally developed intervention designed for children who failed the G4LT four times. Hitherto it had been left to the initiative of teachers to design strategies to remediate those who failed the G4LT (Lewis-Fokum 2011). Failure in the G4LT meant that the student was ineligible for access to the primary exit examination. The ASTEP students (mostly boys) were exposed to a functional academic curriculum designed to prepare them to transition to the regular secondary curriculum after two years. CETT targeted the early primary grades and was designed to improve teachers' reading instruction to children in marginalized communities in Belize, Jamaica, Guyana, St. Lucia, and St. Vincent and the Grenadines.

As in the previous chapter the analysis of the innovations drew on factors identified by Fullan and Stiegelbauer (1991) as affecting implementation: namely *characteristics of the change, characteristics at the school level, the national level* and *factors external to the school system*. Of the fifteen characteristics that favour successful implementation thirteen are present in CETT, with one not applicable as ready-made materials were used. Ten of the fifteen characteristics are absent in ASTEP and three in the case of Literacy 1-2-3 which had the most characteristics "present to some extent" (see table 4.2).

Of the three innovations, CETT was the most successful. Its success is determined on the *effectiveness* standard. According to Cuban (1998) this standard is essentially concerned with the extent to which intended goals have been achieved, as determined by students' test scores and performance at external examinations. Not only has eight additional countries adopted CETT, but the CRSAT developed has since become a standard measure of literacy achievement in the lower primary grades across the CC. Warrican, Spencer-Ernandez and Miller (2013), furthermore, pointed to the likelihood that after five years of instruction, approximately 90 per cent of grade 3 students in participating schools should have mastered the fundamentals of reading and 60 per cent should be reading at or above the grade 3 level.

Conclusion

Factors in favour of successful implementation which were present in CSEC and ROSE and which are also present in CETT are participation of teachers and principals, appropriately trained staff, as well as funding by donor agencies. There are important features to note about CETT which favoured its success.

Table 4.2. Factors Affecting Implementation of Literacy Interventions

	ASTEP (Jamaica)	Literacy 1-2-3 (Jamaica)	Caribbean CETT
Characteristics of the innovation			
Perceived by users as relevant to needs	#	#	Y
Goals are clear to users and means of implementation made explicit	X	#	Y
Perceived by users as not difficult to understand and use	X	#	Y
Materials are of good quality and fit well with teaching situation	X	#	Y
Characteristics at school level			
Change strategy involves participation by teachers and principals	X	X	Y
Principals are supportive	#	#	Y
Staff appropriately trained	X	#	Y
Community is involved and supportive	X	NA	X
Adequate resources (human, physical, material)	X	X	Y
Characteristics at national level			
Support of the government	Y	Y	Y
Realistic time for materials development	X	Y	NA
Provision for evaluation and monitoring of change process	Y	#	Y
Adequate supply of staff to support innovation	X	Y	Y
External factors			
Realistic time frame for funding by donor agencies	X	X	Y
Provision of international technical assistance	N	N	Y

Key: Y = yes/present; # present to some extent X = no/absent; NA = not applicable. Assessments based on data in Ministry of Education (2012), Jennings et al. (2012), Thwaites (2013), Warrican, Spencer-Ernandez and Miller (2013), Chesterfield and Abreu-Combs (2011).

First, being able to use the CRSAT to assess students' reading levels. Second, being able to consult with the teachers and principals to determine the reading material most appropriate for the students. Thirdly, being able to provide sturdy books in a timely fashion. This was possible because CETT selected good quality materials already available. Materials were developed for ASTEP students before their actual reading levels were determined and once developed the materials were late in delivery. The development of L1-2-3 books was timely, but the materials were not suited to the reading levels of all the children. Furthermore, the book covers were so flimsy that by the second year of the programme few were available for use.

A fourth feature which favoured implementation success was CETT's adoption of a training model which involved continuous teacher training throughout the year for two years with follow-up support from reading specialists. This developed the teachers' procedural knowledge enabling them to acquire a good grasp of the means of implementation for the desired reading strategies. This feature was not evident in any of the innovations at the secondary level discussed in the previous chapter. L1-2-3 used a cascade approach to training lasting a few days up to a week for each batch of trainers – an approach also used in the NCERD Skills Reinforcement Guides. Use of the cascade approach did not make explicit how teachers should "open windows" when teaching an integrated lesson so that they could deliver the desired strategies for teaching L1-2-3. Teachers not originally trained had to pick up what they could from those who received training initially. Disenchanted with the proposed salary, the teachers who had been trained to teach the ASTEP students sought work elsewhere. ASTEP students were therefore taught by teachers without the necessary training.

A factor in favour of success which CETT has in common with CSEC and ROSE is its level of funding from donor agencies, but its use of technology is an exceptional feature. Having both the funds and skilfully harnessing the use of technology perhaps in turn enabled CETT to put in place a system for evaluation and monitoring of the change process which was absent in both CSEC and ROSE. Using the CRSAT, CETT was able to report on progress on meeting project goals, and the use of the PSM at the JBTE enabled the monitoring of the progress and performance of the children in the project. Schools could do similarly with children in their classes using the school's PSM. The evaluations done in ASTEP and L-1-2-3 were summative in nature, conducted by the Programme and Evaluation Unit of the Ministry of Education in the case of ASTEP and by international consultants in the case of L1-2-3.

CETT has shown how technology can be harnessed and used successfully for programme monitoring and evaluation. Governments in the CC have championed more ambitious goals for technology such as transforming the education system, changing pedagogy from teacher centred to student centred and even enabling children to teach themselves without the aid of a teacher. In the next chapter we will see how some of these goals were implemented and with what outcome.

5.

Innovations in ICT

Can Technology Revolutionize Teaching
and Learning?

Use of Information and Communication Technologies (ICTs) is widespread in educational systems in the Caribbean; for example, in the British Virgin Islands where the installation of a Wide Area Network has transformed internet access in schools (Dawson and Smawfield 2014), and the Organization of Eastern Caribbean States (OECS), through its education reform strategy, has sought to use technologies to make classrooms more learner centred, more exciting and to improve the quality of instruction (Jules, Miller and Thomas, 2000). In St Kitts/ Nevis, through the One-to One Laptop Computer Initiative, each high school student receives a free computer and there are plans for every teacher to be supplied with a laptop (Bearden 2014). Perhaps common to all these countries in the CC is the belief that the use of ICTs comes with a "leapfrog effect" in that it can have a revolutionary or instantaneous rather than a ripple effect on the country's development. This idea underpins aspirations of Ministries of Education such as "technological innovation provides educators with the opportunity to revolutionize the teaching-learning process" (Ministry of Education, Jamaica 1982, 5) and that "access to these technologies will position a small developing country to take full advantage of the information and developments which are so crucial in a competitive world" (Ministry of Education, Youth Affairs and Culture, Barbados 1998, 135). These aspirations are shared by other developing countries, for example, Cameroon (Ngoungouo 2017) and Ghana (Gyamfi 2017) where governments have made investments in ICT to varying degrees. Overly enthusiastic estimations of the transformative powers of technology are neither peculiar to the Caribbean nor are they new. Thomas Edison in 1913 is said to have predicted that books would become obsolete in schools as they would be replaced by silent films! (World Bank 2018).

Purpose

Has technology, whether traditional or modern, "revolutionized" teaching and learning in CC schools? This question seems all the more pertinent given the momentous decision to resort to online teaching from schooling at home which was taken during the pandemic brought about by Covid-19 in 2020. If the use of modern technology had such powers, then the decision would have been justified. Another question to be addressed, however, is: Did educators carry over to the new millennium what they had learned from the use of traditional technologies in the twentieth century and use this knowledge to inform their preparation for the use of modern technologies? This chapter addresses these questions by critically analysing the expected outcomes of selected innovations in traditional and modern technologies which were introduced into education systems to bring about change in four Caribbean countries: Jamaica, Barbados, Belize, and Trinidad and Tobago. The chapter also discusses the barriers encountered in the implementation of these innovations and points to what educational planners need to do if we are to enable our children to maximize their use of modern technologies.

Theoretical Background

Traditional and Modern Technology

The meaning of technology has varied over time. Rowntree (1988, 1) describes educational technology as "a rational, problem-solving approach to education, a way of *thinking* skeptically and systematically about learning and teaching". He refers to the label "educational technology" once being attached to "tools technology" which emphasized audiovisual aids to the teacher such as film, television and "programmed learning". It was a technology, says Rowntree, that was "devoted to supporting and enhancing the status quo providing teachers with the tools that would enable them to teach the same things more effectively or to larger numbers of students" (Rowntree 1988, 2). Examples of such technology include the blackboard, gestetnered handouts, radio and educational television (ETV), self-instructional materials (SIM). In this chapter, this is referred to as "traditional technology". This tends to be associated with teacher-centredness, that is an image of teachers who with the appropriate "tools" dispense knowledge to the students – the passive recipients of that knowledge. The teachers are implementers in that they receive a curriculum package which they are expected to implement as intended by the developers. These curriculum packages are oftentimes developed to be "teacher proof" and require little input from the teacher in situations where there is a paucity of trained and qualified teachers. An example of this is the use of Interactive Radio Instruction (IRI) in the teaching of grade 2 mathematics in Guyana. The IRI programme compensated for the shortage of teachers qualified to teach mathematics. It required a radio and teachers who, before each radio lesson, wrote exercises from the teachers' manual on the chalkboard. The pupils then copied the exercises into their books (Wintz and Wintz 2015).

The use of modern technologies was expected to replace the teacher-centred forms of instruction associated with traditional technology with a more student-centred or constructivist approach. More specifically this involves students as problem-solvers with their own individual purposes. They are able to find ways of connecting new knowledge to what they have already learned. In this way they "construct" their own knowledge, with the teacher serving as a guide or facilitator. To this end, the teacher is aided by the use of ICT which governments in the CC typically see as a means of bringing about "a paradigm shift in the teaching/learning process" (Ministry of Education, Youth Affairs and Culture in Barbados 1998, 137) from didactic to a student- or learner-centred approach. ICT has been defined as "any technology that allows users to create, store, display information in all its forms or communicate with others over a distance, such as computers, television, handheld computers, radio, audiocassettes, DVD and CD players, cell phones, networks, and the convergence of any of these technologies" (Gaible 2008, 21). ICT is referred to as "modern technology" in this chapter.

Challenges in the Use of Technologies: International Perspective

All over the world the use of modern technology has been seen as having the power to transform education in some way. The unprecedented growth of ICTs has led to the development of a global knowledge society which demands "lifelong learners" who think critically, know how to seek out new knowledge and can respond to the challenges of a rapidly changing world. ICT has been used in Australia for various purposes including the investigation of the real world, increasing student engagement and productivity, and increasing authenticity of assessment, knowledge building, student independence and collaboration (Newhouse 2014). In the United Kingdom, technology is used to "engage and motivate young people and meet their individual needs" (Beastall 2006, 93). The initiators of One Laptop Per Child believed that, with their own laptops, children could teach themselves and their families, without the aid of a teacher (Warschauer and Ames 2010). "The deskilling and depowering of a considerable number of teachers" (Apple 2003, 448) would result, according to Apple, were such a venture to be successful.

Warschauer and Ames (2010), however, describe numerous problems experienced in contexts with high levels of poverty as far afield as Peru and Birmingham, Alabama, which implemented One Laptop Per Child. These problems varied from schools not having electricity and electrical outlets and inadequate access to the internet to limited, if any, training at all for the teachers and lack of technical support. Similar problems were experienced in Birmingham, Alabama, which failed to put the necessary supports in place for the One Laptop Per Child. Within less than two years of use many of the laptops were broken or unusable. "Regrettably" as Warschauer and Ames (2010, 46) maintain, "there is no magic laptop that can solve the educational problems of the world's poor." Ramani (2010) reports that while schools in India may obtain a grant to buy some PCs and a couple servers, their budgets cannot deal with recurrent expenditures for maintenance and software upgrades. Ramani (2010, 12) adds that since "expertise is usually unavailable to block access to undesirable websites by students, anti-virus protection is often missing. As a result, schools prefer to keep PCs locked up." Limitations or barriers to the facilitation of technology use in schools abound even in developed countries such as Australia. Newhouse (2014) highlights research which identifies four barriers: using new technologies in old physical environments where there are inappropriate desks and a lack of power outlets (*technical barrier*), teachers' feelings of inadequacy and limited skill which makes them want to cling to their comfort zone (*personal experience and belief barrier*), the inability of school leadership to create the sort of environment which is technology rich and supportive to teachers and students (*organizational* barrier) and prescriptive curricula that encourages transmission delivery without technology support (*pedagogical* barrier).

How many of the claims about the revolutionary power of ICT have been substantiated by research? Granston and Clayton (2009) conducted a review of the instructional technology subcomponent of the PESP which was designed to achieve quality education through the delivery of the RPC. Fifteen primary schools were selected to integrate ICT into the curriculum. Despite being provided with the necessary tools (desktop and laptop computers, Alpha Smarts, multimedia projectors, colour printers, digital cameras) Granston and Clayton (2009, 17) found that "teachers continued to use traditional, teacher-directed instructional strategies, even when they were teaching with ICT". In contrast, observations of the implementation of a One Laptop Per Child project in two EC institutions in Jamaica showed that the students were mainly interested in a mathematics game and taking photos with the laptop. The researchers noted that "the children expressed an increased interest in numeracy and did better on numeracy tests" (Bailey et al. 2015, 116). These, however, were "initial observations" (Bailey et al. 2015, 122) and not a purposefully designed impact assessment. Feraria (2018) recorded success in the use of a simulated radio station in the classroom of grade 7 Jamaican "at-risk" students. The research, however, only described the responses of twenty students to the "radio-active" classroom. Heeks (2010) is critical of the absence or poor quality of ICT impact assessments and remarks on the little used or abandoned ICT projects and the fact that "something like one-third of such projects were total failures, something like half were partial failures and only a small minority succeeded" (Heeks 2010, 629). Is this true of ICTs in education in CC countries?

The Innovations and Their Expected Outcomes

Traditional Technologies

The four innovations in traditional technologies which are examined are (1) ETV (Jamaica), (2) SIM in the Grade 10–11 Programme (Jamaica), (3) self-instructional materials and "programmed teachers" in PRIMER (Jamaica) and (4) Learning Activity Packs (LAPs) in REAP in Belize. Key elements of traditional technology are a heavy reliance on print, the significance attached to curriculum content and teacher-centred pedagogy. Table 5.1 summarizes the expected outcomes of these innovations.

Educational television. Because there were large numbers of "pre-trained" teachers in the education system in Jamaica post-independence, the quality of education varied across schools. One of the main objectives of Jamaica's Educational Broadcasting Service was to provide print materials in the form of programme guides, workbooks and charts to support the schools' curricula. ETV programmes were designed to disseminate the same knowledge to a wider body of students to ensure equity of access to quality education. The programmes and materials were expected to compensate for the deficiencies in the teachers. The assumption was that the teacher would be able to do the necessary preparatory work prior to each broadcast, supervise the students during the broadcast and do some follow-up work with the students after the broadcast.

Self-Instructional Materials. The Grade 10–11 Programme was introduced into the Jamaican education system at a time when the goal was "the creation of an egalitarian society based on the twin pillars of social justice and equality of opportunity" (Ministry of Education, Jamaica 1977, 5). These ideals were integral to the ideology of the democratic socialist government of the day (Manley 1974). Because of this government's concern with high levels of youth unemployment particularly among those from the lower-income groups in society, the Grade 10–11 Programme targeted this group of students. The programme was implemented in new secondary schools which took in students who had failed the primary exit examination. The developers felt that the Grade 10–11 Programme would make the graduates as competitive in the marketplace, if not even more so than their elite peers in the traditional

Table 5.1. Traditional and Modern Technologies and Their Expected Outcomes

Country	Innovation//Year/Funding	Education Level	Expected Outcomes
Jamaica	Educational Broadcasting Service (ETV) 1963–83/* Funded by Jamaica government supported by Department of Technical Cooperation (DTC) and USAID	Secondary	Quality of education improved by presenting radio and TV programmes to support curricula to large numbers of students/ provision of print/non-print materials/ teachers trained in audiovisual instructional techniques.
Jamaica	Self-instructional materials (Grade 10–11 Programme)* 1974–80 Initially funded as special project in office of prime minister	Secondary	Reduction of education costs by making learning less dependent on teacher. Students developed skills needed to manage their personal and social lives (Life Skills) Students become more self-reliant by exposure to curriculum content relevant to democratic socialism.
Belize	Learning Activity Packs (REAP)1976–mid-1990s* Funded by Belize government/CARE, HPI, US Peace Corps	Primary Secondary**	Students are able to help parents with producing food from their farms and contribute to the development of the agricultural basis of Belize's economy.
Jamaica	Self-instructional materials/"programmed teachers" (PRIMER) 1979–84* Funded by the IDRC	Rural all age schools	Improvement in the quality of education in rural schools through improved instructional management (use of group work, independent learning, flexible scheduling of classes), especially in the areas of language and mathematics. Teachers monitored students' work through effective record-keeping system.

(Continued)

Table 5.1. (Continued)

Country	Innovation//Year/Funding	Education Level	Expected Outcomes
Barbados	ICT infusion in education (EduTech 2000) (1998–2008) # Funded by IDB (40%) /CDB (15%) /Gov. Barbados (45%)	Primary and secondary	A shift in teaching methodology from didactic to child centred. Upgrade of ICT facilities in schools. A workforce capable of managing the emerging technologies.
Jamaica	e-Learning 2006 # Funded by Universal Access Fund (tariff on incoming telephone calls)	Secondary	Improvement in quality of secondary education by upgrading teachers' colleges in educational technology/creating database of test items in 11 CSEC subjects.
Trinidad and Tobago	e-Connect and Learn Programme (e-Cal)# (2010–15) Funded by the government of Trinidad and Tobago	Secondary	ICT infused into teaching and learning. More collaborative teaching and learning. Reduction in the social divide. Students have developed twenty-first-century skills (e.g. problem-solving, critical thinking, creativity, innovation).

Sources of data as in table 5.2 * Traditional technologies; # modern technologies; ** introduced in urban areas post-1983.
HPI: Heifer Project International

high schools. The content of the SIM in some of the academic areas reflected the ideological stance of the democratic socialist government. For example, some of the SIM in social studies projected the "anti-imperialist" stance that the government took against the developed world. The writers were criticized for attempting to indoctrinate students into socialist ideology. There was also public outcry against the images of violence in illustrations in the language arts materials (Jennings 2002). The "Life Skills" curriculum was designed to better prepare the students for managing their personal and social lives. It included areas such as "caring for a child", "how to manage my bank account" and "doing simple electrical repairs in the home". The educational planners felt that this curriculum was to the advantage of the new secondary school students since their elite peers in the traditional high schools had nothing like it.

Self-instructional Materials (SIM) and "Programmed Teachers" in PRIMER

PRIMER was designed as an experimental research project. It sought to improve the quality of rural education in Jamaica by putting in place an efficient instructional management system. It was experimented with in five rural all age schools (i.e. schools with an intake of pupils from six to fifteen years of age) in Jamaica with a focus on grades 1–6. PRIMER focused on improving the language and mathematics skills of children in the rural areas because there was evidence of the superiority in achievement in these areas of students involved in project IMPACT in the Philippines on which PRIMER was modelled (Jennings 1993). It also adopted from IMPACT the use of "programmed teachers" who were the sixth-grade primary school pupils who were tutored to teach specific lessons in language and mathematics to third-grade pupils. In this way they supported the class teachers by freeing up some time for them to monitor the work of the students through a more efficient record-keeping system, thereby enabling them to keep track of each student's progress with the SIM. The SIM were used with the grades 4–6 pupils who were to work in groups to encourage them to develop a more independent approach to learning.

LAPs in REAP

The Rural Education and Agriculture Programme (REAP) was designed to prepare rural children in Belize for a more rewarding life in the countryside and to enable them to participate in the development of the agricultural basis of the national economy. The government of Belize sought to develop positive attitudes towards agriculture through the introduction of a new curriculum which used *LAPs*. These are outlines of lessons for appropriate grade levels, in which teachers were given performance objectives related to a REAP area of study, suggested activities and instructional materials. The LAPs were developed around nine areas of study: land and water, soil, health and nutrition, ecology, animals, village study, weather, plants and agricultural practices. These served as "threads" to integrate the academic subjects – language arts, mathematics, social studies, sciences, the arts and religion (Edmond 1985). Through exposure to this content, it was expected that rural children in Belize would be prepared for a more rewarding life in the countryside with a view to discouraging rural–urban migration in later life.

Modern Technologies

The modern technologies centre on the infusion of ICT into teaching and learning. Some CC countries focus on secondary schools as in the case of e-Learning (Jamaica) and e-Connect and Learn (e-Cal) (Trinidad and Tobago). EduTech 2000 is exceptional in that it focused on both the primary and secondary levels of the education system in Barbados. While traditional technologies sought to help students become more self-reliant, and less dependent on the teacher, invariably in the context of an inadequate supply of trained teachers, modern technology (see table 5.1) was more focused on "the development of 21st century skills in students" (Ministry of Education, Trinidad and Tobago 2010, 3) and changing teaching pedagogy from a teacher-centred transmission model to one that was learner centred and constructivist in approach.

The e-Connect and Learn. e-Cal was designed to supply twenty thousand three hundred laptops to all secondary schools in Trinidad and Tobago and to provide, among other things, a reliable local wireless network structure in the schools, enabling broadband internet connectivity within the students' communities (Mitchell and Harry 2012). In e-Cal, each student was given a laptop for use as a learning tool. The students had access to the internet at school and they were allowed to take their laptops home (Mitchell and Harry 2012). The goals of e-Cal included the improvement of the quality of instruction, the infusion of ICT in teaching and learning and reduction in "the inequity in access to computers and information between the students from wealthy and poor families" (Mitchell and Harry 2012, 50).

EduTech 2000. EduTech 2000 sought to achieve "a shift in teaching methodology throughout the education system from didactic to child-centred" (Ministry of Education, Youth Affairs and Culture, Barbados 1998, 144). It also sought to introduce more project-based learning and to improve teachers' capacities for diagnosing and remediating students' learning difficulties. EduTech 2000 had four components, but only one – integrating learning technologies (IT) – is of concern in this chapter. The IT component entailed eight thousand to ten thousand computers being installed in primary and secondary schools in classrooms, libraries, staff rooms and offices along with the necessary hardware, software and networking infrastructure. According to Pirog and Kioko (2010) the plan was for primary schools with less than 500 children to receive a 30-computer laboratory while larger schools received two such laboratories. Each classroom was to be equipped with a "media centre" which included a television set, a video cassette recorder and a TV-PC converter.

e-Learning in Jamaica. The integration of ICT into teaching in schools was a key objective of the e-Learning Jamaica programme. This programme provided ICT hardware, software and broadband access to all the 166 public high schools, 16 private high schools and 10 teachers' colleges. The programme also included instructional materials in digital format (Miller and Munroe 2014) and targeted the training in ICT of teacher trainers. This proved successful in that it helped the teacher training colleges to include courses on the integration of ICT into teaching in all pre-service programmes.

Barriers to the Achievement of Expected Outcomes of Traditional and Modern Technologies

Table 5.2 analyses the innovations drawing on the barriers to technology use of Newhouse (2014). Some of the barriers have a broader interpretation in this study. *Technical barriers* refer to use of technologies in physical environments which lack needed infrastructure or technical capacity. *Teachers' personal experience and belief* refers to teachers' feelings of incompetence and inadequacy, largely on account of the training received to implement the innovation. It also refers to their beliefs about their role as teacher. Pedagogical *barrier* refers to difficulties with teaching arising from decisions and actions taken which are not in alignment with the curriculum. *Organizational barrier* relates to the inability of school leadership to create the sort of environment in which the technology can be effectively implemented. This includes providing the necessary support for teachers and students. *Resources* is a fifth barrier introduced. It refers to the provision of resources (material, physical, financial, time) to support the innovation.

Teachers' Personal Experiences and Beliefs

Teachers' personal experiences and beliefs appear as a barrier in all of the innovations. This is evident in the fact that the PRIMER teachers were

Table 5.2. Barriers to the Achievement of Expected Outcomes of Use of Traditional and Modern Technologies

Innovation/ Country	Barriers					Sources
	Technical	Teacher's Personal Experience and Beliefs	Organizational	Pedagogical	Resources	
ETV * (Jamaica)	Frequent power outages: lack of skill to repair TVs. Theft of TVs	Inadequate teacher training: inadequate preparation and follow-up after broadcast	Inadequate supervision by principals	Lack of alignment of content of broadcast with curriculum; student unsupervised	Lack of funds to maintain/ service TVs; lack of qualified staff to produce programmes	Jennings-Wray and Wellington (1985)
SIM (Grade 10–11) *Jamaica	No provision for storage of materials	Inadequate teacher training. When supplies of SIM diminished, teachers taught using copies of the SIM	Principals unsupportive	Content of SIM not articulated with curriculum and written above level of students	No funds to replenish stock of materials. Students had to share materials; no time to field test materials Lack of resources for the Life Skills programme	Jennings-Wray and Wellington (1985) Jennings (1994) Jennings (2002)

REAP LAPs * (Belize)	Lack of technical expertise to produce quality LAPs	Teachers unable to make use of LAPs. Inadequate training	Principals unsupportive	Lack of alignment of content of LAPs with academic subjects and primary exit examination	Less funds post-1982 impacted the curriculum integration of LAPs with agricultural programme	Massey (1982) Edmond (1985) Jennings (1988)
PRIMER *(Jamaica)	Technical expertise lacking in many areas (e.g. evaluation). Multi-functional roles poorly executed	Programmed teachers' and students' individual work perceived as "threat". Teachers inadequately trained	Principals unsupportive as expected rewards not received	Materials written above level of students and were of a poor quality. "Organizational chaos" resulted from use of remedial readers	Changes in policy of funding agency impacted negatively on the innovation	Minott (1988) Jennings (1993)
EduTech 2000 #(Barbados)	Computers supplied inadequate. Inability to access the web and school network at home	Teachers not trained to infuse ICT into teaching	(No data on this)	Teachers' inability to integrate ICT into their teaching	No funds for teacher training. Lack of indigenous websites and software	Ministry of Education, Barbados (1998) Gaible (2008) Pirog and Kioko (2010)

(*Continued*)

Table 5.2. (Continued)

| Innovation/Country | Technical | Teacher's Personal Experience and Beliefs | Barriers | Pedagogical | Resources | Sources |
			Organizational			
e-Learning 2006# (Jamaica)	Inadequate infrastructure for use of technology. Poor internet access Problem with access to technology	Traditional high school teachers felt "deskilled"; more training needed to integrate ICT into teaching	Little administrative support	Teachers' inability to integrate ICT into their teaching	Insufficient funds to replace damaged laptops	Butler (2012) Miller and Munroe (2014)
(e-Cal)# (Trinidad & Tobago)	Inadequate physical infrastructure Limited availability of internet classroom space/lack of support from technicians	Teachers felt incompetent to infuse ICT into teaching; heavy workload	Little administrative support	Teachers' inability to integrate ICT into their teaching	Lack of resources (software)	Ministry of Education, Trinidad and Tobago (2010) Mitchell and Harry (2012)

Key: * Traditional technology; # Modern technology.

unwilling to allow the children to work independently. They felt that the correct answers at the end of each self-instructional module encouraged the children to look up the answers and mitigated any real learning taking place (Jennings 1993). Furthermore, the teachers should have welcomed the help offered by the sixth-grade "programmed teachers" whom they were supposed to tutor to teach literacy skills to third graders. However, the teachers did not adequately prepare these "programmed teachers" for the task and in fact perceived them as a threat to their authority. They felt they were "taking over" their role as teacher and invading their territory. An evaluation showed that there was no significant difference in the performance of the third-grade students taught by the "programmed teachers" and third graders without the intervention (Isaacs 1984). The SIM were of poor quality and the teachers did not allow the students to use them independently. This was because students working independently conflicted with the teacher's perception of their role as transmitters of knowledge.

In the case of the grade 10–11 materials, students were not able to work independently using the SIM as the supply of copies of these materials diminished. Eventually teachers taught using the SIM as their source materials. Inadequate training for the task is a persistent belief of the teachers involved in all the innovations. Since the Grade 10–11 Programme was developed over a period of six months there wasn't sufficient time to train teachers for the grade 10 materials to be implemented in 1974. In fact, grade 9 teachers were moved up to teaching at grade 10 and those in the lower grades were replaced by primary school teachers "who could not competently implement the grades seven to nine curriculum" (Ministry of Education, Jamaica, 1977, 38–39). Jennings-Wray and Wellington (1985) cite data from the Ministry of Education, Jamaica, which shows that in 1975–76 the new secondary schools which delivered the Grade 10–11 Programme had 15.13 per cent pre-trained teachers compared with 5.3 per cent in the traditional high schools. The SIM were expected to compensate for the deficiencies of the teachers in the new secondary schools.

Both teachers and students were introduced to the use of the SIM through the media. For example, model classes were selected to demonstrate the new methodology using ETV. The guides which the teachers should have used as the students worked through the SIM were sent to the teachers *after* the students had covered the materials in their individualized booklets. When the grade 11 materials were implemented in 1975, seven implementation officers were selected from among classroom teachers who were judged "model teachers" in their use of the grade 10 materials. A remarkable achievement perhaps, given that they were trained to teach up to the grade 9 level!

The teachers in REAP struggled with the LAPs as was to be expected given that about 64 per cent of rural primary school teachers in Belize at the time were untrained (Edmond 1985). At the workshops the teachers received training in such areas as agricultural skills, principles of curriculum development and the writing of performance objectives. The teachers developed the LAPs at the training workshops which lasted from two days to two weeks. The LAPs were generally of a poor quality and the teachers had difficulty articulating work in the school garden with the use of the LAPs and with the academic subjects. Massey (1982) found that teachers made little use of the LAPs. Jennings (1988) suggests that this was due to an underestimation of the level of expertise required to develop materials that effectively integrate academic areas, traditionally taught separately, with agricultural study. "It is a task for a team of disciplinary specialists of the highest competence with the able assistance of classroom teachers" (Jennings 1988, 122).

Was the training of teachers for the modern technology interventions any better? According to Miller and Munroe (2014), 4,662 high school teachers were trained in the integration of ICT in instruction. The usefulness of e-Learning in schools is perceived differently by teachers with some considering it helpful in improving their pedagogy, while others perceived it as having a deskilling and erosion of authority effect (Butler 2012). According to Butler, many teachers expressed the need for more training to properly equip them to integrate technology in their teaching, since they did not feel competent enough to use the equipment and materials provided.

The cascade approach was used to train teachers for both e-Learning and e-Cal. Basically this involved training the trainers of teachers in a two-day workshop and these teachers were then expected to train other teachers in the schools. This approach proved ineffective in both e-Cal and e-Learning. Mitchell and Harry (2012) point out that teachers in e-Cal felt that the training provided was inadequate and expressed the need for "ongoing, on site, in-depth training" (Mitchell and Harry 2012, 64) that is responsive to the concerns and needs of the teachers. The teachers did not feel that they had the competence to infuse ICT into their teaching and so the change in teaching pedagogy envisaged in e-Cal did not materialize.

No plan was in place to train new teachers who entered the system after the initial training with the result that such teachers had limited information about the programme (Onuoha, Ferdinand and Onuoha 2015) and just had to "muddle along". Granston and Clayton (2009) reported a similar experience with the training of teachers to integrate ICT into the primary school curriculum in Jamaica.

Several problems were experienced with the teacher training component of EduTech 2000. The training was done by the local teacher training college and a number of consultants. There was much variation in the training, and this resulted in the teachers becoming confused especially in relation to the integration of IT. The fact that training was also voluntary and conducted after school hours resulted in timing and logistical problems as communication between the teacher training college, the Ministry of Education and the schools was deficient. Training in IT took place even when there was no IT available in the teachers' classrooms (Pirog and Kioko 2010)! These writers contend that "there was a huge gap between the mastery of basic computer technology and the ability of the teachers to integrate the technology into the curriculum and the classroom" (Pirog and Kioko 2010, 89). So much of the budget was spent on capital works that none was left for the training of the teachers to change their pedagogy. Most surprisingly, there was no training in alternative assessment of students and child-centred/constructivist approaches to teaching which was such a central feature of the innovation. Thus, as Pirog and Kioko (2010, 89) maintain "teachers who went through the training may have gained little pedagogically".

Pedagogical Barriers

Possibly, since most involved curriculum change, the traditional technologies illustrate how decisions can be taken in a project which cause real difficulties for teachers to implement. How can teachers be expected to use materials which are not appropriate for the grade level being taught? Yet this was the case for teachers of both PRIMER and the Grade 10–11 Programme. The materials for both programmes were written above the level of most of the children for whom they were designed. In the case of PRIMER this was because a reading test, administered after the SIM were written, revealed that about 80 per cent of the pupils were reading at or below grade 2. A remedial programme called "Marching On" was developed for the students, but this only increased the teachers' confusion when they had to use these alongside the revised version of the SIM. The teachers "kept moving pupils backwards and forwards, out of and into selected groups of module users. . . . There was 'organizational chaos'" (Minott 1988, 134).

The SIM for the Grade 10–11 Programme were developed largely by people outside of the Ministry of Education who had little knowledge of the varying abilities of the students who attended the new secondary schools. The SIM were written at the level expected of students in grade 10, but few would have reached the expected level because an estimated 53 per cent of these students entered these secondary schools barely functionally literate (Ministry of Education, Jamaica 1977). The teachers did not adequately monitor the students' progress in using the SIM, so they raced ahead from one module to the next with the minimum of understanding.

The teachers in Belize had difficulty using the LAPs in REAP because their training did not give them the skills to use the nine areas of study as "themes" or "threads" to integrate the content of the LAPs with the other subjects in the curriculum. Teachers in Jamaica were faced with several problems in making use of ETV. The timetable for programmes from the Educational Broadcasting Service always arrived late and so the preparation on the part of the teachers before the broadcasts was poor, if done at all. The content of the ETV invariably was not properly aligned with what the teachers taught in the regular classes, and this caused some confusion for the students. Added to this the teachers failed to adequately supervise the students during the broadcast and to do the necessary follow-up work after the broadcast (Jennings-Wray and Wellington 1985).

Teachers using modern technologies had real concerns about the effect of having to use the laptop on their accustomed mode of teaching. A typical view is captured in the study by Mitchell and Harry (2012, 58):

> It means I have to change how I used to teach . . . I have to understand the use of the laptop and how to integrate it . . . find ways of using it that's comfortable for me. Not sure if the new role is easy, it seems difficult.

Organizational Barriers

The principal plays a key role in making educational reform work at the school level and yet in none of the innovations was any provision made for even orienting the principals into strategies for their successful implementation. The teachers were trained to implement the innovations; the principals were not. Often, they did not understand what the innovation implied for changes in teacher behaviours and many times they were required to implement innovations in their schools without the resources to do so. In the Grade 10–11 Programme, for example, the principals of the newly created new secondary schools did not have the funds to purchase sewing machines and other tools and equipment needed for the Life Skills programme. Nor did they have the resources to make new copies of the SIM. If principals see that their teachers are having difficulty integrating ICT into their teaching, or integrating the content of the LAPs with subjects in the curriculum, should they not have organized additional training and ongoing support for their teachers? Admittedly, they should have, given their key role in educational reform, if they saw those things as their responsibility. The problem is that they didn't. The innovations were introduced using the power-coercive or "top-down" approach and so principals saw themselves as carrying out mandates "from above". In their eyes the Ministry of Education was responsible for providing the schools with the needed resources. While to the researcher, the principals should have monitored the teachers' supervision of the students during the ETV broadcasts (Jennings-Wray and Wellington 1985); however, from the perspective of the principal the problem lies in the lateness of the Educational Broadcasting Service in sending the broadcast programme to the schools.

The kind of support that teachers need to integrate technology into their teaching is not provided most of the time. Teachers need time to prepare beforehand. This is multiplied if they teach several classes. Time is also needed to set up in the classroom, get the cords, contact a technician in cases of difficulty, change classroom if a plug is not working. This can mean time lost in a teaching period allotted a specific time. The cumulative effect of this, according to a teacher interviewed, is that "out of 100 per cent of work for the term, I may only complete 40 to 50 per cent . . . so the whole curriculum with me will not be delivered" (Mitchell and Harry 2012, 59). Teachers in e-Cal received little support from their principals. In fact, one reported complaining to the administration, "and what administration told me, they have little control over that" (Mitchell and Harry 2012, 65).

Technical Barriers

It should have occurred to the educational planners of the Grade 10–11 Programme that space needed to be provided for the safe storage of the SIM. This was not done and could account for why the materials fell into disrepair and copies disappeared. In the case of REAP, the physical conditions of work in the school gardens proved problematic. The REAP students did not have the proper clothing for agricultural work. Washing facilities in the schools were inadequate and this caused the students discomfort when they had to return to the classroom after work in the school garden. Personal safety was also an issue because first aid provisions were minimal in case of injury. Another pressing problem was "praedial larceny". This is the theft of crops from the school garden invariably by persons outside the rural community (Jennings 1988).

A number of technical barriers were also encountered in the use of ETV. Frequent power cuts, poor maintenance, vandalism and theft of TV sets undermined the attempt to improve the quality of education which was an important goal of the use of ETV. In fact, Jennings-Wray and Wellington (1985, 177) maintain that the television programmes produced "have not been of the best quality because of a lack of qualified staff to produce them". ETV succeeded in reaching a wider student body, but most teachers claimed that ETV "does not improve basic scholastic ability" (Jennings-Wray and Wellington 1985, 176) and described the use of ETV as having resulted in "utter failure".

Butler (2012) reported that Jamaican teachers did not think that the e-Learning materials were practical in all the subjects of their schools' curriculum. The e-Learning materials were also not readily accessible. Almost 50 per cent of the teachers sampled said that more e-Learning equipment, materials and laboratories needed to be made available to teachers. The fact that the teachers also suggested that a maintenance unit should be made readily accessible to the schools indicates that the malfunctioning of computers was a problem. This was also a problem experienced in EduTech 2000. Pirog and Kioko (2010, 90) conclude that "due to frequent malfunctioning of the computers, long delays with respect to repairs, limited memory and storage capacity, lack of indigenous websites and software, and inability to access the web and school network at home, computers were not generally incorporated into the learning process of students".

Similar problems were experienced in e-Cal. Mitchell and Harry (2012) reported that infrastructure proved to be a major challenge in the implementation of e-Cal. The traditional classroom was not equipped to accommodate infusion of ICT into teaching and learning. Some classrooms did not have the electrical outlets required and the size of the classrooms did not allow for flexible arrangements of desks for collaborative work or for free movement within the space.

Resources

Time proved to be an important resource in the Grade 10–11 Programme. The democratic socialist government of the day (Manley 1974), as part of its political manifesto, had pledged to solve the youth unemployment problem summarily. Since the Grade 10–11 Programme was the solution, it had to be developed and implemented quickly. Slated to be developed in one year, the development of the grade 10 curriculum was squashed into six months. Because of such speed the time given for the field testing of the materials was inadequate because improvements to draft units were sometimes not incorporated into the finished product because of the pressure to meet deadlines (Jennings 2002).

Mitchell and Harry (2012) report that teachers in e-Cal complained about not being supplied with the necessary resources. As one teacher in their study reported, "The problem seems to be related to resources and infrastructure as we have crowded, cramped classrooms, no Internet access and so this makes it difficult to use the laptops" (Mitchell and Harry 2012, 60). Internet access at school proved highly problematic not only for the students but also for the teachers. Classrooms did not have adequate electrical connections and teachers experienced problems in getting easy access to projectors, multimedia and other equipment. After about two years of use the laptops became damaged and were not replaced. As noted by a teacher in another study on e-Cal, "It is usually difficult when you come to class and only five boys have functional laptops and three quarters of the class do not have working laptops" (Onuoha, Ferdinand and Onuoha 2015, 11).

In relation to EduTech 2000, Pirog and Kioko (2010) noted that most teachers said that more equipment and materials were needed in their schools as what was provided was insufficient to meet the needs of all the classes. Perhaps this is not surprising given that much of the technological hardware and software promised did not materialize. According to Pirog and Kioko (2010, 76) "IT is the most expensive component of EduTech, initially budgeted at $68.9 million. However, by the end of the seven-year loan period only 23.6 per cent of the technology had been installed (although 41 per cent of the funds had been spent)".

A critical resource is funding. What is evident from table 5.1 is that all the innovations, except for the Grade 10–11 Programme and e-Cal, received funding from international aid agencies or private enterprise. REAP and EduTech 2000 were exceptional in the amount of funding they received. International aid agencies provided REAP with the capital and technical assistance which the government of Belize could not have afforded by itself. REAP was well financed from 1976 to 1982 when the transfer of the support role from the international organizations to the Belizean government and local organizations took place. Strong ideological support from the minister of education of the day ensured some funding. Nevertheless after 1982 the schools began to experience difficulties in obtaining supplies of feed, chicks and rabbits as well as farm implements (Edmond 1985) and in 1984 REAP's strongest advocates lost the general election (Jennings 1988).

The importance of strong ideological support for funding an intervention is underscored by the Grade 10–11 Programme. The budget allocation for education was increased by over thirty-six million Jamaican dollars for the 1974–75 fiscal year and most of this was spent on the Grade 10–11 Programme. So critical was this programme to the democratic socialist government which saw it as the fulfilment of an election promise to stem youth unemployment that the programme was made a "special project" in the prime minister's office with its own budget and specially recruited staff. Alas, this was only affordable for two years! When the programme was moved to the Core Curriculum Unit in the Ministry of Education the programme ran into difficulty. Instead of being distributed on a one-to-one basis, because of shortage of supply of the SIM over time, the grade 10–11 materials had to be shared among the students thus defeating the self-pacing rationale for self-instruction. The Life Skills curriculum was poorly implemented. Topics such as "how to repair garments" or "how to fix an electrical fuse in the home" required resources which many schools did not have: for example, sewing machines and electrical supplies. Because of the various problems encountered, there was no evidence that the use of SIM led to a reduction in education costs due to less reliance on the teacher.

The per capita income of Trinidad and Tobago is almost four times that of Jamaica. Given its oil-rich economy, it is understandable that it should be able to finance its own educational innovations. Like the Grade 10–11 Programme, e-Cal was part of the government's manifesto promise. The laptops were distributed within a short space of the new government assuming power, but the problem with the internet filter software to prevent students from accessing undesirable websites soon became apparent and proved difficult to fix. The fact that damaged laptops could not be replaced indicated that the recurrent costs of e-Cal were beyond the education budget.

EduTech 2000 was funded by the IDB, the Caribbean Development Bank (CDB) and the government of Barbados to the sum of US$213 million over seven years – "a massive investment for a school system with approximately 48,000 primary and secondary school students" (Pirog and Kioko 2010, 72). But even this massive financial outlay proved insufficient. Although the IT component was allocated the largest sum in the project, it was only sufficient to install less than 25 per cent of the technology. The amount allotted to capital works proved insufficient to cover the amount of infrastructural work that had to be done to schools to make them ready for the technology.

Summary

Traditional technologies had goals ranging from equity of access to quality education (ETV) and creating as many opportunities for children from poor social and economic environments to access jobs on leaving school as their more-well-to-do peers (SIM Grade 10–11). There was also the goal of improving the educational opportunities of rural children by strengthening their language and mathematics skills (PRIMER) or their agricultural knowledge and skills (REAP). These goals were to be achieved through new curricula delivered by well-trained, if not exceptional, teachers who would ensure effective learning on the part of the students. For example, the best teachers were to deliver the classes via ETV so that *all* students benefited, and teachers were to guide students as they learned at their own pace, with the assistance of teachers' aides, in the case of PRIMER. Because agriculture was integrated in all their areas of study, students in REAP schools were able to apply their new knowledge in their home gardens and farms and so were able to see the relevance of their learning to their daily life.

Modern technologies, in contrast, were more focused on changing teaching pedagogy from a teacher-centred transmission model to one that was learner centred and constructivist in approach. By improving the quality of instruction, through the infusion of ICT in teaching and learning, e-Cal sought to reduce the inequity in access to computers and information that existed between the students from wealthy and poor families. A key objective of both EduTech 2000 and e-Learning Jamaica was to shift the teaching methodology in schools from teacher centred to learner centred. In all of these innovations the schools were provided with computers and laptops and in the case of EduTech 2000 a civil works component was designed to improve infrastructure in schools to make them "technology ready".

Both traditional and modern technologies encountered five barriers to the achievement of their goals: namely, *teachers' personal experience and beliefs, pedagogical, organizational, technical* and *resources*. In PRIMER, for example, teachers did not allow the students to use the self-instructional materials independently because this conflicted with their perception of their role as a teacher which was to stand in front of a class and deliver. The teachers felt that the training they received to implement the innovations was inadequate. The teachers in *e-Cal* felt they needed more ongoing, on-site and in-depth training that was responsive to their concerns and needs. All the innovations experienced resource constraints. For example, by the end of the seven-year loan period for EduTech 2000 the schools had been provided with less than 25 per cent of the computers and laptops expected. In the absence of funds to reproduce the self-instructional materials, teachers in the Grade 10–11 Programme used the few that remained as their own source materials.

Pedagogical barriers encountered in the use of traditional technologies included the fact that curriculum materials developed were written above the level of the students and proved difficult for the teachers to use. In the case of REAP the teachers found the integration of agricultural knowledge into subject curricula far too difficult and therefore made limited use of the LAPs. Due to weaknesses in their training, for the most part, teachers were unable to integrate ICT into their teaching. Technical barriers such as the absence of electrical outlets to accommodate the technology, the malfunctioning of computers and the inability in some cases to access computers or laptops when needed only served to frustrate teachers even further. There was a tendency for teachers to perceive school principals as being unsupportive when they saw no attempt to alleviate their difficulties. However, there was no instance of principals being provided with any training that would empower them to give teachers the support they needed in implementing the innovations. In the case of the Life Skills curriculum in the Grade 10–11 Programme, the principals did not have the funds to provide the resources the teachers needed to implement it. Unsurprisingly, by 1980 when a new government came to power in Jamaica the Life Skills curriculum had been dubbed the "Dead Skills" (Jennings 1994).

Conclusion

So, what have we learned from our experiences in using traditional and modern technologies? What this chapter has shown is that traditional and modern technologies had different goals, but they experienced similar implementation problems. This suggests that policy decisions on modern technologies were made with little or no reference to experiences of the education systems with traditional technologies. But transfer of learning from the past to inform present decision-making can only occur if the knowledge of those experiences is made available. This knowledge comes from formal evaluations. The problem is that formal evaluation is rarely built into efforts to bring about change. Of those discussed in this chapter only two – REAP and EduTech 2000 – were formally evaluated. PRIMER had provision for an evaluator, but the position was never filled. A thorough research of the local institutional contexts into which the innovations were to be implemented should have been done. Clearly insufficient, if any, research was done to inform decision-making as is evident in the case of PRIMER where tests of students' abilities were done *after* the materials were developed (Jennings 1993). In e-Cal the need for an internet filter software only became apparent *after* the students were seen accessing undesirable websites (Mitchell and Harry 2012) and in EduTech 2000 there was gross underestimation of the physical conditions of schools which had to be updated to accommodate the new technologies (Pirog and Kioko 2010).

The big question is: What does the use of technology look like without the barriers identified? We cannot say because the use of technologies in schools has been so fraught with barriers to implementation that they were not given a fair chance to "revolutionize the teaching-learning process" (Ministry of Education, Jamaica,1982, 5). Cuban (2008, 191) puts it more graphically, "Partially baked breads seldom rise sufficiently to taste good. And half-done policy implementation means that the question of whether the reform-driven policy works well seldom gets answered." PRIMER succumbed under the weight of its implementation problems and offered no solutions to the improvement of learning in rural schools (Minott 1988, Jennings 1993). In fact, as one researcher noted "one has to look very hard to detect the innovation in use within Project PRIMER" (Stromquist 1982, 7). PRIMER was the only IMPACT-related project that closed at the end of the initial funding period (Cummings 1986).

Where do the learners fit into all of this? What is noticeable about the innovations studied in this chapter are the ambitious goals they had for the students – goals relating to equity of access to quality education, equalizing work opportunities for children of the poor and revolutionizing teaching pedagogy. Can we reasonably expect such goals to be achieved within the limited time span for funding by the international aid agencies? If they sought to do less, could the innovations have achieved more, for example, in terms of improvement in student learning? In fact, little attention was given to this in the cases examined in this chapter. Exceptions were REAP and EduTech 2000 which show mixed results. The evaluator of REAP (Massey 1982) took pains to underscore that students in REAP schools performed as well in the Belize National Primary Examination as their peers in non-REAP schools. On the performance in the Barbados Secondary School Examination the evaluators of EduTech 2000 conclude that "the most innovative component of EduTech, the infusion of technology, has no significant impacts on student test scores" (Pirog and Kioko 2010, 88). All these findings support the point made by Cuban (2008) that access and use of ICT has not led to any changes in teaching pedagogy or improvement in academic achievement. He reminds us that the technology is the medium or the machine and should not be confused with the teacher's instructional methods. There is little difference between the use of PowerPoint with notes and writing the same notes on a chalkboard.

Online Teaching during a Pandemic

How does our past experience with modern technology inform online teaching from schooling at home during the pandemic? We do not have any example of the use of modern technology in this way at the lower levels of the education system. There is a wealth of experience at the tertiary level, as in the Open Campus of the UWI, but our concern here is with the lower levels of the education system. However, our past experience with the use of modern technology raises some concerns which are pertinent to the online teaching with the school-at-home approach used by Ministries of Education in the region.

The first concern is that this approach necessitates that the learners assume more responsibility for their own learning. The teacher is cast in the role of a facilitator. That this represents what teachers expect is evident from a parent who reported that because of a glitch in the computer programme, the students could not upload a file with a diagram as required and so they emailed the completed homework to the teacher. The teacher was heard "complaining bitterly that they must go and learn how to use and manoeuvre the system and stop e-mailing her work" (Hibbert 2020). Our experience with modern technology has shown that it has not resulted in teaching becoming student centred and so students continue to rely on the authority of the teacher.

This leads to the second concern. Teachers may have been trained to integrate technology into their teaching, but this is not the same as being trained to teach online. This requires more complex skills and competencies in preparation of materials, managing online discussion or chat groups and interacting with students online, individually as well as in groups. The students themselves need training in how to use the technology to maximize their learning and this includes learning how to "manoeuvre the system". Admittedly, this may not be difficult as the children of today are digital natives. The greater concern is for the parents or guardians, because of the greater demands being made on them. They too need training in the use of the online learning platform so that they can more readily help the children when in difficulty.

The third point concerns resources. All of the innovations in technology experienced resource constraints. Preparing the infrastructure of schools to make them "ready" for the technology is a huge cost, the extent of which is often underestimated, as in the case of EduTech 2000. Providing each child with a laptop is also an enormous expense – and a recurrent one as laptops have a relatively short life. Some countries cannot supply each child with a laptop and choose to give to the most needy[1] with the onus being put on parents to provide laptops for their children. This has increased the hardships on parents already finding it difficult to cope due to job losses caused by the pandemic. Many parents from low-income homes cannot afford to pay for internet in their homes and those who live in rural and remote areas may not even have electricity on a regular basis. The fact that parents from high-income homes will be able to provide their children with all the essentials for online learning underscores the potential for schooling at home using online teaching to further widen the gap between the rich and poor. This is happening in the context of countries that embrace educational goals of social equity and quality of education for all.

The fourth concern is for children with special needs. None of the innovations in technology have addressed them specifically. In the onset of the pandemic, while provision is made to give laptops to the poorer children, nothing is said about provision for children with special needs. Yet materials can be written at multi-levels using graphic tools, voice, animation and other devices to cater to children with learning difficulties. Technology can be adapted in other ways to respond to the needs of children with hearing impairment or loss of sight.

It could, of course, be argued that the pandemic came upon us so unexpectedly in 2020 that there was no time to do the necessary preparations to provide the needed resources, do the necessary training and prepare the materials required for online teaching. However, the fact that there has been so much investment in modern technology indicates that we envisioned a time when technology would play a leading role in education, but our policymakers and educational planners did not clearly articulate that role, apart from emphasizing the need for teaching to become student centred. It took a pandemic to thrust upon us what it meant for the education system to undergo "radical change which will place the student at the centre of the teaching/learning process" (Ministry of Education Youth and Culture (1998, 142)). It meant freeing learning from the boundaries of the school walls and opening it up to homes and other places in the wider society with the necessary technology for access to learning. It meant broadening the range of facilitators of learning to include parents, guardians, caregivers and other stakeholders in education who are able to assist the children with online learning.

Our children live and have to learn in an age of rapidly advancing technology. This chapter has underscored the long road along which Caribbean school systems still have to travel in order to enable our children to maximize their use of modern technologies. In the words of Newhouse (2014, 480): "If we want to create more student-centred learning environments based on constructivist understandings, and if we want to empower children as learners, then we know we can use such devices to support these aims; assuming we also have reliable networks, adequate technical support, appropriate software, informed and effective school leadership, relevant curriculum, well-prepared teachers, and connected local communities."

6.

Using Technology in Training to Teach

Case Studies from Jamaica and Guyana

The previous chapter focused on the integration of technology into teaching and learning at the school level. An analysis of the case studies presented found several barriers that inhibited successful integration. We questioned what the use of technology without implementation barriers looks like and concluded that because of these barriers the use of technologies in schools was not given a fair chance to achieve the objective of revolutionizing the teaching-learning process. The question then is: In the Caribbean experience was the use of technology more successful at the post-secondary and tertiary levels? It is to this question that we address our minds in this chapter through an examination of two innovative programmes that used technology to train teachers through distance education. The two programmes are the Bachelor of Education Secondary Distance Education (BEdSecDE) (Jamaica) and the Guyana In-Service Distance Education (GUIDE) programme. The BEdSecDE was initiated by the Ministry of Education in Jamaica in 2001 and funded for ten years. GUIDE was offered over twelve semesters commencing in 1995 in two regions of Guyana with the largest numbers of untrained teachers. It was funded by the governments of Guyana and the United Kingdom.

Many governments and tertiary institutions in the Caribbean have responded to challenges to increase access to teacher education using distance education (DE). For example, in a study that informed the development of distance education programmes in Guyana, Hamilton (1999) underscored the concern for the number of untrained teachers who do not have the minimum requirement for entry into a teacher training programme. She observed that "in-service training is therefore an increasing priority and for the hinterland and deep riverain areas where teachers are scattered over an expansive terrain, distance education is a necessary strategy" (Hamilton 1999, 3).

DE is a modality described as a "flexible multi-media delivery system which is highly sensitive to social realities" (Koul 1999, 106). Features of DE delivery systems include learner-centredness in that the technology used has the flexibility to respond to the learner's needs; open and flexible entry requirements to increase access and equity; work–study combinations; multimedia course packages which accommodate different learning styles and techniques; and courses prepared by teams of experts "to provide up-to-date and rich content and specialized instructional design for easy access, grasp, retention and retrieval" (Koul 1999, 110). The two programmes studied are examples of the distance education modality. Why look at these programmes now, the reader may ask, given that they were initiated some time ago and we are now well into the digital revolution?

It is indeed true that since then technology has had a strong impact on tertiary education as many courses and programmes are offered online and "open universities" and "open campuses" are prevalent. But how did we in the CC get to this point? Jennings (1999, 121) describes how dual mode (face to face and by distance) delivery of courses and programmes at the University of Guyana was hailed as "the most significant development in the twenty first century" but academia was hesitant in embracing the new technology. The response was similar at the UWI (Kingston, Jamaica campus) when the UWI Distance Teaching Experiment was first introduced in 1983. The Faculty of Education was one of the few that responded and offered its Certificate in Education to nine CC countries via a telephone link-up for interactive communication and use of print materials. Frequent breakdown of the telecommunication system, late arrival of print materials, difficulty on the part of students to balance full-time work and study and shortage of reference materials were among the difficulties experienced.

Were any of these difficulties experienced in the two programmes discussed in this chapter or had the developers learned from past experience? The two programmes have been deliberately chosen for three reasons. First, at the time of their initiation they were innovative in that they represented new ideas being used in their respective education systems for the first time. Second, they offer a contrast between the use of traditional and modern technologies at the post-secondary and tertiary levels to serve as comparisons with those at the secondary level discussed in the previous chapter. Third, they underscore how the choice and use of technology are mediated by contextual considerations, even though countries in the CC have so much in common.

Purpose

This chapter compares the experience of using traditional technology to train teachers in the more remote parts of Guyana with that of training teachers in Jamaica who were exposed to more sophisticated and modern technology. The programmes are the BEdSecDE (Jamaica) and the GUIDE programme from

Guyana. The case studies of the programmes will show how effectively they were implemented and with what measure of success. Using the effectiveness criterion of Cuban (1998), the extent to which the goals of the programmes were achieved will be examined with reference to the following indicators: (1) *inputs* (i.e. the qualifications and experience of staff in the programmes, and resource provisions), (2) *process* (including the quality of interaction between students and staff, student preparedness for interactive sessions) and (3) *outcomes* (that is throughput and student performance). In the remainder of the chapter the writer will pinpoint similarities and differences between the two programmes and discuss the extent to which they remained faithful to the principles of distance education. Towards the end of the chapter some lessons learned from the case studies which need to be considered by those planning similar change in their education systems will be pointed up. Some background information will first be given on Guyana and Jamaica to set the context of the discussion.

Background to the Case Studies

Guyana, "the land of many waters", and Jamaica, "the land of wood and water", both former British colonies, are countries which have much in common and yet are different in many ways (see table 6.1). Guyana is situated on the South American continent, surrounded by Spanish-, Dutch- and Portuguese-speaking neighbours, while Jamaica is an island in the Caribbean Sea whose nearest Spanish speaking neighbour is Cuba. Guyana faces greater challenges than Jamaica in terms of its level of poverty, the variety of its ethnic groups, including an indigenous population of nine tribes scattered over a vast terrain of 24,970 square kilometres for which it has to provide trained teachers. Much of the hinterland and deep riverain areas are difficult to access. During the 1990s modern technology was not available in these areas.

According to the government of Guyana (2002, 13) "Amerindians, the indigenous people of Guyana, represent less than 10 per cent of the population but account for 17 per cent of the poor because they live in the geographically isolated and inaccessible rural interior". The government of Guyana (2002, 4) further acknowledges that "the educational and other services provided to hinterland and deep riverain regions are clearly below national standards". The hinterland and deep riverain areas are largely inhabited by the Amerindians. In these areas 69 per cent of teachers are untrained and unqualified. Potential teachers from the deep rural and remote parts of Guyana would have to leave their homes to spend three years in the city of Georgetown where the sole teacher training college is located (Jennings 1996). It runs counter to the cultural values of the Amerindians for their girls to live away from home. Leaving the

Table 6.1. Area, Population and Economy of Jamaica and Guyana

Country	Area (Sq.km)	Population (2020)	HDI/ Rank** N = 157 (2016)	Economy *
Jamaica	10,991	2.9 million	73.0 (82)	Tourism, bauxite production and remittances are the mainstay of the economy; GDP per capita US$9,447; 1.4% growth; public debt is 99.4% of GDP. 9.5% unemployment; corruption and high levels of crime impact growth of economy. **Government spending on health and education 11.4% of GDP
Guyana	214,970	0.8 million	63.8 (107)	Exports of timber, gold, diamond, sugar, bauxite, rice; commenced oil production in 2020; 3.4% growth; GDP per capita (2015) US$8,519.00; public debt is 57% GDP; 12.2% unemployment; widespread corruption in government, police and judiciary. **Government spending on health and education 8.4% of GDP

*Source: 2020 Index of Economic Freedom the Heritage Foundation.
**SDG Index and Dashboards Report 2017: Global Responsibilities.
HDI: Human Development Index

quiet seclusion of the rain forest for life in a bustling city is a culture shock to the Amerindian (Jennings 2011). Very few of the African- and East Indian-Guyanese teachers are attracted to teach in the hinterland where working and living conditions are deplorable. Some of the houses provided for teachers have neither water supply nor electricity. Being unaccustomed to Amerindian culture and not speaking the language would result in culture shock for them too. The solution was to provide teacher training in the hinterland regions. GUIDE was the pilot programme that informed the design and delivery of training in these regions.

Jamaica neither has an indigenous population, nor the variety of ethnic groups of Guyana, and even though it has much less land space (10,991 square kilometres) it also faces inequities in educational provision. Teachers can readily obtain initial training at some nine teachers colleges located in different parts of the island, but for many years to obtain a degree they had to access the campus of the main university – the UWI – which is located in the capital city, Kingston. This posed hardships particularly for teachers who live in rural areas which are relatively inaccessible. Heavy rainfall invariably results in flooding in rural parishes which cuts them off from the rest of the island. In these areas computers, internet facilities and libraries are not as readily accessible to teachers as to those who live in the larger towns and cities.

Case Studies

The Bachelor of Education Secondary Distance Education Programme

Context/Goals

The ROSE programme in the mid-1990s ushered in the rationalization of secondary education which attempted to remove the barriers between different school types in Jamaica. What were formally known as new secondary and comprehensive high schools were reclassified as "secondary high schools" (referred to as "upgraded high schools" to distinguish them from the traditional high schools). A change of name alone was insufficient to erase the differences in quality and competence of teachers and raise levels of achievement in all schools. This alongside the GOJ's commitment to universal secondary education created the demand for more qualified and competent teachers at the secondary level. In 2003, 53 per cent of secondary school teachers were graduates of the teachers colleges. Only 22 per cent were trained university graduates (Ministry of Education and Culture Jamaica 2003).

In 2001 the Ministry of Education and Culture awarded a ten-year project to the UWI to develop and implement through its Distance Education Centre a bachelor of education degree programme which targeted three thousand teachers especially those from the newly upgraded high schools. These teachers were to be trained in five cohorts admitted between 2003 and 2007 and each cohort was expected to complete the programme in four years at the rate of six credits per semester and summer. The expectation was that by 2011 all three thousand teachers would have been trained and graduated and performance in the Caribbean Secondary Examination Certificate (CSEC) would have improved, particularly in the newly upgraded high schools.

Inputs

The programme offered the following areas of specialization: biology, chemistry, physics, mathematics, geography, computer science, history, English language and literature, French and Spanish. A coordinator was assigned to each specialization. Training was organized for both the coordinators and course writers. One year was devoted to the preparation of courses for delivery by distance in the following year. For example, courses to commence in 2003 were prepared in 2002. This involved developing course manuals which students needed to read before meeting with their course tutors. Course writers were commissioned to write the course packages consisting of a course guide: course outline, course material, readings and tutor's guide. For the first two years a blended approach of online, video conferencing and face-to-face delivery was used. Course tutors delivered the courses via teleconferencing from the UWI Distance Education Centre (UWIDEC) on the campus. UWIDEC was linked to ten sites located throughout the island. Face-to-face courses were offered in the summer on the UWI campus over a six-week period.

Over time, however, the demands of the numerous courses on UWIDEC far outweighed the available physical and timetable space for tutorials and teleconferences. In the 2004–05 academic year, therefore, UWIDEC took the decision to move away from the dependence on synchronous technologies (i.e. teleconference and face-to-face tutorials) to a greater use of asynchronous technologies (e.g. email discussion lists, audio/video recorded lectures). This would enable students to complete their programme without the need for face-to-face attendance. However, provision was made for those who needed it early in the programme to have face-to-face contact or other synchronous support. UWIDEC commenced a blended learning/asynchronous delivery in the 2005–06 academic year with a limited number of courses.

The students in the programme did not have to pay tuition costs. That was borne by the GOJ which also covered instructional materials and accommodation costs for the face-to-face summer component. Students only paid small fees for books, meals and transportation. In return, the students were bonded to serve for three years after graduation.

Process

Many students came to the interactive sessions unprepared because they did not manage to read the materials beforehand. In an earlier course delivered by distance, Jennings (1999) reported that lecturers sometimes had to abandon interactive sessions as the students had not done the necessary preparation beforehand. The situation did not change for the better after the introduction of blended learning. Because of difficulty with access to a computer and internet, many students tended to log into the online Virtual Learning Environment provided by the UWI and download course materials and assignments only. Because they were not doing enough reading, they tended not to make use of the opportunity to post questions, engage in chat sessions and other forms of online communication with the lecturers. And yet they complained about missing the ability to interact with the lecturers and get immediate feedback which the face-to-face students enjoy (Xeureb and Peart 2006). At the same time, however, many teachers did not get the support they needed from their schools. For example, when teleconference sessions were set in the early afternoon during school hours, some principals refused to allow the teachers release from their duties to attend the interactive sessions at the UWIDEC sites.

Outcomes

With a projected five intake for training three thousand students, it was expected that the BEdSecDE would attract six hundred students per intake. But the yearly intake ranged from 213 in 2004 to 143 in 2006. The total number of students admitted was 858 (B. Ed Secondary Distance Programme Office 2007). Reasons for this included weak advertising of the programme and the attraction of offshore universities which offered teachers a much shorter period for obtaining the same degree.

A major problem, however, was that many of the teachers in the upgraded high schools were not qualified for entry into the BEdSecDE. Many were trained to teach at the primary level but were teaching in a secondary school. Others were trained to teach at the secondary level but were not teaching the subject that they were trained for. For example, a teacher trained to teach history may be employed to teach physical education. It was a requirement that to be admitted into the programme, the teacher had to be teaching the subject in which further training was being sought.

The graduates of the DE programme were expected to have sufficient content knowledge to enable them to teach the subject to grade 11 in preparation of students to take the CSEC. Content input into the programme was increased from eighteen to thirty credits (where one credit equals fifteen hours) in courses delivered by faculty members outside education. But there were complaints about the lack of depth of subject knowledge of the B. Ed students whether face to face or by distance. This resulted in courses having to be adapted to suit the students' level of ability. The overall effect of this was that many graduates emerged who did not have adequate content knowledge for teaching effectively at the CSEC level (Xuereb and Peart 2006).

Table 6.2 shows that 195 of the students enrolled in the programme dropped out of the programme for reasons varying from ill health, an inability to balance study and full-time teaching simultaneously and the absence of the kind of support services (e.g. online peer support groups, seminars, hotline numbers for depression) provided for their peers who studied in the traditional face-

Table 6.2. BEdSecDE: Student Admission and Status 2011–12

Option	Admission	Enrolled in 2011	Drop out	Transfer out	Total graduates	Percentage of students completing (%)
Biology	114	13	24	4	72	63
Chemistry	34	13	17	2	12	35
Physics	21	2	6	3	10	48
English	218	15	54	9	140	64
French	4	1	2	1	0	0
Spanish	51	1	8	4	37	73
History	97	7	15	3	71	73
Geography	64	10	14	11	28	44
Computer Science	80	8	18	5	49	61
Mathematics	175	20	37	3	115	66
Total	858	81	195	45	534	62

Source: Adapted from Annual Report B. Ed Secondary Distance Education Project, October 2012.

to-face mode. At the time that the programme ended, there were still eighty-one students enrolled and arrangements had to be made for them to transfer to the face-to-face delivery of the programme offered by the department that delivered the programme. Instead of three thousand newly trained teachers after ten years of the project, there were only five hundred and thirty-four. This represented 62 per cent of the total admitted, but only 17.8 per cent of the original target.

The Guyana In-Service Distance Education Programme
Context

According to Guyana's 2003–07 Strategic Plan, the target was to increase the proportion of trained teachers in the hinterland regions by 50 per cent by 2007 (Government of Guyana 2003). This was easier said than done because in the hinterland regions Amerindians have access only to primary education and three years of lower-secondary education in schools known as "primary schools with tops". These schools do not provide them with the level or quality of education needed for entry to the teacher training college on graduation. At the initiation of GUIDE 69 per cent of teachers in the hinterland were untrained/unqualified (Government of Guyana (2002)). This underscores what the government of Guyana (2002, 5) stated, "that the majority of pupils in the hinterland are exposed to unqualified and under qualified teachers".

A precursor to GUIDE was the Hinterland Teacher Training Programme (HTTP) which provided training in English language, mathematics, social studies and integrated science to the level required for entry to professional training and "to effectively teach at several grade levels in their own communities" (Jennings 1996, 62). In all, 159 trainees were admitted to the programme, of whom 132 (83 per cent) completed the programme, but only 122 trainees actually sat the final examination. Thirty-seven trainees dropped out of the programme, largely on account of domestic difficulties. However, less than 50 per cent of the students passed the HTTP and became eligible for formal training at the college of education. An explanation offered by Jennings (1996) is that most of the trainees were from "primary schools with tops" which only offer secondary education up to grade 9 (age fourteen plus) and so the few who took the Caribbean Secondary Examination Certificate (CSEC) obtained failing grades. The level of attainment in mathematics and English of the trainees was weak. The question is: Did GUIDE learn from the experiences of the HTTP?

Goals

GUIDE was an upgrading programme which sought to enhance the learning experience of secondary school children by improving the quality of teaching using distance education methodology. GUIDE focused on teaching skills and methodology while upgrading the teachers' knowledge of the content of the three areas of greatest need: mathematics, English and science. The students also did a course in education. The programme was piloted in regions five and six (Mahaica-Berbice and Corentyne) of Guyana, where the main economic activities centre around rice farming, cattle rearing and sugarcane production.

Inputs

One hundred untrained teachers with four CSEC passes at grade 3 or above were the original target group for GUIDE. They were expected to be teaching at the lower secondary level (forms one, two and three) in primary schools with tops, community high schools or junior secondary schools in the hinterland. However, as there were no other options open to them, trainee-teachers from nursery schools in the coastal plain of region five were also admitted. At the inception of the programme in 1995, a total of ninety-four trainee-teachers were admitted. Later in the year this increased to one hundred and twelve. However, one year later this had reduced to eighty-nine. Almost 72 per cent of the trainee-teachers entered with CSEC Grade 3 passes, but some were at the Basic Proficiency, not the General Proficiency level. Students who had not completed secondary school or had taken part in the Secondary School

Proficiency Examination in the third form of the community high school were admitted to the programme (Jennings 1999). The functional literacy of students from the community high school was found to be particularly low (Jennings et al. 1995). Perhaps it is not surprising that after one term of the 1995–96 school year, principals of the GUIDE schools removed most of the trainee-teachers from teaching in the forms to teaching in the primary grades because they were too weak academically to teach in the forms. Only about 33 per cent of the trainee-teachers taught in forms 1–3.

There were eight tutors in each region. Of these 75 per cent had a Trained Teachers Certificate while the remainder had a bachelor's degree from the University of Guyana. The tutors were either head teachers, deputy heads, senior teachers or heads of departments. Their responsibilities included holding tutorials every two weeks, invigilating examinations and liaising with the regional coordinators. The responsibility of the latter included the recruitment of students, tutors and mentors, arrangements for meetings of tutorial groups, the administration of tests and examinations and submission of monthly reports to the Head of Distance Education at NCERD who had direct responsibility for managing GUIDE.

Curriculum materials produced for distance education programmes should be developed by experts who can "provide up-to-date and rich content and specialised instructional design for easy access, grasp, retention and retrieval" (Koul 1999:110). Importantly, they need to have good lead time for development and should be available to the students before the commencement of the courses. GUIDE met the latter condition because the developers used ready-made materials including modules in child development and teaching methods which were part of a distance teaching programme in Belize (Jennings 1999). They also used pre-university materials used for training in English. In addition to these materials the students were to have access to current textbooks and other reference materials at learning resource centres which were to be readily accessible in their communities.

Process

The Ministry of Education and Cultural Development (MOECD) granted trainee-teachers release from teaching two half days per week to study. They were required to remain in their schools during this period and once it was convenient, to meet with their mentors who were usually a trained teacher in the school. The trainee-teachers attended tutorial sessions fortnightly on Saturdays normally at the nearest learning resource centre. Since these centres were in schools, they were of variable quality. Some were in spacious accommodation and well supplied with textbooks, a computer and photocopying machine.

Others were merely one room with books stacked, unsorted and inaccessible to the students. Some students relied on their tutors to provide them with photocopies of required reading materials (Jennings 1999).

A feature of GUIDE valued by the trainee-teachers is that they were able to put new ideas into practice in their classrooms as they learned them. Given the dearth of materials, the trainees used the GUIDE modules to teach in their classrooms. Exceptions were the nursery teachers and those in the lower grades in primary schools who reported not being able to use the mathematics and science modules as they were "at too high a level for the students" (Jennings 1999, 48). They also had difficulty coping with multi-grade classes. Some students went to tutorial sessions unprepared as the following comments from the tutors show: "Many students do not read the modules or if they do, they do not read them carefully. At tutorial many students would make excuses that they did not have time, the modules are too difficult or there was too much to read."

The lack of comprehension of concepts is due in part to teachers not reading the modules properly and, in most cases, not conceptualizing the matter (Jennings 1999, 96).

Outcomes

Of the 112 students who registered in the programme, 73 completed within 4 to 8 semesters. This represents an overall completion rate of 65.2 per cent (Dalgety, Kellman and Thomas 1999). Table 6.3 shows the overall completion rate by subject. Table 6.4 shows that the lowest level of achievement of the trainee-teachers was in education and English. The scope of content of the education modules proved to be too much for the GUIDE trainees (Jennings 1999) and this was reflected in their achievement. Close to 58 per cent of the trainees received grades in the "C" band, with most of the others receiving "B" grades. Their level of achievement was worse than in mathematics where only 18 per cent of them received grades in the "C" band despite the fact that they complained about the level of difficulty and scope of the mathematics modules.

Table 6.3. Overall Completion Rates in GUIDE by Subject

Subject	Number (73)	%
Education	58	79.5
English	61	83.6
Mathematics	37	50.7
Science	70	95.9

Source: Adapted from Dalgety et al. 1999.

Table 6.4. Overall Percentage Achievement in GUIDE by Subject

Subject	A–/A+	B–/B+	C–/C+
Education	1.3	40.8	57.9
English	14.1	42.3	43.6
Science	54.3	35.8	9.9
Mathematics	35.6	46.6	17.8

Source: Adapted from Dalgety et al. 1999.

Table 6.5. Overall Awards Achieved by Trainee-Teachers in GUIDE

Level of award	Number (73)	%
Distinction	8	11.0
Credit	38	52.0
Pass	27	37.0

Source: Adapted from Dalgety et al. 1999.

The English course pursued by the trainee-teachers in GUIDE was not at the level of the CSEC English and although the trainees appeared to have done well in science (e.g. all of them in one centre achieved "A" grades) the integrity of the assessments in this area was questionable (Dalgety et al. 1999).

Table 6.5 shows that most of the trainee-teachers were awarded credit (52 per cent) or pass (37 per cent). These graduates were awarded the NCERD In-Service Assistant Teacher Certificate Level 1. The eight trainee-teachers who achieved distinction were awarded the NCERD In-Service Assistant Teacher Certificate Level 1-with distinction. They were the only ones guaranteed a place at the college of education to pursue the trained teacher's certificate.

Although the trainee-teachers reported that since their involvement in GUIDE they had observed that their students tended to ask more questions, observations of these teachers' lessons revealed that the instructional strategies they mostly used were expository teaching, practice and drill and teacher-initiated questions (Jennings 1999). The mentors assessed the trainee-teachers as being more confident in their teaching, having developed better relationships with their students and generally more proficient in class management. Their weak areas were evaluation of lessons, an inability to provide for the varying abilities in their classrooms and providing little opportunity for the students to initiate questions.

When compared with untrained (and in some instances trained) teachers, the trainee-teachers in GUIDE schools demonstrated superior performance in the classroom (Jennings 1999). This, however, did not impact on the achievement of their students. When a comparison of the achievement in mathematics of forms two and three students in GUIDE schools was made with their counterparts in the control schools, the difference between the students was not significant and the overall achievement of all the students in mathematics was low. This was not altogether surprising because the GUIDE teachers themselves were weak in mathematics. An analysis of the overall results by subject showed that the lowest percentage completion for the trainee-teachers (50.7 per cent) was in mathematics (Dalgety et al. 1999). Worth noting is the fact that only fifteen teachers entered GUIDE with passes in CSEC mathematics at grade 3 and below at the Basic Proficiency level! (Jennings 1999) The teachers' weakness in mathematics reflected in the achievement of their students. While the students in both GUIDE and the control schools were found to be achieving at a low level in science, those in the GUIDE schools did better than those in the control schools. Jennings (1999) suggests that this may be due in measure to the GUIDE teachers using the science modules to teach from in their classrooms. These materials would not be available to the control schools. The same reason may account for the significant differences in achievement in English between GUIDE students in all the school types and their counterparts in the control schools. The GUIDE students were better in Standard English grammar and style of expression.

Discussion: Commonalities and Differences

Both GUIDE in Guyana and the BEdSecDE in Jamaica sought to address inequity issues in their education systems. The BEdSecDE specifically targeted teachers who were in schools implementing the ROSE in Jamaica which sought to address the inequity in educational offering between the upgraded high schools which catered to children from the lower-socioeconomic class and their middle/upper-class peers in the traditional high schools. Graduates of the BEdSecDE were expected to prepare the upgraded high school students up to CSEC level.

GUIDE prepared teachers in the hinterland to implement the Secondary School Reform Project (SSRP) which was modelled on ROSE. Jennings (1999, 80) noted that the community high schools used in the GUIDE project "are pilot schools in the SSRP". However, most of the trainee-teachers in GUIDE taught in the "primary schools with tops", which catered to children from the lower-social and economic class. The same applied to the community high schools. Ultimately these were the children who were to benefit from the improvement in teaching provided by GUIDE.

Failure to Capture the Target Group

While both the BEdSecDE and GUIDE succeeded in increasing access to teacher training, many teachers in both countries were unable to benefit from the opportunities made available. In the case of Guyana, the root of the problem lay in the deficiencies in the secondary education provided to students in the hinterland regions. Like the HTTP, GUIDE was designed to make up for these deficiencies but failed to bring many potential candidates to a level which qualified them for entry to the college of education. This was due in part to their low level of entry and ultimate achievement particularly in mathematics.

Lack of adequate employment opportunities in their area of abode caused some teachers in Jamaica to take jobs teaching at levels of the education system for which they were not trained and to teach subjects which were not the main area in which they had been trained. For the secondary teachers who were in primary schools, an upgrading programme designed by some teachers colleges in Jamaica failed to attract sufficient numbers of these teachers to make the programme viable. The extent of this problem was either unknown to or underestimated by the Ministry of Education with the result that less than one thousand teachers were trained in the BEdSecDE over ten years, although three thousand were targeted.

Deficiencies in the Modules

Because of stability of funding guaranteed for the life of the project, the availability of technical expertise, incentives for the writers and stricter quality control, including the payment of peers to review the materials, the DE materials for the BEdSecDE were of a very good quality. In fact they were highly sought after by other training programmes including those delivered face to face. The trainee-teachers in GUIDE had to use materials which were not prepared specifically for the programme: for example, the education modules which were written for Belizean teachers. The quality of the materials to which learners are exposed has been shown to be a significant factor in learning achievement. Heyneman and Jamieson (1984) emphasize that the success of the Philippine's Textbook Project in the late 1970s was due to textbooks being of high quality and produced on time. The GUIDE modules were ready on time because they were produced for other programmes. While using ready-made modules may have saved on cost, the losses may have outweighed the benefits. Some of the modules were clearly too difficult for the students, such as in education and mathematics.

Not only were the English modules not designed to bring the trainee-teachers up to the standard of the CSEC but they also did not address deficiencies in the approach to teaching Standard English in the school system generally. Furthermore, the modules did not prepare the trainee-teachers to teach children whose first language was not English. The typical Guyanese teacher speaks a Guyanese Creole vernacular which, according to Craig (2006), differs significantly in grammar and idiom from Standard English with which it shares a considerable amount of the same vocabulary. Craig argues that the Guyanese Creole, like other Creoles in the Anglophone Caribbean, interferes with and complicates the learning of Standard English. The work of teachers in the Guyanese hinterland is exacerbated by the fact that they, as Creole speakers, must teach Standard English to children whose first language is an Amerindian language and for whom in some cases English is their third language. This situation has arisen because whereas in the past Amerindian children were largely exposed to teachers who were missionaries and from whom they learned to speak Standard English, Amerindian children increasingly are getting their first exposure to English from African- or Indo-Guyanese working and living in the hinterland who speak Creole. Some of these teachers who are untrained (sometimes even trained) are poor models as speakers of Standard English for the children. Thus, Amerindian children whose first language is Macushi "pick up" non-standard English (Creole) from their community and then have to learn Standard English in school. Teachers not only have children like this to contend with in their classes but may also have some children who understand no English whatsoever and others whose first language may be Portuguese or Spanish. Some parents in Venezuela and Brazil send their children to schools in the Guyanese hinterland to learn English. Consequently, it has long been recognized that Teaching English as a Second Language should be a key component of a teacher training programme and especially for teachers destined for the hinterland (Fanfair and Van Dongen 2003). Teaching English as a Second Language was not a feature of the English module used in GUIDE.

Resource Constraints

Being given only the modules, the GUIDE trainee-teachers complained about the lack of access to reading materials, including those recommended in the modules themselves. This was not such a problem with students in the BEdSecDE as they were given a book of essential readings along with the course guide. Furthermore, they could more readily access the internet which brought libraries to their doorsteps. In contrast, material resources were a severe constraint in the Guyanese context, with some teachers even finding it difficult to access such as were made available in the learning resource centres.

Teacher (In)Effectiveness

In Jamaica, Guyana and other parts of the Anglophone Caribbean, teachers are expected to "occupy an irreplaceable position in transforming education, in changing teaching practices within the classroom, in the use of teaching and technological resources, in facilitating relevant and quality learning" (CARICOM 2005, 10). For teachers to change their teaching practices, they need teacher educators who can model the new practices. There was no modelling of any teaching strategies by teacher educators in GUIDE because the programme did not have a teaching practicum. The teacher trainees were not adequately prepared to teach in their particular context. Children in the hinterland start school at different ages and so in a first-grade primary school classroom, a teacher is likely to find children with ages ranging from six to nine or beyond. As McEwan (1998, 437) maintains, "the multi-grade classroom is a demanding environment for the teacher, the greater the student diversity the greater the need for careful planning and organization". For this the teachers needed to be trained in multi-grade teaching which includes training in group learning and delivering an integrated curriculum appropriate for children at different developmental stages. Because this was not done in GUIDE it was hardly surprising that the teachers used the only resource they had – their distance education modules – for teaching the children in their classrooms. What quality of learning does this signify for the children, given the teachers' own academic weaknesses? Jennings (1999) noted the heavy reliance of the teacher trainees on tutorial sessions at the regional resource centres and attributed this to their generally low level of ability which led to them having difficulty comprehending written material and relying on the tutors for explanations and clarifications. The same observation was made of the HTTP (Jennings 1996). Although the GUIDE trainee-teachers performed better in the classroom than their peers in the control schools, "chalk and talk", practice and drill with little or no opportunities for the children to initiate questions were their typical instructional strategies. GUIDE was supposed to focus on "teaching skills and methodology while at the same time helping teachers to master the content of three core areas" (Jennings 1999, 2). If the education modules dealt with teaching skills and methodology, these were not demonstrated to the teachers. The evaluator observed teachers who "made most use of the lecture method", "put too much in one lesson and used up much of the lesson giving practice and drill exercises" (Jennings 1999, 63). Another teacher "took ten minutes to write a comprehension passage on the chalk board. She had her back turned to the children all the time and left them with nothing to do in the meantime" (Jennings 1999, 71).

The BEdSecDE had a strong teaching practicum component which, like the B.Ed. secondary degree delivered face to face, focused on developing the teacher's skills as a reflective practitioner (Feraria 2000). The teachers were taught by experts who modelled best practices in their areas of specialization.

Evidence suggests that the BEdSecDE had a positive effect on student achievement. Statistical data from the Ministry of Education showed an increase in the percentage of trained university graduate teachers in secondary schools from 22 per cent in 2001 to 40.7 per cent in 2009 (Doreen Faulkner Consultancy 2010). The 2007–08 CSEC results for traditional high schools that had teachers in the BEdSecDE showed a 10 per cent increase in passes for mathematics, biology, chemistry and geography and a 50 per cent increase in physics (Doreen Faulkner Consultancy 2010). It should be borne in mind that the BEdSecDE originally targeted the upgraded high schools, but there was no monitoring of the schools in which the graduates taught. They were not bonded to serve in particular schools and so the Ministry of Education did not follow through on its aim to address inequity.

The achievement of students taught by the GUIDE teacher trainees was not significantly different from those taught by teachers not in GUIDE. But then candidates were admitted to GUIDE who did not meet the original criteria set; for example, GUIDE was not meant for nursery school teachers or persons who had essentially dropped out of secondary school.

Fidelity to Principles of Distance Education

Table 6.6 indicates that both programmes combined work and study and the courses for the programmes were written by experts, except that in the case of GUIDE insufficient attention was given to the cultural relevance and level of difficulty of the modules. GUIDE used standard print materials which could readily be photocopied in large numbers. Their appeal to different learning styles was not an objective in GUIDE. When the BEdSecDE was put online, with the availability of more technical expertise in using varieties of software, lecturers were able to present their materials in ways that appealed to different learning styles.

Table 6.6. Programmes' Adherence to Distance Education Principles

Principles of Distance Education	GUIDE	BEdSecDE
Responsive to learner needs	√	#
Open and flexible entry requirements	√	X
Work–study combinations	√	√
Multimedia course packages responsive to different learning styles	X	#
Courses developed by team of experts	#	√

Key: √ = present; # = present to some extent; X = absent

Another principle of distance education referred to earlier in the chapter is learner-centredness in the sense that the technology used should have the flexibility to respond to the learner's needs. Both programmes responded to learners' needs in some way. Persons in the Guyanese hinterland who wanted to teach, also wanted to be trained without having to leave their cultural environment. GUIDE provided them with this opportunity.

The BEdSecDE responded to learners' needs in some respects but not in others. Teachers in Jamaica normally had to wait their turn to apply for leave from their job to undertake full-time study for two years at a university. They would have to incur the expense of tuition and accommodation fees as well as the challenges of being away from home and family. The BEdSecDE offered them the opportunity to be trained without having to leave their jobs or their homes. Furthermore, they did not have to pay tuition fees. While the teachers welcomed this, many objected to being bonded to serve for at least three years after the completion of their training, on the grounds that they had already been teaching for many years, in some cases. Furthermore, they objected to having to do the teaching practicum on the grounds that they had done one already in their initial training at the teachers college. So strong was this objection that it deterred many candidates from seeking entry to the programme.

The final principle of DE in table 6.6 is "open and flexible entry requirements" to increase access and equity. At the outset the entry requirement for GUIDE was inflexible: four CSEC passes at grade 3 or above. However, they became flexible. Most candidates were admitted with what was considered as "failing grades" in CSEC and even students who had not completed secondary school or had taken a part of the Secondary School Proficiency Examination in the third form of the community high school were admitted. Although the programme was not designed for them, teachers in nursery schools were granted admission. In contrast, the entry requirements for the BEdSecDE were rigidly applied. Many candidates could not gain entry because they were not teaching at the appropriate level, or they were teaching in areas for which their training had not qualified them. The inflexibility of its entry requirements was perhaps the factor that contributed most to the failure of the BEdSecDE to attract the three thousand students anticipated by the Ministry of Education (Doreen Faulkner Consultancy 2010).

Summary

This chapter compared the experiences in two programmes using traditional technology for in-service training in the remote hinterland of Guyana (GUIDE) and the use of modern technology to do the same in Jamaica

(BEdSecDE). GUIDE sought to upgrade the knowledge of trainee-teachers in mathematics, English and science while improving teaching skills and methodology. Admission requirement was four CSEC passes at grade 3 or above. On completion of the course, successful participants would be able to proceed to the college of education to do the trained teacher's certificate. The BEdSecDE was a ten-year project funded by the Ministry of Education in Jamaica which was designed to increase the number of university-trained teachers particularly in the more disadvantaged secondary schools. To qualify for admission candidates had to be teaching the subjects in which they were seeking training in a secondary school. Specialist training was offered in ten subjects examined in the CSEC.

Initially delivered via teleconferencing and face-to-face tutorials, after three years, the BEdSecDE used blended learning and asynchronous delivery. GUIDE used print materials and face-to-face tutorials. Both programmes incorporated principles of distance education in that they combined work and study, their materials were developed by experts and while the GUIDE materials were standard, the technical skills made available to course writers for the BEdSecDE enabled them to use modern technology to appeal to different learning styles. Both programmes were learner centred in that they responded to the needs of the students. GUIDE enabled trainees in the Guyanese hinterland to do teacher training without having to leave their homes. The BEdSecDE did the same for teachers in Jamaica and saved them the cost of both tuition and accommodation fees.

Its original target of one hundred having dwindled due to dropouts, of its seventy-three trainee-teachers GUIDE achieved an overall completion rate of just over 65 per cent but the level of achievement was low, particularly in mathematics, with the result that only eight graduates were guaranteed a place at the college of education by the end of the programme. An explanation for this is that many of the students admitted did not satisfy the entry requirement. The BEdSecDE also failed to capture its target group. Although 3,000 were targeted, only 858 were admitted largely on account of the inflexible admission requirements and students' objection to being bonded in return for non-payment of tuition fees.

GUIDE shared a common barrier with traditional technologies used at the secondary level: namely, pedagogical. The materials were either written at too high a level for the students or lacked cultural relevance. In fact, because of their low entry level, much of the content of the GUIDE modules was a challenge for the trainees. Like modern technologies used at the secondary level, the BEdSecDE experienced technical, organizational and resource constraints: for example, difficulty in accessing computers and the internet and the unwillingness of some principals to allow teachers release from their duties to attend interactive sessions at the UWIDEC sites.

Conclusion

So, was the use of technology more successful at the post-secondary and tertiary levels? Judging the success of both the BEdSecDE and GUIDE is problematic, on the one hand, given their failure to attract the number of students targeted and the various problems experienced. On the other hand, the BEdSecDE evolved into the B. Ed (online) offered by the UWI Open Campus which began in 2007 when the final cohort of the programme was admitted. The programme administrator for the B. Ed (online) played a seminal role in the BEdSecDE and incorporated the best practices of the latter into the B. Ed (online) (Doreen Faulkner Consultancy 2010). The BEdSecDE became institutionalized, though under a different name. GUIDE was incorporated into the post-secondary level of Guyana's education system and served as a model not only for upgrading programmes that followed but also for the Trained Teachers Certificate later offered by distance by the Cyril Potter college of education (Jennings 2011). The fact that both programmes were institutionalized in some way signals some measure of success.

Space permits the highlighting of only two lessons that we have learned from the case studies presented in this chapter which need to be considered by all involved in introducing change into school systems. The first relates to the symbiotic relationship that exists between levels of the education system. Success at one level depends on the efficiency of preceding levels. We have noted in Guyana that resources at the post-secondary level had to be used in an effort to correct deficiencies at the secondary level. Weaknesses in the achievement of GUIDE teacher trainees have been linked to weaknesses in achievement at the secondary level. The problem is an interplay of access, equity and cultural issues in Guyana because of the inability of the disadvantaged groups who live in the remote hinterland areas to readily access secondary schools that have the resources and suitably qualified teachers to prepare them for the secondary school exit examination. A good secondary education system is the bedrock of teacher training programmes. Failure to put the necessary resources into the secondary system will only increase the costs at the post-secondary level.

A second lesson is the need for innovations to be informed by research. The experience of both GUIDE and the BEdSecDE underscores the importance of feasibility studies to be undertaken *before* an innovation in the education system is introduced. Important objectives of a feasibility study are to determine the likely level of entry of the candidates targeted, their views on the requirements of the programme, and in fact to ascertain if the numbers targeted are indeed feasible. The admission of nursery schoolteachers "to make up numbers" signalled a departure from initial standards set for GUIDE – that is to prepare teachers to teach in the forms (lower secondary level). This complicated the process of measuring GUIDE's outcomes against set goals. In the case of the BEdSecDE a feasibility study would have informed the Ministry of Education of the number of teachers in the system who would actually satisfy entry requirements. Such information was ascertained instead *during* the implementation of the programme by the programme coordinator.

Following their training, teachers begin their professional careers in educational systems into which changes are frequently introduced. How well are the teachers prepared to respond to the challenges of change? This question is particularly pertinent given that teachers in the BEdSecDE did not want to do a teaching practicum as they felt they had done one already in teachers college. This is akin to equating training with a vaccine. Once you've had it, you don't need to have it again, as you are immune. But is this so? This is a question that we will address in the next chapter which focuses on how teachers in CC countries are trained to implement innovations introduced into school systems.

7.

Teachers as Agents of Change

The Ideal and the Real

The vision of teachers in the CC is that of being "agents of change" who occupy "an irreplaceable position in transforming education, in changing teaching practices within the classroom, in the use of teaching and technological resources, in facilitating relevant and quality learning" (Mark, Joseph and Remy 2005, 9). This is a vision shared by many developed countries. Most CC countries strive to become "developed". Jamaica, for example, has targeted 2030 for achieving that goal. Barbados, on the other hand, was designated a "developed country" in 2010 based on the quality of life of its citizens (UNDP 2013). With being or becoming "developed" in mind, CC countries target educational achievement such as that attained by countries like Singapore and Finland. "Finland is the world's number one performer in literacy, math, and science in the PISA rankings for 15-year-old students. It boasts some of the narrowest achievement gaps in the world" (Hargreaves and Shirley (2009, 33)). To achieve these goals, Finland controls teacher quality by only admitting the best into the profession. Applicants to teacher education programmes have only a one in ten chance of acceptance. "Within broad guidelines, highly qualified teachers created curriculum together in each municipality for the students they know best. The sense of delivering a curriculum devised by others from afar is utterly alien to Finnish teachers" (Hargreaves and Shirley (2009, 33)). How close are CC countries to achieving this ideal aspect of "development"?

The answer to this question depends in part on one's understanding of what it means to be an "agent" of change. Priestley et al. (2012) in their exploration of agency point to those who have an individualistic view of agency wherein the teacher acts autonomously. Teachers are therefore able to "critically shape their responses to problematic situations" (Priestley et al. (2012, 195)). In contrast are those who have an ecological view of agency whereby "agency is a matter of personal capacity to act, combined with the contingencies of the environment within which such action occurs" (Priestley et al. 2012, 196). The implication here is that policymakers, educational planners and school leaders need to be cognizant of the contingencies of the environments in which teachers as change agents must function. Society's perception of the teacher and how teachers are treated in the change process are aspects of that environment.

Innovations are developed with a particular image of the teacher in mind. Rarely in the CC are teachers seen as curriculum *makers*, as "problem-solvers" who have the knowledge and expertise to develop curricula for the students they teach. The dominant view of the teacher is that of *curriculum implementer*; not a musical composer, but one who plays music composed by others. Doyle and Ponder (1977–78) identify three images of the curriculum implementer: that of rational adopter, stone-age obstructionist and pragmatic sceptic. The most widely held image of the teacher is that of a rational *adopter* as the change strategy adopted normally involves giving the teacher information about the innovation including research data explaining its need and relevance and providing the necessary training for implementation. "The weight of scholarly evidence, together with an appropriately inspirational rhetoric, will compel any 'reasonable and intelligent' teacher to rush out and try the latest 'new idea' in education" (Doyle and Ponder 1977/78, 4). In CC countries, however, teachers do not enjoy the privilege of choice. They are mandated to implement innovations. Indeed, some policymakers and educational planners are of the view that adult behaviour is difficult to change and so teachers are likely to obstruct the change effort. Particularly in situations where the teachers are untrained or inadequately trained, it is best to by-pass these "stone-age obstructionists" and render the innovation "teacher proof".

Decades of educational policy have tried to bring about change in schools: for example, the change from the view of the student as a passive recipient of knowledge and the teacher as the authority to impart that knowledge to a view of the teacher as a facilitator who can unlock the potential of the students to construct meaning for themselves. Numerous innovations to achieve this ideal have made little difference to what happens in classrooms. In a study carried out in eight CC countries, Jennings (2001) found that the dominant view of the teacher emphasized in their training programmes was that of knowledge-giver, organizer/manager and an instructor/evaluator. Failure to change is invariably blamed on the teacher, being as they are "the final arbiters of classroom practice" (Doyle and Ponder 1977–78, 2) working in relative isolation and functional autonomy. Because this gives them the power to close their classroom doors to change, policymakers have over time acknowledged the need to make teachers more central to the change process, through consultation and involving them in the innovation, for example, in the development of the curricula they will teach. Despite this the innovations often fail to impact classroom practices.

The work of Hall and Hord (2006) on the reaction of teachers to innovations provides some insight into why this happens. Building on the earlier work of

Francis Fuller (1969), they found that the concerns of teachers differ at various stages in the implementation of the innovation. At the outset they question their competence to handle the tasks (*self-concerns*). They are concerned about how best to manage their time (*task concerns*) as they start to implement the innovation. Some may implement the innovation so well that they begin to think what to do to improve their students' performance (impact *concerns*).

Doyle and Ponder (1977–78) contend that teachers are more likely to try to incorporate into their classroom procedures change proposals that they perceive as "practical". There are three conditions of practicality: instrumentality, congruence and cost. *Instrumentality* basically means that the new procedures and behaviour patterns associated with the innovation need to be clearly communicated to the users. This is supported by Fullan and Stiegelbauer (1991) who emphasized the importance of clarity of goals and means in the implementation process. The second condition of practicality is that the proposed change should be *congruent* with the way that the teacher normally conducts classroom activities; it should be compatible with the teacher's self-image and preferred mode of relating to students. Cost from the teacher's perspective is not primarily a matter of monetary remuneration. It more has to do with the ease with which the new procedures can be implemented (or what Rogers (2003) refers to as the *complexity* of the innovation), and the reward that teachers get in terms of incentives and praise for the effort and time that must be expended.

Purpose

In this chapter we explore how well our teachers are prepared to become agents of change by asking the questions: (1) What images of the teacher do innovations in the CC reflect and are these images consistent with the new demands being made on teachers? Are these new demands compatible with the teacher's accustomed behaviour and classroom practices? (2) How do we train our teachers to implement innovations? How effective are the different approaches used? In examining training, particular attention will be paid to whether the new procedures to be implemented in the classroom were clearly explained to the teachers (*instrumentality*). (3) Whether the innovations were easily and effectively implemented by the teachers (*cost/complexity*). The innovations are set out in table 7.1.

Images of the Teacher

Most of the innovations involved a top-down or centre-periphery approach to change which cast the teacher in the role of implementer of decisions from

Table 7.1. Role of Teacher in Curriculum Change: Approaches to Training for Implementation

Curriculum Change/ Innovation	Country/ Education Level	Change Model	Level of Success	Role of Teacher	Training for Implementation
REAP 1976–99	Belize (rural primary)	Centre-periphery	*	Integrate LAPs with academic subjects.	**Project-based workshop training incorporated into pre-service training.** Training workshops; study of REAP in pre-service training at Belize College of Education (Jennings 1988).
PRIMER (1980–83/4)	Jamaica (grades 1–6 in rural all age schools)	Centre-periphery	X	Instructional supervisors; keep records of students' progress; prepare "programmed teachers" (older primary school pupils) to teach some lessons in mathematics and literacy to younger pupils.	**Project-based workshops.** Teachers given 5 weeks in-service training in use of (SIM) and new approaches to classroom management (McKinley 1982). Teachers received 10 days orientation in use of SIM (Cummings 1986). Training in 11 workshops by members of project team (Minott 1988).
NCERD (SRG) (1988–92)	Guyana (Primary grades 1–5)	Centre-periphery	X	To reinforce literacy and numeracy across the curriculum.	**Cascade approach.** Principals trained in workshops (one per principal) to "cascade" training to teachers in their schools. One teachers' guide per school (Craig 2006/07).

Project (period)	Territory/level	Model		Role of teacher	Training approach
Literacy 1-2-3 (2005 to present)	Jamaica Primary (grades 1–3)	Centre-periphery	#	"Opening window" for discrete treatment of literacy in integrated curriculum; constructivist approach to teaching.	**Cascade approach.** Training of Master Trainers' workshops. Provision of support materials explaining the literacy intervention model (Ministry of Education & Youth (2005)) and support from RPC Curriculum Implementation Teams (Jennings 2011).
CCETT (2001–09)	Belize, Guyana, Jamaica, St Lucia, St Vincent and the Grenadines (primary)	Centre-periphery	*	Use effective reading methodologies and classroom management techniques; diagnose and address students literacy needs.	**Regional/cluster/school level training.** Regional workshops for training reading specialists (RS). In-service training at the cluster and school level of teachers supported by RS visiting schools every 2 weeks (Warrican, Spencer-Ernandez and Miller 2013).
CSEC (1975 to present)	14 Caribbean territories **(secondary)	RD&D/ proliferation of centres	*	Teacher as "curriculum developer" (as member of subject panel). Knowledge-giver, organizer/manager, instructor/evaluator (Jennings 2001).	**Cascade approach /Pre-service training.** Training through the SCDP/country-level workshops. Subject organizations may offer some training at the national level, but these are often limited by resources available.
Sixth Form Geography (1979–81)	Jamaica (traditional high schools)	Problem-solving	X	Adopt enquiry approach to "A"-level teaching.	**No training.** Orientation to the project workshop, but no training in curriculum development (Morrissey 1981).

(Continued)

Table 7.1. (Continued)

Curriculum Change/ Innovation	Country/ Education Level	Change Model	Level of Success	Role of Teacher	Training for Implementation
ROSE 1 (Resource & Technology) 1993–98	Jamaica (non-traditional secondary schools)	RD&D/ Centre-periphery	#	Cooperative planning; guiding students through the design process. Infusion of career education into R&T (Jennings 2012).	**Cascade approach/incorporation into pre-service training.** Training workshops held in summer (cascade approach). ROSE lecturers appointed in teachers colleges.
ASTEP (2011–13)	Jamaica Secondary (grades 7–8)	Centre-periphery	X	Facilitator of learning using constructivist approach in student-centred classrooms.	**Project-based workshops** that focused on specialized training in key features of the ASTEP curriculum, personal empowerment. Teachers' feedback on their use of curriculum guides to aid revision of the guides.
EduTech 2000 (1999–2008)	Barbados Primary & secondary	Centre-periphery	#	Integrate technology into teaching and learning.	**Voluntary training after school hours.** Insufficient funds for effective training in IT (Pirog and Kioko 2010).

** Antigua, Barbados, Belize, the British Virgin Islands, Cayman Island, Dominica, Grenada, Jamaica, Guyana, Montserrat, St Kitts/Nevis, Anguilla, St Lucia, St Vincent and the Grenadines, Trinidad and Tobago, Turks and Caicos Islands, the Cayman Islands withdrew in 1977.

Key: * successful; X = not successful; # successful to some extent.

"the top". This approach implies that the teacher must be told what to do and trained how to do it. CSEC could be viewed as an exception in that teachers were cast in the role of decision-makers in both curriculum development and the examination process. The syllabus for each subject examined was developed by a panel of six members of the education system, three of whom had to be practising teachers of the subject at the level of examination. These three teachers may have been decision-makers, but the teaching body as a whole had to implement their decisions. School-based assessment, however, involved all the teachers as this is the teachers' evaluation of students' coursework assignments which can account for up to 40 per cent of the final examination mark.

Except perhaps in one case, the teachers were not perceived as "stone-age obstructionists", but rather as rational adopters. The assumption was that, once explained to them, they would understand the new ideas and strategies sufficiently to be able to use them appropriately in their own classrooms. In the case of REAP, for example, the Belizean teachers had to use their own initiative to integrate the LAPs into their teaching of the academic subjects. Jamaican primary school teachers using an integrated curriculum had to know when to "open windows" for the discrete teaching of literacy (i.e. the Language Arts Window (LAW)). CETT is exemplary in that the teachers were treated as partners or collaborators, illustrating a blend of "top-down initiative and bottom-up participation" (Fullan and Stiegelbauer 1991, 83). CETT sought the opinion of teachers and principals on what needed to be done to improve teaching of reading and student achievement in literacy in their school. The reading specialists, based on the information received, worked with teachers and principals to design action research interventions for different classes in their schools. In a real sense they were treated as *rational problem-solvers* who, *with* some outside help, were able to solve their own problems.

The teachers in the Sixth Form Geography Project were also perceived as rational *problem-solvers*. After all they were teachers of Advanced Level Geography and were expected to be highly intelligent and knowledgeable about their discipline. That is why they could be trusted to develop their own curriculum. This is in contrast with the teachers in PRIMER who were perceived by the project staff as inadequate, incompetent and difficult to deal with. In fact, the teachers' inability or unwillingness to follow instructions was perceived as obstructing the project staff's desire "to see the project 'succeed' at all costs" (Minott 1988, 179). In the minds of the project staff, the teachers were like "stone-age obstructionists".

Demands on the Teacher: New Roles, Skills and Behaviours

Despite viewing the PRIMER teachers as incompetent, the project team nevertheless expected them to take on the new role of *instructional supervisors* who served as managers of instruction and provided needed direction to students who worked at their own pace in the use of the SIM. For this they needed to be skilled in record keeping and more adept at facilitating greater flexibility in the scheduling of individual learning. They also needed to prepare the selected upper-level primary students (programmed teachers) who would assist them in teaching literacy skills to students in the lower grades.

Having been brought up on a diet of rote learning, ASTEP teachers, like those in PRIMER, were accustomed to being the givers of knowledge in their classrooms, writing notes on the chalkboard to be diligently copied by the students and asking questions to which the children responded in unison. ASTEP teachers now had to adopt a constructivist approach to teaching and learning. They were expected to design interactive lessons which catered to multiple intelligences and create an inquiry-based classroom environment in which students felt free to converse, discuss and question. They were to engage the children in problem-solving activities and collaborative group work and integrate the use of technology into their teaching. Furthermore, because weak literacy and numeracy skills were at the root of the students' low achievement level, ASTEP teachers were required to integrate literacy and numeracy in their teaching. Because their low level of achievement had impacted their self-confidence, the task of each teacher was to nurture the students' self-esteem. Given that the ASTEP teachers were to be selected from those who had specialized in "special needs", these demands were not considered unreasonable.

Teachers of L1-2-3 shared some of these demands because they functioned in a RPC which too was steeped in constructivism. Accustomed to using paper and pencil tests for summative assessments, both teachers of L1-2-3 and the ASTEP were asked to adopt a formative approach to assessment that helped students to learn (*assessments for learning*). Use of journals, portfolios and media that incorporated different learning styles was encouraged.

Considerable demands were also made on teachers of R&T. The subject was organized into five elements (agriculture and the environment, home and family management, product design and development, resource management (including IT) and visual arts). Hitherto working alone, the teachers of these elements were expected to plan their teaching together so that the five elements formed a cohesive whole. Furthermore, they had to be able to guide students through the *design process*. This involved five stages: (1) identify needs/

problems, (2) consider a range of resources to produce design proposal and develop ideas for solving the problem identified, (3) plan the work, (4) make the product or design a system which solves the problem identified and (5) evaluate the success of the solution to the problem. The teachers also had to prepare the students to do mini-enterprise projects.

What is clear from all these demands is that the innovations were expected to change the way that the teacher normally conducts classroom activities and were not designed to be compatible with the teacher's preferred mode of relating to students. The question is: Were the teachers adequately trained to implement these new skills and behaviours?

Training Teachers to Implement Innovations

What is evident from table 7.1 is that several of the innovations used the cascade approach to training. "Cascading" involves selecting teachers with the ability to be "master trainers" to be trained at a central location for about one week or more (depending on the availability of funds). One week away from regular school was quite an incentive for these teachers, especially if this was spent at a popular tourist resort. These teachers were then expected to return to their schools to train teachers in their own and neighbouring schools in the new ideas and skills learned. To do this they needed the assistance of the principals of the schools and the resources for organizing the training. Such support may be forthcoming in the "master trainer's" own school, but unlikely in the neighbouring schools. This may explain why some six years after implementation, some teachers reported never having received any training in the use of the L1-2-3 (Jennings-Craig et al. 2012). This is despite the fact that a manual had been prepared for the teachers clearly outlining the strategies to be used for "opening windows" for literacy instruction, including various ways in which groups could be organized for single-grade and multi-grade teaching. But did these manuals ever reach the teachers? Feedback from teachers at the ASTEP workshops revealed that support manuals prepared for the students never reached them (Jennings-Craig 2011a). What makes the NCERD Skills Reinforcement Guide an interesting case is that it was the principals who were trained as "master trainers", but in only one workshop. The principals had the power to organize the necessary training but particularly those in the rural and hinterland areas lacked the necessary resources, for example, electricity or printers to provide copies of the curriculum guides for the teachers.

The training of teachers in the various techniques of assessment related to the CXC syllabi and examination was a major objective of the SCDP which was funded by the USAID. The training was organized in workshops held at the regional, sub-regional and country levels. Regional workshops were held in Barbados and Jamaica and attended by teacher representatives from the participating countries. These teachers were then expected to cascade the training received to teachers in their respective countries. The workshops organized by the SCDP triggered local workshops organized by subject associations, individual schools or groups of schools which generated a highly desirable multiplier effect (Griffith 1981).

A second approach to training for implementation is evident in table 7.1. This is training which is voluntary and done after school as in the case of EduTech 2000. The main teachers college in Barbados assumed responsibility for the training of teachers to implement EduTech 2000. Particularly in the first seven years of the programme, training in the infusion of IT into teaching was done for the most part without the availability of IT in the classrooms! Although teachers were expected to use alternative student assessment approaches and child-centred constructivist approaches to teaching, they did not receive training in these areas due to the lack of funds (Pirog and Kioko 2010).

A third approach is to offer no training at all, as in the Sixth Form Geography Project. The assumption was made that these teachers ought to have skills in curriculum development as they were all trained teachers. Furthermore, were they not all teaching at the advanced level? The teachers identified "a lack of confidence in their curriculum skills" (Jennings-Wray 1984, 52) as one of the reasons for their failure to produce any materials at all in "A"-level geography.

A fourth approach to training evident in table 7.1 is that of project-based workshop training as in REAP, PRIMER and ASTEP. This approach ensured that all the teachers who were to teach in the particular programme were actually trained. The Ministry of Education in Belize trained teachers in the REAP pilot schools in ten workshops between July 1976 and February 1979 (Massey 1982). PRIMER involved only five schools and the teachers were given in-service training in the use of SIM and new approaches to classroom management. This was according to the project director. The evaluator of the programme referred to the teachers having only ten days orientation to the new ideas (Cummings 1986). What went on in the workshops was described as "something of a mystery" (Minott 1988, 173) since the real issues of actual use of the new methods and materials and the new roles to be adopted were not made clear. ASTEP teachers had four one-day workshops held in hotels or conference centres. The workshops addressed various aspects of the methodology of ASTEP, obtained feedback from the teachers on the curriculum materials they had been asked to review, and engaged the teachers in writing learning and assessment activities which could be included in the revised curriculum guides.

A fifth approach to training which was used by CETT is tiered in that it offered training at the regional/cluster/school level. It illustrates important features of successful training for implementation. "One shot workshop prior to and even during implementation", write Fullan and Stiegelbauer (1991, 85), "are not very helpful." They add that what is needed is "ongoing, in-service cumulative learning to develop new conceptions, skills and behavior". The teachers in CETT were given ongoing in-service training at both the cluster and school levels followed up with support from a reading specialist (RS) who visited each teacher at least fortnightly. The RS worked with the teachers, supported by the principal, to design and develop action research interventions to address specific needs within their classrooms. The RS themselves were trained at regular regional workshops "in the most up to date teacher training strategies, as well as matters related to testing and technology" (Warrican, Spencer-Ernandez and Miller 2013, 9).

A sixth approach to training evident in table 7.1 involved the combination of the cascade approach or project-based training for implementation initially which was later absorbed into the curriculum for training teachers at the teachers colleges. For example, ROSE lecturers were appointed in the teachers colleges of Jamaica and all institutions that prepare secondary school teachers use the syllabi developed for CSEC. The study of REAP was made an integral part of the pre-service training of teachers at the Belize Teachers College (which has since been incorporated into the University of Belize). Worthy of note is the fact that this approach to training involved the use of various strategies to inform not only the teachers but also the general public about the innovation. In the case of REAP, for example, a newsletter was started in 1977 and a twice-weekly radio programme on REAP was initiated in the same year. A REAP agricultural manual (*Lets Reap Together*) was produced in 1979, and in 1981 another radio programme – The *REAP Experience* – came on stream. ROSE had a newsletter – ROSEGRAM – which has issues published between 1995 and 1997; there was also ROSE PRESS, a leaflet that updates on the programme sent out by the public relations officer. These only lasted as long as the ROSE secretariat was funded. In the early days, the CXC issued leaflets such as "Fact Sheet", "CXC News" and "CXC questions and answers" to inform teachers and the general public about the examinations. Currently a wealth of information about the CSEC is available on the CXC website. Acquiring information is particularly important at the early stage of use of the innovation (Hall and Hord 2006).

Clarity of Explanations to Teachers

What Doyle and Ponder describe as *Instrumentality* proved to be a problem in a number of the interventions. The Belizean teachers were asked to integrate the

LAPs into their teaching of academic subjects, but it was found that "teachers in REAP schools are having difficulty in articulating work in the school garden with the use of the LAPs and with the academic subjects" (Jennings 1988, 122). The teachers were confused about what it means to "integrate", being more familiar with the term "correlate". This general confusion has been highlighted by Beane (1997, 3) who states that "correlations across various subject areas . . . has often been referred to . . . as an 'integrated curriculum'".

Although at the time "integration" and "correlation" were being emphasized in teaching at the primary level in schools in the CC, in Guyana NCERD avoided the confusion by using the term "reinforce". In the training of the principals to use the Skills Reinforcement Guides, reinforcement was explained as setting the learning of English and literacy "as an important objective in all other activities and subjects in the school curriculum" (Craig 2006/07, 13). The same applied to the reinforcement of mathematical concepts and skills.

How well the principals explained this to the teachers is questionable. Craig (2006/07) highlights a study which evaluated the use of the Skills Reinforcement Guides (SRGs) in a sample of schools in which the researcher reported that the teachers were unclear about the difference between "integration" and "reinforcement". "Some apparently felt that being asked to reinforce language and mathematic skills was the same as being asked to integrate the subjects" (Craig 2006/07, 26). The teachers who had to implement the SRGs did not have any opportunity to meet with the developers of the SRGs to clarify the meaning of reinforcement and so they muddled on in their state of confusion.

The teachers' guide for Literacy 1-2-3 clearly outlined the four-stage strategy to be used for "opening windows" for LAW. The strategy involved spending fifteen minutes at the beginning of the class with a whole group activity, after which the teacher divided the class into four groups and worked with two groups for fifteen minutes each (second and third phases) while the other two groups engaged in collaborative learning in groups or pairs. The final phase is a whole class discussion and evaluation during which the children discussed what they had learned and shared their work. Despite such clarity, Jennings (2009) found that some teachers interpreted group work to mean dividing the class into groups of three, then lecturing to one group while the other children, though sitting in two groups, worked individually.

Even more confused were the teachers in the PRIMER schools especially after it was discovered that the materials written for the students were above their reading level. Instructions they were given changed from one workshop to the next and the project staff were not clear on how to proceed. Teachers reported that although they listened at the workshops, it was never clear to them what they were supposed to do (Minot 1988). Perhaps it was because the project team members were themselves confused. In fact, the project director admitted to not being familiar with rural primary schools. The fact that the project team was based in Kingston which was some sixty miles away from the project schools resulted in them "having difficulty in comprehending the rhythm of life and the constraints on education found at the site" (Cummings1986, 59).

Ease and Effectiveness of Implementation

Teachers in the REAP schools had difficulty articulating work in the school garden with the use of the LAPs and integrating the LAPs in the teaching of the academic subjects. This partly had to do with the quality of the LAPs themselves. Teachers' participation in the development of the LAPs themselves did not result in them having a better understanding of the LAPs. In fact, the assistance of subject-matter experts eventually had to be sought to improve the LAPs (Massey 1982). Furthermore, because of difficulty in hiring an expert in REAP to teach at the Belize Teachers College, in the early years the graduates who had been trained in REAP were found to be no better in implementing REAP than those who had not received the training (Thompson 1982).

The PRIMER teachers fared even worse. The teachers' attempt to implement what they had learned at the workshop resulted in "chaos and confusion" (Minott 1988, 174). Tests administered to grade 4 students during the first two weeks of the 1980 school year revealed that 80 per cent of them would not be able to read the modules prepared for them because they were reading below grade 2 level. Having been trained to carry out their new roles, the teachers were now advised "to continue in their traditional roles" (Minott 1988, 133). So accustomed were they to their teacher-centred "chalk and talk" behaviour that they did not even want the children who could use the SIM on their own to do so. "The pupils could not be trusted to work on their own", they said, "they would waste time" and "the answers to the exercise which were included in the modules would militate against real learning" (Minott 1988, 134). In the second year of implementation, after the modules had been revised, there was still "organizational chaos" because the level of the content was still too difficult for most students. The teachers "kept moving pupils backwards and forwards, out of and into selected groups of module users according to whether or not pupils could or could not cope with particular aspects of the content" (Minott 1988, 134).

As for ASTEP, the Programme Monitoring and Evaluation Unit (2012, 3) noted "the lack of fidelity in the implementation of ASTEP" and attributed this to the fact that most of the teachers who delivered ASTEP had not received the specialized training necessary. The specialist teachers trained in the workshops found employment elsewhere as they were dissatisfied with the salary offered to teach in ASTEP. Those who actually delivered the programme did not have the knowledge and skills needed to cater to the learning difficulties and psycho-social challenges faced by the students. The quality of their teaching was poor and because they assessed the students in an ad hoc manner instead of using the guidelines in place, it was not possible to determine in an objective way any gains made by the students in literacy and numeracy.

How effectively teachers were able to implement the NCERD Skills Reinforcement Guides (SRGs) depended on the training and guidance given by the principal. Some principals simply handed the teachers the SRG with instructions to prepare their lesson plans from it. Others planned regular staff development sessions which resulted in the teachers at particular grade levels planning lessons together and discussing strategies for integrating the teaching of a particular concept across the different subjects. Most teachers, however, had difficulty with "reinforcing" language and mathematics as they felt that this compromised and diminished the teaching of concepts in the other subject areas (Ganesh 1992). The teachers of Literacy 1-2-3 had a similar perception. To them, to "open a window" to teach literacy in a class where they were focusing on what they knew to be a concept related to social studies or science compromised the teaching of those subjects. Research on the implementation of L1-2-3 did not find any instances where the teacher implemented the four-stage strategy outlined for teaching literacy (Simms 2010, Mascoe-Johnson 2012). Teachers tended to adapt the use of L1-2-3 to suit their own purposes. As one teacher said, "I select from the topic (of the Big Book) the content that matches what I am doing in Integrated Science" (Simms 2010, 71).

The teachers perceived R&T as complex and were not clear on how to use themes to integrate the elements. In fact, most schools only had enough teachers to deliver three of the five elements which in most cases excluded resource management. This was an important part of the curriculum because mini enterprises were part of this element. Involvement in mini enterprises was supposed to be the students' introduction to the business world and, in essence, initial training in entrepreneurship. However, many students were deprived of this opportunity. Jennings (2012) found that of the thirty-five lessons observed, only eight attempted to teach R&T in an integrated way. For the most part the individual elements were taught discretely. Even though R&T is a practical subject, lack of land space and equipment in some schools resulted in agriculture and the environment being taught in classrooms in lessons centred on theory. In home and family management, a shortage of space resulted in a practice of rotation. This involved approximately a quarter of the class doing practical work one week while the rest of the class was set written work to do in another room. In the following week a quarter of those who did theoretical work did practical work. And so, it went on until each quarter had its turn.

A study of reading specialists attached to CETT pinpoints some difficulties that they had in carrying out their role. The distances they had to travel between the schools impinged on the time they could spend supporting the teachers. They needed to have less teachers to service. Some principals, furthermore, "hide the resources that have been sent to the schools by CETT and teachers are unaware of what is available to improve literacy" (Charles 2011, 47). Others take the liberty of including and bringing "greetings at a graduation function, representing the district in all kinds of things" (Charles 2011, 50) as part of the reading specialist's duties. An evaluation of CETT found that CETT trained teachers demonstrated effective teaching practices, but the teachers' knowledge of content did not deepen over the two-year period of training (Chesterfield and Abreu-Combs 2011). This is important given that there is a significant relationship between teachers' knowledge and student achievement (Glewwe et al. 2013).

Discussion

Invariably when innovations fare badly, blame is put squarely on the shoulders of the teacher. But would it be fair to blame the teachers of ASTEP who "filled in" for those who had received the specialized training but went elsewhere when the salaries they had been promised did not materialize? Blame for failure tends to be levelled at the teacher without consideration of the factors that inhibited their effective implementation of the innovation. For example, teachers face hidden challenges which escape the attention of project leadership and there are weaknesses in the model most often used to train for implementation. Resources that the teachers need to implement the innovation effectively are often not provided and some principals fail to give them the support that they need. But first a question before considering these factors: How do teachers feel being on the inside of these innovations? How are they treated?

The PRIMER teachers spoke of being disillusioned, being treated like guinea pigs, being made to feel like children, of feeling that a "battle was being waged", as they never seemed able to please the project director. They felt inadequate and constantly criticized. They were afraid of failure and certainly did not want their pupils to fail. "Teachers felt threatened . . . pressured. They were constantly reprimanded when they failed to cover the work set for a specific time" (Minott 1988, 182). Furthermore, "petty jealousies and bad feeling were generated as teachers became defensive and the project staff became anxious to see the project succeed at all cost. . . . It became a project of resentment rather than experiment" (Minott 1988, 179).

Even though "interventions to facilitate change need to be aligned with the concerns of those engaged with the change" (Hall and Hord 2006, 138), the Programme Monitoring and Evaluation Unit (2012) does not give any insights into the experiences of the ASTEP teachers. However, one can imagine the teachers' frustration at having to deliver a curriculum for which they had not been prepared. There is a tendency to view teachers who have to teach children with learning difficulties as if they themselves are slow learners.

Hidden Challenges Faced by Teachers in Implementing Innovations

In their evaluation of the one-day training workshops, the ASTEP teachers voiced such concerns as "too much information crammed into limited time", "needed more time to process the programme" (Jennings-Craig 2011a, 17). These concerns are understandable because of the demands that introducing change makes on teachers. Change initiatives are not typically centred on a single innovation, as "several innovations will be frequently masquerading as one" (Hall and Hord 2006, 8). What may be seen as a single innovation is usually comprised of a *bundle* of innovations. For example, catering to multiple intelligences, teaching language and literacy skills across the curriculum, building the students' self-esteem are among the *bundle* of innovations that ASTEP teachers were expected to do. Functioning as instructional supervisors, preparing "programmed teachers", keeping records of students' achievement comprised a *bundle* of innovations for the PRIMER teachers. Furthermore, teachers sometimes find themselves having to cope with more than one "innovation bundles" at a time. For example, Literacy 1-2-3 was part of the RPC which was grounded in constructivism. The teachers of Literacy 1-2-3 not only had to develop expertise in using the language experience and awareness approach but they also had to master the bundle of innovations in constructivism (e.g. student-centred teaching, active participation, student-initiated questions, collaborative learning). It takes *time* to move from the "teacher as transmitter of knowledge" model to one in which children are guided to construct their own knowledge. It takes *time* furthermore to process the information needed to master one innovation, much less two or even more. It is not unusual to find that in a particular school a teacher must grapple with two innovations simultaneously. Jennings (2011b) reported that during a training session for L1-2-3, some teachers expressed concern over the conflicting demands being made on them by having to implement L1-2-3 and another innovation – the New Horizons for Primary Schools – which also sought to improve levels of literacy. While for the L-1-2-3 the teachers had to prepare lesson plans using the language experience and awareness approach, a different approach was required for the New Horizons for Primary Schools. At the same time their principals insisted that they were to prepare their lesson plans in accordance with the accustomed practice of the school. Because the principals reviewed and approved their lesson plan, it does not take rocket science to figure out the choice the teachers had to make.

Weaknesses in the Training Model

The difficulty experienced by teachers in processing a multiple of new ideas thrown at them in a one-week workshop either escaped the educational planners or they themselves were constrained by limited funds to organize more extensive training. CETT was exceptional in that it had the funding needed to organize training which provided "ongoing, in-service cumulative learning to develop new conceptions, skills and behavior" (Fullan and Stiegelbauer 1991, 85). Training was extended over two years and the use of reading specialists to work with individual teachers enabled them to respond to the needs and concerns of the teachers, for the most part. Collaborating with the teachers on action research provided them with opportunities to help teachers diagnose problems specific to their context and to develop interventions to address the problems. This is particularly important because in the other innovations studied there was a tendency to paint all teachers with the same brush. Even though they may be working in the same school, each teacher functions in a different context. Their pupils differ, so does their learning milieu. There are also differences in the level of training of the teachers: some have teachers college diplomas (TCD), others have bachelor of education degrees. Of concern are the specializations in the TCD and degrees obtained by some primary and secondary school teachers. One of the reading specialists in the study by Charles (2011) was not trained in reading but in educational administration. While most primary school teachers are trained as generalists, in certain schools literacy is taught by primary school teachers who have been trained to teach at the secondary level in such areas as agriculture, business studies, food and nutrition (research cited by Jennings 2011b), physical education, guidance and counselling (Jennings-Craig et al. 2012). The implication of this was underscored in a focus group discussion with principals, one of whom noted: "We really need to look at the pedagogical content of the teachers we have at the primary level. When you think that the integrated curriculum 1-2-3, they open a window and there are many days when that window stays closed, for the teacher's fear of it" (Jennings-Craig et al. 2012, 297).

This is also a problem at the secondary level. For example, in some schools in Jamaica many of the teachers preparing students for CSEC English, although they have a degree, "they were not trained in the discipline of Language education, so they did not have the requisite academic background or pedagogical skills to effectively deliver English" (Jennings-Craig et al. 2012, 94). These researchers found that teachers trained in management studies, public administration and library and information studies were teaching CSEC English.

The cascade approach to training does not compensate for any deficiencies in teachers' academic background. Nor does it address their specific needs or concerns. It is a multi-tiered model in which training is a "one size fits all". Information is passed on from one tier to the next – that is from the project consultants/specialists to "master trainers" and then to the teachers. Its main advantage is that it can produce many "trained" teachers within a short period of time in a cost-effective manner. This is particularly attractive to international funding agencies and the governments who report on the use of funds to these agencies. The main disadvantage is that information passed down the tiers becomes distorted and by the time it reaches the teacher the messages are unclear and confusing. At the training workshops, furthermore, the tendency is for the master trainers to be *told about* the innovation rather than being shown *how to* do all the new things required of them. The master trainers then train the teachers as they were taught. Thus, a typical comment of teachers evaluating an L1-2-3 training workshop was: "We would love to see someone demonstrate a lesson for us instead of just telling us" (Jennings 2011b, 93). The ASTEP teachers wanted "more practice in the subject areas", "more hands-on activities" (School of Education UWI (2011)). Follow-up support is not built into the model and so the new skills, behaviours and practices are rarely mastered.

Despite the strengths of CETT, the evaluators recommended that if in-service training is offered over two years, the second-year curriculum should be well defined and focus on deepening the teachers' knowledge (Chesterfield and Abreu-Combs 2011). Reading specialists who had worked with CETT were of the view that CETT did not have the capacity to train them in the knowledge and understanding they needed to effectively carry out their role and suggested that a master of education degree in reading was the ideal qualification for reading specialists (Charles 2011).

The Issue of Resources

For many teachers, implementing an innovation is like being given a basket to carry water. Inadequacies in the funding of the innovations impacted on teacher training. Teachers were expected to integrate technology in their teaching even though the funds for EduTech 2000 had been exhausted before training in IT could be done (Pirog and Kioko 2010). Literacy 1-2-3 was part of the PESP which received funding from an international agency. Only a limited amount of funds from PESP was earmarked for a literacy intervention in selected schools but this was stretched to accommodate the entire primary system since the literacy problem affected all schools (Jennings 2009). Understandably the funds for training teachers to use the L1-2-3 were limited. Limited funding influenced the choice of the principal rather than the teachers to train in the use of the NCERD SRGs and the absence of funding made it impossible to train the Sixth Form Geography teachers in curriculum development.

Studies on the implementation of L1-2-3 in primary schools using a constructivist approach to teaching and learning revealed that teachers persisted in their use of traditional "chalk and talk" with children giving choral responses to questions initiated by the teacher. Traditional "chalk and talk" was how these teachers were taught in school and how they were trained at the teachers college (Marshall 2006/07). The classrooms in which they taught had remained unchanged since their own schooldays: unwieldy wooden combined desk and bench seating two or more children in classrooms separated by chalkboards. Jennings (2009, 100) describes a classroom which was so crowded that "in order for the children to move around they had to climb over desks or other children had to get up from their seats to allow them to (literally) squeeze through". These classrooms were designed for the "banking concept" of education not for active learning associated with constructivism involving such things as use of role play, drama and various grouping strategies that required space in the learning environment.

The principals of primary schools in the Guyanese hinterland were sceptical about implementing the SRGs and gave the following reasons to the director of NCERD: "Their buildings and classrooms were dilapidated, poorly furnished. They were forced to operate without even the most basic of educational materials such as paper, chalk and writing materials. There were no books for reading" (Craig 2006/07, 18).

To make matters worse, for the training of the teachers in using the SRGs, the principals were each given only one curriculum guide.

PRIMER was plagued with staff shortages: the project director had to also function as a curriculum analyst. The curriculum materials were poorly edited due to the lack of a full-time editor among the project staff. The use of part-time editors proved counterproductive due to lack of communication with writers of the modules. The teachers suffered from the problems in R&T relating to physical resources. In the use of rotation, for example, the teachers found repeating the same thing to four different groups not only tiresome but it also caused disruption in the students' learning due to the lack of completion of work scheduled for the rotation period. Teachers of the product design and development element had to resort to teaching as theory an element that should have been very practical and focused on developing skills. A lesson on tools, for example, involved the teacher drawing the tools on the blackboard and the students then copying them in their books (Jennings 2012).

Principal Support

"As implementer of change", writes Sarason (1971, 131), "the principal is in a crucial role". NCERD underscored this point by making the principals the "master trainers" with responsibility to train the teachers in their schools to implement the SRGs. On reflection this was a wise move because data from the Planning Unit of the Ministry of Education and Cultural Development in Guyana showed that in the early 1990s most teachers at the primary level (close to 50 per cent) were untrained and unqualified (Jennings 1998). Teachers look to the principal for support as they grapple with innovations they have to implement. But rarely are principals themselves trained in the innovation. They receive information about it from the Ministry of Education but are often left in the dark about the specifics of the new behaviours and practices required of the teacher. As a result, they are prone to make demands of teachers which conflict with the requirements of the innovation. When teachers had any problems with "opening windows" for teaching L1-2-3, they could not rely on their own principals to offer guidance. A typical view expressed by the primary school principals was: "When I went into the system and I heard about those windows, I still have a problem with this windows business, how to open the windows and what it is really about" (Jennings-Craig et al. 2012, 299).

When teachers of the elements of R&T wanted to meet to plan their lessons so that R&T would be presented to the students as a cohesive whole, the principals in several schools refused to allow the teachers to do the planning in school time (Jennings 2012). Meeting after school was not possible for teachers who had other commitments. There was an unhealthy relationship between the principal of the PRIMER schools and the teachers, and the project team expressed dissatisfaction with the leadership of the principals. Project team members felt that the principals were unsupportive and did not give the teachers the help they needed. The principals of the PRIMER schools practically washed their hands of PRIMER once they realized that it had not "put their schools on the map" (Jennings 1993, 532) and community support had waned after they saw the government making no effort to construct new buildings or refurbish old ones as promised (Minott 1988).

CETT is exceptional in that in-service training was organized at the school level and various strategies were used to involve stakeholders in the project, in particular the parents. Separate workshops were held for principals and teachers to ensure that they "own the management, leadership and instructional strategy by which they achieve success" (Warrican, Spencer-Ernandez and Miller 2013, 8). These workshops were also the venue for the discussion of the results of annual performance tests as well as the effectiveness of action research interventions which involved both principal and teachers.

Summary

Teachers in the CC "occupy an irreplaceable position in transforming education" (Mark et al. 2005, 9). But the image of the teacher as an agent of transformation is hardly consistent with the image of "teacher as curriculum implementer". This is associated with the top-down strategy used by the centralized education systems of the CC to introduce change into school systems. Because teachers are the ones with power at the classroom level, blame is levelled at their feet when innovations fail: for example, when they refuse to allow children to use self-instructional materials independently and instead use them as text. Using SIM as text is the teachers' way of *adapting* an innovation to be congruent with their image of "teacher" and how they prefer to relate to their students. Project directors, like policymakers, are not interested in adaptation (or some may say *obstruction*) of innovations. They want teachers to honour fidelity implementation: that is to use the innovation as intended by the developers. But these intentions are often not clearly communicated to the teachers; the innovations are complex to understand and pose considerable problems to the teachers as they grapple with the new ideas.

This chapter has drawn attention to the teachers' experiences on the inside of the innovations which gives us an insight into why they fail to implement innovations as expected and why they tend to revert to their accustomed way of teaching. CC countries use a variety of approaches to training for implementation, with the cascade approach being most widely used. Other approaches are project-based workshop training, voluntary and out-of-school hours, no training at all, a tiered approach (regional/cluster/school level) and a project-based workshop/cascade approach followed by the training being incorporated into the pre-service training of teachers.

Weaknesses in the use of the cascade approach to training include the lack of support and resources for the "master trainers" to disseminate the training they received: the failure of this approach to address the needs and concerns of teachers in their particular contexts. The cascade approach paints all teachers with the same brush, indifferent to the fact that they have varied levels of training and some even teach out of field. Training in the cascade approach is short term and does not offer the ongoing support to the teacher that fosters cumulative learning; the focus of the training is on telling rather than demonstrating or "showing how to do". Because innovations come in "bundles", the teacher is not given enough *time* to acquire and master all of the new learning. Furthermore, information often becomes distorted as it is passed through the "tiers" of the cascade approach resulting in a lack of clarity on the part of teachers in their understanding of new concepts. Workshop-based training by a project team encounters most of these challenges and can become stymied by personal animosities as well as shortcomings in project leadership, as in the case of PRIMER. Because principals invariably receive no training in implementing the innovations, they do not have a clear understanding of the new requirements of the teacher and so can make conflicting demands on the teacher. Consequently, the support that teachers look up to the principal to provide as they implement the innovation is often not forthcoming. Left to implement innovations without the resources required, often in classrooms which were designed to foster the achievement of the very objectives that the innovation has abandoned, teachers become disillusioned, fearful of failure and experience feelings of inadequacy.

Conclusion

Producing teachers who are agents of transformation who have shed their didactic pedagogy for a more student-centred constructivist teaching has proven to be a remarkably difficult task in the CC. Explanations for this range from the disconnection between the theories of teaching and learning that are taught to trainee-teachers and the practice required of them in the classroom (Evans 1997), the failure on the part of teacher educators themselves to model what they demand of the teachers (Marshall 2006/07), the fact that the change proposals fail the teacher's "practicality ethic" (Doyle and Ponder (1977/78)) and that proposals for change are not aligned with teachers' concerns (Hall and Hord 2006). To these explanations, this chapter has added another: the experiences of the teachers on the inside of the innovations and the quality (or lack thereof) of training to implement the innovations.

Teachers in the CC have a long journey before they can achieve that degree of professionalism that makes them agents of transformation. That journey must begin by revisiting (1) our approaches to introducing change into school systems, (2) the image of the teacher associated with these approaches and (3) the approaches that we use to train teachers to implement change. We need to move to a plane where we have confidence in our teachers as professionals who can develop curricula to suit their particular contexts or at least *adapt* centralized developed curricula to meet the needs and interests of the students in the situations in which they teach, with as much support from specialists as they require. CETT, though not without its flaws, exemplifies an approach to training for implementation which respects the teacher as a professional, in that teachers were seen not just as rational adopters but as problem-solvers who, with support from the reading specialist and with the aid of the principal, could design and implement action research which informed the solution to the problems they identified in their teaching. In this regard, it is interesting to note that Finnish teachers "receive generous specialist support as needed" (Hargreaves and Shirley 2009, 33). The Academy of Singapore Teachers has been established by the Ministry of Education to "drive a teacher-led culture of professional excellence" (Hargreaves 2012, 15) and this underscores the fact that "it is teachers' sense of professionalism that ultimately drives the impetus for change" (Hargreaves 2012, 13).

Hargreaves and Shirley identify three principles of professionalism which are relevant to our discussion, particularly in the context of CC countries which have set "developed status" as a goal. First, *high-quality teachers* who are not only accorded high status in society but "are trained to a rigorous intellectual and practical standard" (Hargreaves and Shirley 2009, 36). Finland and Singapore ensure that persons entering their teaching profession are highly qualified with postgraduate qualifications to the master's level. CC countries have a long way to go in this regard because it is only in the last decade that they have made a first degree a requirement for the initial training of teachers. The second principle is powerful *professionalism* fostered by Teachers' Associations that become "profound agents of systemic change" (Hargreaves and Shirley 2009, 36). Teachers' Associations in CC countries tend to focus more on teachers' salaries and working conditions rather than on professionalism. The third principle is that teachers form lively *learning communities* "in which teachers learn and improve together in cultures of collaboration, trust and responsibility" (Hargreaves and Shirley 2009, 36). The R&T teachers could well have formed the nucleus of such a learning community had they been encouraged and supported to work collaboratively in developing integrated lesson plans. The same could be said of the Sixth Form Geography teachers had they received rigorous training which included the skills to develop their own curriculum. It is one thing for policy to frame teachers as agents of transformation, and quite another to put in place the systems necessary for this to happen. Teachers may be able to "critically shape their responses to problematic situations" (Priestley et al. (2012, 195)) but their ability to do this in the CC countries is limited by the constraints of the environment in which they function.

The next chapter further illustrates how teachers function under the constraints of their environment as they implement an innovation in an impoverished rural area in Jamaica.

8.

When Fidelity Implementation Fails

A Case Study in Early Childhood Education

In this chapter we want to probe further into the factors that affect or influence the implementation of an innovation by focusing on an innovative project from BSPS[1] which provides an interesting contrast to other innovative projects explored in earlier chapters. The BSPS was designed to better prepare three to five years old from impoverished backgrounds in a rural area of Jamaica to transition to primary school. "Transition to school is more difficult for rural children who are usually not adequately provided for", writes Yeboah (2001, 12). In a study that focused on schools in rural Jamaica, Cook and Ezenne (2010) found that the children in these schools are from poor families with limited means and some are unable to send their children to school because they cannot afford the school uniform, transportation costs or provide breakfast or money for school lunch.

In Jamaica education provision for children in the three to five years age group falls into three broad categories which are for the most part differentiated by social class. Children from the lower-social class attend community-based *basic schools*[2] which are privately owned and minimally subsidized by the government. The government operates less than 10 per cent of the schools that cater to three- to five-year olds (Kinkead-Clarke 2018). Services for this age group are especially significant for children from low-income families as they can compensate for gaps in the child's development resulting from deficiencies in the home environment. This is underscored in longitudinal research in Jamaica known as the Profiles Project which in 2003 followed up 69 per cent of a national sample of six-year olds who had entered primary school in 1999 and had attended basic, infant or preparatory schools. The children from parents of lower-socioeconomic status performed significantly weaker than their peers of parents from the higher-socioeconomic status (Samms-Vaughan 2004). Children in basic schools need a high-quality curriculum that better prepares them to do well at the primary level.

The start of primary school is one of the most important transitions in a child's life as it entails moving from the familiar to a strange physical environment, getting accustomed to different teachers, to new ways in which classrooms are organized, all of which can be a source of great anxiety for the young child. Researchers have therefore emphasized the need to bridge the gap of discontinuity between the preschool and the primary school and to prepare the ground for a smooth transition (Fabian and Dunlop 2002, Margetts 2007). This was the main objective of the BSPS.

The purpose of this chapter is to elucidate the key factors that impacted the fidelity implementation of an innovation designed to smoothen the transition to primary school of children from an impoverished rural area in Jamaica. The BSPS had several innovative features which were new to the rural schools in which it was implemented. These features included the use of literature-based activities to integrate the children's experiences in core areas of the curriculum and novel approaches to assessment using portfolios and checklists. It was also enriched with resources not normally found in public preschools. The theoretical underpinning of the evaluation will be discussed before outlining the innovation itself and elaborating on the methodology used for the case study.

Theoretical Framework

According to Carroll et al. (2007, 1), "Implementation fidelity refers to the degree to which an intervention or programme is delivered as intended". They contend that a principal reason why fidelity implementation needs to be measured is that it may impact the relationship between the intervention and its intended outcomes. Elements of fidelity implementation are (1) programme differentiation, (2) adherence, (3) exposure, (4) quality of delivery and (5) participant responsiveness (Carroll et al. 2007, Shaughnessy 2015). The elements which are distinct and essential to the innovation should be made clear (*programme differentiation*). The innovation should be implemented as intended (*adherence*) and users should have access to and be able to use the various inputs that comprise the innovation (*exposure*). *Quality of delivery* relates to how the teacher delivers the innovation and enacts new approaches to delivery as intended. *Participant responsiveness* relates to how the users respond to the innovation as well as how they judge aspects of it. Carroll et al. (2007, 2) contend that the elements that are measured in fidelity implementation "have certain overlaps with process evaluation".

Evaluation here is seen as a process of obtaining and providing useful information to guide decision-making. The approach used to evaluate the fidelity implementation of the BSPS draws on the framework developed by Stufflebeam and Shinkfield (2007) which comprises four elements: context, input, process and product. *Context* is interpreted as the environments and conditions in which the innovation is implemented. *Inputs* are the resources (human, material, physical, financial) which are necessary to ensure fidelity implementation. The *process* element focuses on the innovation as it is implemented and contrasts what was *expected* by the designers of BSPS with *what actually happened* as gleaned from the observations of experts and feedback from stakeholders. Product is equated with the *outcome* of the BSPS as measured by the students' achievement in standard tests. Cuban (1998) identifies the fidelity standard as a measure of the success or failure of a reform. "The fidelity standard", he writes, "places great importance on implementers, who invariably are teachers and principals, following the designer's blueprint. When practitioners add, adapt, or even omit features of the original design, then policy makers . . . say that the policy and programme cannot be determined effective because of these changes" (Cuban 1998, 158). The approach to the evaluation is set out in table 8.1.

The BSPS Innovations

The BSPS involved (1) workshops for the training of teachers, principals and education officers in (a) use of an integrated approach to teaching literacy, science and drama instruction through literature-based activities, (b) the use of a variety of assessment strategies including portfolios and checklists, use of worksheets and work books and (c) the setting up of learning centres; (2) provision of resource materials including play dough, crayons, floor mats, large pencils, slates, paints and brushes, as well as a computer and printer with some CDs for each school; (3) equipping parents of children in the project schools with knowledge and skills to support their children's literacy development and science learning; (4) improvement of the learning environment with the provision of hexagonal desks and chairs to allow for flexibility in classroom arrangement, folding cupboards, provision of a variety of storybooks appropriate for the age group.

Lecturers in a teachers college that focused on EC education trained teachers, principals and education officers to create a child-centred environment and to build children's early literacy experiences by reading stories to them, engaging them in shared reading and writing activities and encouraging children to read, write about and draw their experiences. The teachers were also trained to use questioning techniques with an emphasis on encouraging the children to ask questions and to work in groups. The project coordinator had responsibility for the improvement of the learning environment in the schools, coordination of all activities, programmes and workshops, supervision of teachers and head teachers, procuring all project materials and equipment, and equitable distribution of these to the transition basic schools. The coordinator also had responsibility for parent and community orientation, support and training.

Table 8.1. From Basic School to Primary School Project: Context, Input, Process and Outcomes

Context	Input	Process (Implementation) Expected (Fidelity)	Process (Implementation) Actual (Observed)	Outcomes
8 Transition **basic schools** in sugarcane farming area. No. of children in each school ranged from 16 to 78. No. of boys = 190. No. of girls = 197. No. of teachers in each school = 2/3 (total = 20) 1 teacher in each school served as the head teacher. 2 or 3 classrooms separated by chalkboards. Two schools housed in a church where all materials and furniture have to be removed on Fridays. Schools have piped water, boy/girl toilets, but some schools have pit latrines. Some have electricity. None have outdoor playground equipment. Some classrooms poorly ventilated, with leaking roofs left unrepaired since the last hurricane.	Project coordinator 23 training workshops for teachers; 22 (for parents) 10 (for head teachers/education officers). Workshops conducted by lecturers in training college specializing in early childhood education. New curriculum Learning centres Variety of assessment strategies (e.g. portfolios) Resources (e.g. story books, crayons, sand computer, printer, new desks /chairs) International funding. Parental education	*Change in teaching approach* Use of new integrated curriculum. Teachers create a child-centred environment; read stories to children/encourage children to ask questions and work in groups. Integration of IT in teaching. Teachers use new assessment strategies (e.g. portfolios). Children write about and draw their experiences. Improved learning environment. Use of moveable desks and chairs for flexible classroom arrangement. Use of learning centres. Resource-rich lessons using variety of books Sand and water play. Rest area. Environment conducive for learning Parental involvement in children's education: interaction with teachers/principals	Persistent use of worksheets and copying from chalkboard. Teacher-initiated questions. Group work possible in only 2 schools. Group seating in most schools but not group work. TV kept in teacher's home. No starter pencils. No evidence of integrated approach. Paper pencil tests mostly used. Learning centres in all the schools but children not allowed to use some books. Toys unused and still packaged. Insufficient blocks for children to use. No water play area. Only one classroom had sand. No rest area for children in some schools. Most classrooms poorly lit/ventilated Improved interaction between teachers and parents. Parents better able to assist children with homework.	Grade 1 Reading Inventory *Visual-motor coordination mastery* CP = 46.8; TP = 29.02; NA = 86.4 *Visual Perception* CP = 16.97; TP = 13.39; NA = 61.0 *Auditory perception* CP = 21.43; TP = 19.2; NA = 64.6 *Number and letter knowledge* CP = 24.1; TP = 22.32; NA = 68.0 Caribbean Reading Standards Achievement Test (CRSAT) (Mastery attainment levels) *Non-mastery* CP = 0, TP = 7 *Approaching mastery 1* CP = 4, TP = 22 *Mastery level 1* CP = 26, TP = 10 *Approaching mastery 2* CP = 16, TP = 10 *Mastery level 2* CP = 4, TP = 1

1 Control basic school in same area. No. of children = 135. Separate classrooms.	No innovation inputs.	Teacher-centred approach to teaching; choral response from children; paper pencil tests.	Toys and blocks placed in learning centres for children to use.	
1 Transition primary school* No. grade 1 children = 112. Grade 2 = 139. Separate classrooms in grade 1. Only school with trained head teacher.	No innovation inputs.	Constructivist approach to teaching using an integrated curriculum in grades 1–3. Group work. Continuous assessment practices using portfolios/journals. Less reliance on paper/pencil tests.	Blocks available but not used by children.	The control primary outperformed the transition primary on both the GRI and CRSAT.
1 Control primary school No. grade 1 children = 145 Grade 2 = 121	No innovation inputs.	Same as above.	Blocks used by children.	

Source: Jennings (2005). *Key:* CP = control primary; TP = transition primary; NA = national average.

Methodology

Two specialists in early childhood education from the teachers college observed how the teachers implemented the innovations in the transition basic schools. They also conducted observations in the control basic school, but there were limited observations in the other schools. An evaluator assessed the effectiveness of the interventions. In so doing Jennings (2005) sought to find out how the transition basic school children who entered the transition primary school (i.e. the feeder school for the transition basic school children) performed on (1) the Grade 1 Readiness Inventory (GRI) and (2) the Grade 2 Caribbean Reading Standards Achievement Test (CRSAT) compared with their peers in the control primary school. The CRSAT is the test developed by CETT. The GRI is a diagnostic test designed to assess the readiness of the students to meet the demands of the grade 1 primary curriculum. It was administered during the first two weeks of the children starting primary school in 2004. The CRSAT was designed to determine whether students had met the demands of the grade 2 curriculum but for the purposes of the BSPS, it was used to compare the performance of the students in the transition primary (who had attended the transition basic schools) and students in the control primary school who had not been subject to any of the innovations. The CRSAT was administered in early May 2005.

Questionnaires were administered to the principals to ascertain their perception of the effectiveness of the innovations in terms of the provision of resources, their observations on changes in the teachers' methodologies, the smoothness of transition from the basic to the primary schools, the helpfulness of the training they received. Structured interviews were conducted with the project coordinator to assess how effectively project responsibilities had been carried out. The questionnaire for parents sought to ascertain whether the training received had resulted in them becoming more involved in their children's education, whether they felt that there had been improvement in the performance of the principals, in the learning environment and in the relationship between the basic and primary schools.

Findings

Process

Expected Implementation

From a synthesis of research on the quality of early childhood care and education services in selected Caribbean countries, Davies (1998) concluded that the schools had insufficient play materials and equipment for children to interact with. Particular effort was made to ensure that this was not the case in the schools in the BSPS. Therefore, the transition basic school classrooms were to be provided with ample supply of materials such as blocks of different colours, construction materials, puzzles, large pencils, paints and play dough and chalkboards. All transition basic schools were to have an adequate supply of developmentally appropriate storybooks and provided with moveable furniture that could facilitate group work. Teachers were expected to establish learning centres in each classroom and areas for sand and water play. An area for rest was also to be designated. The teachers were expected to use the instructional approaches in which they were trained with particular attention to the children's natural love of play, the development of their interests and curiosity, the use of group activities and an integrated approach to the curriculum.

Actual/Observed Implementation

Classroom observations revealed that all the transition basic school classrooms had chalkboards, chalk, small pencils and writing books. The presence of these indicates a strong emphasis on writing but they were given small pencils which did not help to develop the fine motor skills of the children. None of the schools had large (starter) pencils. The chalkboards were also used as partitions in all schools with the exception of the grade 1 classrooms in the transition primary school and the control basic school. In the control basic school there were five individual rooms, completely blocked off from each other with firm partition material. In addition, although a number of books were placed on shelves or in cupboards in the transition basic school classrooms, it was evident that the children were not allowed to use some of them. In fact, many were still packed away in boxes. A few commercially made toys were seen in the transition basic schools, but most were still packaged. At one school, for example, two doctors' kits, still wrapped in cellophane, were placed on display on the wall. A car, still in the box, was displayed on the table. In contrast, in the control basic school toys were placed in the learning centres in all classrooms and it was evident that they were being used by the children. An adequate supply of blocks of different colours was in use in the control basic and primary schools, while there were very few in the transition basic schools. When a second-grade teacher in the transition primary school was asked if blocks were available in her classroom, she responded that they were in the adjoining classroom as they had to be shared between two classes. They were, however, seen stacked in a cupboard unused.

While the schools had mobile furniture, limited space made flexibility in organization difficult. Chairs were organized in rows and in only two of the transition basic schools were they organized in a circle or in a way to make group work possible. Only three of the classrooms could be described as well ventilated and lit, and pleasant and conducive for learning.

Only learning centres were well established and in a defined area in all the transition basic schools. There was no water play area in any of the transition basic schools and in two of the schools where there was evidence of sand, it was in small containers and tucked away under cupboards. In the two transition basic schools housed in a church, a rest area was created by placing a piece of sponge over two benches. Three of the other transition basic schools had only one child-sized bed for all students on roll. The beds, however, in all schools were only used to accommodate children who were ill. For rest, the children placed their heads on their desks.

While the project coordinator reported that assessment strategies, such as portfolios, checklists and worksheets were developed for use by the teachers, observations revealed that most teachers were not using portfolios with the children, neither were skills checklists completed. There was evidence though of the use of worksheets and a strong emphasis on copying from the chalkboard.

Seventy-eight per cent of the transition basic school head teachers reported that the teachers' methodology had improved. However, observation of the teachers' practices revealed the consistent use of the "chalk and talk" method in the classrooms with an emphasis on whole class teaching, memorization and limited opportunity for the children to ask questions. Neither in their planning nor instruction did they show an understanding of the integrated approach to teaching which includes group work and encouraging the children to ask questions.

Outcomes

Readiness for Transition to Primary School

The control primary school outperformed the transition primary school students in all of the GRI subtests. These comprise visual-motor coordination, visual perception, auditory perception and number and letter knowledge. Both the transition and control primary schools performed below the national average in the GRI. For example, while the national average in the mastery of number and letter knowledge was 68.0, the average for mastery in the transition primary school was 22.32 compared with 24.1 for the control primary school. In the CRSAT, the students in the control primary school outperformed those in the transition primary. The transition primary had a larger number of the students operating at the non-mastery level and approaching mastery levels. The majority of the students at the control primary school were operating at mastery level 1 and approaching mastery level 2 (see table 8.1).

Given that the results of the GRI showed that the readiness for grade 1 of the children who had been exposed to the BSPS was below standard, the BSPS has fallen short of adequately preparing basic school children for a smooth transition to the primary level. The performance of the students in the CRSAT shows that even at grade 2 they were still performing below standard.

Over 80 per cent of the parents of children in the transition basic schools said the schools conducted workshops to guide them in assisting their children with their schoolwork, compared with only 23 per cent of parents in the control basic school. In the transition basic schools, parents reported that they were given opportunities to discuss their children's work with their teachers and they were able to better help their children with their homework. However, they needed more help with how to develop the children's mathematics and reading skills. Sixty-two per cent of them felt that the performance of the principal and teachers had improved as a result of the BSPS.

The head teachers were of the view that the BSPS had facilitated a smooth transition from the basic to the primary school. They pointed to the interaction between teachers from the transition basic school and the transition primary school and the fact that children from the transition basic school had opportunities to visit the transition primary prior to their admission.

Discussion

How do we account for the fact that the control primary school students outperformed the transition primary school students in both the Grade 1 Readiness Inventory and the CRSAT given that the intake of the transition primary was from basic schools in which innovations had been introduced to facilitate a smooth transition? Three possible explanations will be considered: the contexts in which the BSPS was implemented, the children themselves and the training of the teachers.

The Contexts for Fidelity Implementation

For an innovation to be implemented as intended (*adherence*), the situations in which the innovation is to be implemented should be "ready" for it. Schools should be able to provide the engaging learning environments that the new approach to teaching requires. Poor physical facilities in the transition basic schools indicated that they were not "ready" for the children. Conditions in the control basic school appeared to be better in that they had classrooms which were more conducive for learning. They had individual classrooms completely blocked off from each other with firm partitions. The transition basic schools had chalkboard partitions between the classes. This encouraged distractions and noise interference. Some of the transition basic schools had been badly affected by Hurricane Ivan in September 2004 and they still had leaking roofs. New furniture promised to the schools were late in arrival.

In fact, they came close to when the project was due to terminate. Having only unwieldy chairs and desks made it difficult to create the child-centred learning environments that the BSPS required.

The sanitary facilities in the schools were generally inadequate. Some of them had pit latrines with no separate facilities for the boys and girls, and in one case the children and teachers shared the same facilities. In one school there was no piped water and hands had to be washed from water poured from buckets filled at houses near to the school. These conditions pose serious challenges for basic schools which need to lay the foundations for appropriate health and hygienic practices and the development of appropriate social skills. While all but two of the transition basic schools had adequate outdoor space for play, none had any outdoor playground equipment for the children.

Fidelity implementation requires that users should have access to and be able to use the various inputs that comprise the innovation (*exposure*). In the control basic schools, the resource materials and toys were used and readily available to the children, whereas the opposite applied in the transition basic schools. More costly items like the television, computer and rug for the use of the children for story telling were all kept at the head teachers' homes. Three of the transition basic schools were located on church premises and in one case the teachers had to remove all classroom materials out of the church two or three times per week to make way for the church services. In this case it could be, as the head teacher explained, that the teachers had to take materials and equipment home for "safe keeping". At the same time, it must be borne in mind that computers cannot be used in schools without electricity and internet connection as was the situation in a number of the transition basic schools.

Both principals and parents were concerned about the adequacy of resources provided to the schools. Only 14 per cent of these respondents were satisfied with the physical facilities, including building and playground facilities. In contrast 40 per cent of the respondents in the control basic and primary schools expressed satisfaction with resources and facilities in their school. Although more so in the transition schools, it was clear that in the control schools also physical conditions and resources needed to be improved to make the environment more conducive for learning.

The Children and Their Disadvantaged Backgrounds

The performance of the children in the transition basic schools in a developmental screening test showed that many were at a disadvantage developmentally and this clearly impacted on their learning ability. Results of the Denver 11 developmental test revealed suspect cases in the schools ranging from 8 to 45 per cent. The four-year-old age group had the highest frequency of suspects (32 per cent) and the items with which children failed most frequently were related to language (*names colours, counts blocks, defines words and actions, defines adjectives*) (Ashby, Evans and Thorburn 2004). The administration of the Denver II tests in June 2005 produced similar results. For example, the results showed that the four-year-old age group had the highest percentage (32 per cent) of suspects and 77 per cent of the failure was in the language domain. Most of these children have difficulty naming colours, counting blocks, defining words and actions, and defining adjectives. Their language development was deficient from the start. If the deficiency is not corrected in the basic school, they move to the primary school with this disadvantage. This explains their performance in both the GRI and the CRSAT.

While the Denver II tests were not conducted on the children in the control basic school, it seems likely that they too suffered from similar developmental disadvantages as the transition basic schools by virtue of them being in the same location in the same parish which was disadvantaged both socially and economically. The schools were all located in an area where families relied on the sugarcane industry in which employment is seasonal and there are few jobs for women. Many of the children were from single-parent homes where mothers were the breadwinner and often could not provide their children with breakfast or money for school lunch. At the time of conducting this study, the transition basic schools charged a tuition fee that is equivalent to US$10 per term, and they provided a cooked lunch which costs about US$3 per week. Even so most parents could not afford this and so absenteeism in the schools was high. In fact, while in the country generally there has been an increase in enrolment in preschools, there are still a disproportionate number of children from lower-income homes not enrolled in preschool. In the parish in which this study was conducted, more than 20 per cent of the three- to five-year olds from low-income homes are not enrolled in schools. The BSPS sought to improve enrolment and attendance, but whether it was successful in doing so could not be assessed as record keeping was not systematic. In fact, physical conditions in some of the schools made the accessibility of records problematic. The effect of all of this is evident in the overall performance of the children. Those in both the transition and control primary schools performed below the national average on the GRI.

Level of Training of Teachers and Head Teachers

The *quality of delivery* is another important element of fidelity implementation. That this would be problematic is evident from the level of training of the head teachers and teachers. Jennings (2005) noted this as cause for concern. Only the principal in the transition primary school was trained, but not formally trained in educational administration and leadership. Over 80 per cent of the transition basic school teachers were aged forty to sixty and functioned as "pre-trained" teachers, meaning that they were teaching without a trained teacher's certificate. Thirty-three per cent of them had been teaching around eleven to thirty years. This is not untypical of what applies in basic schools throughout Jamaica. While the teachers in the infant schools and kindergartens are usually trained at teachers colleges, many of those in the basic schools are "pre-trained" and few have a trained teacher's certificate, but they attend monthly workshops where they share ideas and learn from each other's experiences (Daley and Thompson 2004). Davies (2015, 15) sums up the situation in Jamaica thus: "college trained diploma teachers comprise less than ten per cent of practitioners in all early childhood facilities, and less than one per cent of all practitioners in the EC sector have a first degree."

Twenty-three workshops are unlikely to have much of an effect on changing the accustomed ways of teaching of these teachers, especially as only 33 per cent of them attended around eleven to twenty of the workshops. The two education officers involved in the project did not attend the workshops at all and complained of not being able to assist the teachers and principals as much as they had wished largely because of their workload.

Furthermore, the use of workshops outside their school contexts was not the most appropriate method for training the teachers to implement the innovations in the transition basic schools. These teachers needed in-service training which was ongoing, interactive and provided adequate time and opportunities to develop new conceptions, skills and behaviour (Fullan and Stiegelbauer 1991). Abdul-Majied and Chin (2013) arrived at similar conclusions in their study of the quality of teaching at the infant level in a newly built primary school in Trinidad and Tobago. They found that while the school sought to be a model for high-quality teaching and learning, this objective could not be achieved by simply providing nice physical facilities and resources. The teachers needed ongoing support to deal with the problems that children brought with them from the home as well as indiscipline in the school.

The importance of ongoing support is underscored by the fact that what the teachers encountered in the BSPS was "innovation overload". As mentioned in the previous chapter, several innovations are embedded in one innovation. In the BSPS the use of literature-based activities to integrate the teaching of literacy, science and drama, new assessment strategies, integrating technology into teaching, establishing learning centres, parental education are but five of the new ideas they were using for the first time. The teachers needed time to get to grips with each of these, and to do this they needed ongoing support in their schools. The education officers could not provide such support as they only visited these rural schools around five to ten times per year. How the teachers were to integrate technology into their teaching was not at all clear given that the computer was kept at the head teacher's home for safe keeping. The elements which are distinct and essential to the BSPS are the integrated approach to the teaching of literacy, science and drama (*programme differentiation*) but the training in this area was inadequate as the teachers did not understand how to implement the integrated approach.

Summary

The BSPS was designed to better prepare three- to five-year olds from impoverished backgrounds in a rural area of Jamaica to transition to primary school. Teachers in eight transition basic schools were expected to implement an innovative integrated approach to teaching in classrooms which were to have learning centres, a variety of resources including story books, a computer and a printer with CDs and moveable furniture that facilitated group work. Teachers were expected to adopt a child-centred approach to teaching, using more varied assessment techniques. Training workshops were held for the teachers, head teachers and education officers who supervised them. Parents were also trained to support their children's learning in the new curriculum. A project coordinator managed the BSPS including the organization of the workshops, procurement and distribution of materials and resources.

The use of a model that drew on the work of Stufflebeam and Shinkfield (2007) enabled the evaluation of the contexts in which the BSPS was implemented, the inputs, how the BSPS was implemented (process) and its outcomes. The findings revealed that some elements for fidelity implementation were absent in the BSPS. It was found that new furniture for the classrooms did not arrive until near the end of the project and resource materials provided for teaching were unused (*exposure*). The teachers did not show any understanding of the use of an integrated approach to teaching, which was the most unique and essential aspect of the BSPS (*programme differentiation*). Observations of teaching revealed a persistence in the practice of children copying from the chalkboard and no use of new assessment techniques was observed (*quality of delivery*). Despite the difficulties incurred, participants responded positively to the BSPS: for example, the head teachers felt that the BSPS had facilitated a smooth transition from the basic to the primary school and parents were satisfied with the support they received from the transition basic schools (*participant responsiveness*).

The outcome of the BSPS was measured by a comparison of the performance in two tests of the children who attended the transition basic schools with those in the control basic school. The tests were the GRI and the grade 2 CRSAT. The students who attended the control basic school outperformed those who attended the transition basic school in both tests. This indicated that the innovations of the BSPS had not made them "ready" for transition to the primary level and that even after one year at primary school they had not yet attained the required level. The head teachers and parents of children in the basic schools, however, were of the view that the BSPS had prepared the children for a smooth transition to the primary school. That the children were able to visit the primary school prior to admission and teachers in the basic and primary schools were able to meet and talk about the children were factors that contributed to this.

Conclusion

Although the parents and head teachers assessed the BSPS favourably in that they felt that the project had facilitated the smooth transition of the children from the basic schools to the primary school, evidence shows that fidelity implementation did not occur in the BSPS. Participants were not given exposure to various elements of the innovation: for example, children did not have access to resource materials which were stacked away in unopened packages. Perhaps this is the way the teachers dealt with scarce resources: used them sparingly or packed them away because once they were used up the school had no money to replenish the stock. With regard to *quality of delivery*, the teachers could not reasonably be expected to change their teaching method, given the difficult physical conditions in which they had to work and the fact that the new furniture which would have helped to create the milieu favourable to the new teaching method they were expected to use did not arrive until near the end of the project. Questions can also be raised about the nature of the training they received given that there was no evidence from their teaching that they understood the new approach they were supposed to use. The workshop-based training provided to the teachers was clearly inadequate. They could not rely on the persons with responsibility to offer them guidance in their teaching on an ongoing basis – the education officers – because they themselves did not participate in the training provided.

What this case study has clearly shown is that the onus cannot be put solely on the teacher when fidelity implementation fails. The contexts in which they are expected to work, the nature of the training they are given and even the *time* when needed resources are made available to them frustrate any effort on their part to meet expectations. Attention also needs to be given to the children themselves, their socioeconomic background and how this impacts their development as well as their ability to attend school regularly. As Lewin and Stuart (1991, 16) affirm: "In many educational systems in developing countries the losers in the change process are those clients on the margins of the existing system. Rural children and teachers in isolated, under-resourced and neglected schools, with many unqualified teachers and little access to information, are those least prepared for change."

9.

Lessons Learned

Drivers for Change

Our journey has ended. It is time to reflect on where we have been and what we learned along the way. What first came to mind is the title of a paper written by Elliot Eisner which began with "Those who ignore the past . . ." In the paper he reflected on fifty years of US education and elaborated on lessons learned from attempts to reform schools and change teaching practices. Eisner's title reminded me of a main purpose of this book highlighted in the introduction and captured by London (2002, 69), "When practitioners are better able to understand the past, chances are that they will be able to impart greater sensitivity to their plans for change and as a result improve the probability for success in their programmes." Like Eisner, my hope is that what we have learned on our journey in this book "may promote debate that might decrease the likelihood that the past will be repeated" (Eisner 2000, 343). Perhaps this should be amended to "ill-conceived decisions and actions of the past", because there are a number of good things that we have learned from past attempts at change in the Commonwealth Caribbean. An example of this is the systematic rather than piecemeal attempt at change in Barbados' EduTech 2000 which sought to address simultaneously the factors that impact student achievement, namely, infrastructure, technology, curriculum,[1] teacher and staff training and treated with primary and secondary education at the same time. Innovative features of the CSEC (e.g. school-based assessment) have influenced practices even in developed countries such as Canada, Australia, the United Kingdom and Hong Kong. CETT has shown how technology can be used in the evaluation of change and ROSE underscored the importance of research to change.

Based on lessons from the past, can we formulate a theory that could guide policymakers and educational planners in the future? On a theory of change Sarason (1971, 53) notes that

> theories are practical, particularly in relation to the change process, because they tell one what one has to think and do, and not what one would like to think and do. A theory of the change process is a form of control against the tendency for personal

style, motivation, and denial of reality to define the problem and its possible solutions along lines requiring the least amount of personal conflict.

My interpretation of a theory of change, then, is outlining some key points that policymakers and educational planners need to consider when they plan to introduce change into school systems. Doing this will not guarantee success as change is so unpredictable; it will nevertheless ensure that the approach to change is informed. These key points will be discussed in this chapter as "drivers for change". What is significant about the theory presented is that it applies to centralized education systems which are characteristic of the CC. In these systems curriculum development for public schools from EC to the lower secondary level (up to grade 9) comes under a central authority (i.e. the Ministry of Education).[2] Mandates for implementation are handed "top-down" to teachers, principals and other stakeholders.

Purpose

This chapter, therefore, seeks to do two things: (1) to summarize the process used in CC countries to introduce innovations into their school systems with key points that need to be considered at each stage, as became evident from the case studies and (2) to discuss the drivers for change.

The Change Process

The first principle of change highlighted by Hall and Hord (2006, 4) is that "change is a process, not an event". "Process" implies a series of continuous actions. As figure 9.1 shows, we can identify these actions in the stages that we move through as we engage in the process of change. It begins with the *initiation* or invention of a new idea (innovation) which is then designed. The *design* stage articulates the rationale for the change process. Designing is a way of organizing thinking about all matters that are important to the change process. It involves outlining what the innovation consists of, what its important elements are, its intended outcomes, how these will be realized, by whom, when and under what conditions. How will we know that these outcomes have been achieved? The design stage requires forward-thinking about and planning for subsequent stages (e.g. implementation and institutionalization), thereby underscoring the inter-relatedness of the different stages. This also ensures that needed supports will be provided for at the different stages. An advocate who can articulate the vision, the goals and intended outcomes and "sell" the new idea to stakeholders and users would be an asset as the innovation takes shape. Feedback from stakeholders can inform the design.

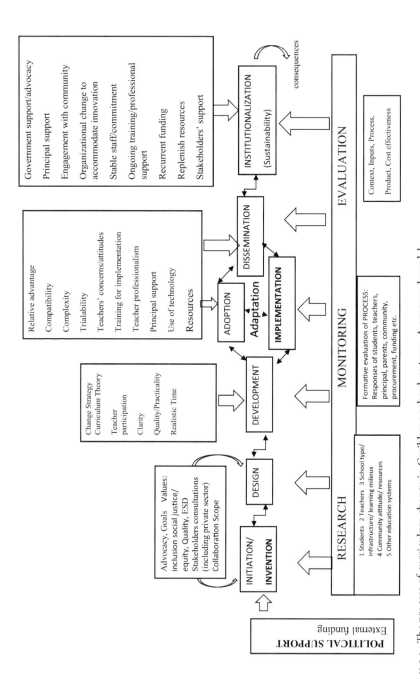

Figure 9.1. The process of curriculum change in Caribbean school systems: A proposed model.

Key: CP = control primary; TP = transition primary; NA = national average.

As is evident from the direction of the arrows, the path from *invention* to *design* is not a direct one because it can be thwarted by controversy, disagreements or lack of clarity about the ultimate goal and how to attain it. ASTEP, for example, started out as ASEP. Some officials of the Ministry of Education in Jamaica were certain of the need for an Alternative Secondary Education Programme (ASEP) for students who would not attain the level to sit the primary exit examination. These students, they felt, should stay on in the all age school. There were other officials, however, who felt that despite their level of achievement, the students would be of secondary school age and for their own self-esteem at least some of them should be allowed to transition into grade 8 of a secondary school (ASTEP) after one year in the all age school. The case of ASTEP underscores the importance of stakeholder consultations as deliberations on the initiation and design of the innovation are ongoing. Had such consultations taken place in the case of the NCERD Skills Reinforcement Guides, it is unlikely that the first workshop would have been "immediately greeted by a most unexpected series of negative statements and protests" (Craig 2006/07, 18) from the head teachers.

After the design stage, the innovation is then developed *(development)*. According to Hall and Hord (2006, 6) "development includes all of the steps and actions involved in creating, testing and packaging an innovation, whereas implementation includes all of the steps and actions involved in learning how to use it". Because the development of curricula is centralized in CC countries, a top-down or power-coercive strategy for change has been used, sometimes involving teacher participation as in the case of REAP and CETT. The development of the product should be guided by principles of *clarity, quality* and *practicality*. There was only one case study (the Sixth Form Geography Project) which involved a problem-solving approach to change which put control in the hands of teachers. In contrast to the teachers of geography who would have chosen to use the product they developed, in the top-down approach the users are mandated to adopt *(adoption)* and use the innovation *(implementation)*. It may be argued that because adoption implies choice, this stage does not apply in centralized education systems, since change is mandated. But people cannot be forced to change. They have to be persuaded to see the value of the change. This is where an advocate, opinion leaders or "influencers" have such an important role to play because their power of persuasion for the fidelity implementation of the innovation will come up against the teacher's "practicality ethic". This is the "teachers' perceptions of the potential consequences of attempting to implement a change proposal in the classroom" (Doyle and Ponder 1977, 5). Teachers do not feel comfortable steering far from their comfort zone.

There is a tendency on the part of educational planners and change facilitators to focus on what change *should* do and what teachers *should* do to make this change happen. The expectation is that the teachers, being "rational adopters" (Doyle and Ponder 1977) will be so impressed that they will bend over backwards to implement the new ideas. When they fail to do so they are dismissed as "stone-age obstructionists" who are resistant to change. Little attention is given to what teachers think about the change proposal and how they perceive its demands in terms of their perception of their role. Doyle and Ponder (1977, 1) urge attention to be given to "the decision-making processes which appear to underlie teacher reaction to change proposals". Teachers make decisions about whether the change is better than what they were doing before (*relative advantage*); whether it is consistent with their values and accustomed way of doing things (*compatibility*) and whether it is easy or too difficult (*complexity*) to implement. What teachers decide on these things will influence their attitude towards the mandate to adopt and use the innovation.

The case studies presented in this book underscore the importance of paying attention to the factors that influence teacher decision-making and in turn form attitudes which are/not receptive to the change. For example, the teachers in the PRIMER schools were really not receptive to the "programmed teachers", that is, the older primary school pupils who were expected to assist them in teaching language arts to the children in the lower grades. They perceived these "teachers" as a threat to their authority and did not give them the pre-training they needed to carry out their role (Minott 1988). In other words, these "teachers" were *incompatible* with their perception of themselves as teachers. To them there is a "hallowed ground" between themselves and the students they teach. The principals of many traditional high schools in Jamaica did not see the need (*relative advantage*) for ROSE 1 as they perceived it as below their standard. Equity and social justice were the concern of the Ministry of Education, not theirs. On the other hand, in e-Cal "the teachers all viewed the initiative as serving a need. They acknowledged that the use of technology served to motivate students to learn and fostered their engagement in the teaching/learning process" (Harry and Mitchell 2015, 1062).

The ease of implementation will depend on the approach used for training for implementation. Problems associated with the use of the cascade approach have been noted, but CETT has illustrated an approach to training which is ongoing, extending over a long period of time thereby enabling the concerns that teachers have to be addressed. Difficulties in implementation are eased by teachers having the resources they need and the support of the principal. Many principals were not convinced of the need for the Life Skills curriculum in the Grade 10–11 Programme. They were mandated to implement it without the schools being provided with the necessary resources. The principals therefore went through the motions of implementation by putting the programme under the charge of inexperienced teachers whom they knew would be quite ineffective. The Life Skills curriculum was short-lived.

The implementation phase leads into the *dissemination* of the innovation throughout the level of the education system for which it is designed. As figure 9.1 indicates there is an interconnection between or overlapping of the adoption, implementation and dissemination stages. This underscores the fact that the change process is not a linear one but one which, as it were, loops back on itself. Jamaica's ROSE programme provides a good illustration of this. Schools entered the programme in phases, including schools which were built as part of the civil works component. While the curricula for certain subjects were being implemented, others were just being developed. For example, Davis (1994) noted that the implementation of six curricula was taking place in seventy-three schools, while physical education, dance and music were being piloted in six schools. Five new subjects were to be developed during the school year.

According to Rogers (2003) an innovation that can be tried out (*trialability*) is more readily adopted by users because they can see the results of its use. Innovations are piloted for similar reasons. Through formative evaluation, the quirks can be ironed out and improvements made before being finalized for system-wide use. Of the case studies, the BSPS and PRIMER were pilots. In ROSE the subjects that make up the curriculum were pilot tested in phases, commencing with five subjects in September 1991 in four all age schools. An additional seven schools joined in September 1992. Revisions were made to the subjects before additional schools joined. Approximately 150 schools were expected to join ROSE between 1993 and 1998 (Davis 1994). GUIDE was piloted in regions 5 and 6 in Guyana (1995–97); region 3 came on board in 1998 and regions 4 and 10 in 1999 (Hamilton 1999). The findings of the evaluation of GUIDE informed the delivery by distance of the teacher training programme of the Cyril Potter College of Education. CSEC was piloted in five subjects in 1979 and since then the number has increased to thirty-three. Some innovations were implemented system wide without piloting. The NCERD SRGs, for example, were implemented all at once in 423 primary schools spread over 10 administrative regions in a country of 83,000 square miles. Of these schools 303 were known as "primaries with tops" because they included secondary departments with low-achieving grades 7–9. Because these followed what was essentially an extended primary curriculum, they were included in the innovation from 1990 to 1991. This was a massive undertaking in a context of scarce resources of all kinds.

Innovations become *institutionalized* when they become internalized in the continuing operations of the school and mechanisms are in place to sustain them. Such mechanisms include funds to replenish resource materials, continuing government support, administrative support at the school level and organizational change to accommodate the innovation.[3] These are examples of conditions that "successful" innovations need to satisfy, but as shown in an earlier chapter, successful innovations do not get ticks in all the boxes. ROSE is an interesting case. The development objectives of ROSE 1, according to the World Bank (2001, 3), "can be considered to have been achieved", suggesting some reservation about its success, and yet the principles that underpinned ROSE 1 (e.g. improvement in quality and equity) have been incorporated into policy which guides Jamaican education to the present day. In fact, the World Bank (2001, 24) in justifying the sustainability of ROSE noted that the government had "adopted policy and set targets that are not only consistent with ROSE but also push the agenda much further beyond the original conception to ensure the sustainability of reform in all levels of education in Jamaica". Worth noting is the fact that the multi-level nature of the ROSE curriculum (Foundations 1 and 2, Normative and Enrichment) based on differences in reading level has been carried over into the Alternative Pathways for Secondary Education (APSE) (SP 1, 2 and 3).[4] Learning skills for the twenty-first century (such as problem-solving, creative and critical thinking, collaborative, and other kinds of group work) which were embedded in the ROSE curriculum (Ministry of Education and Culture, Jamaica 1993) are also developed in APSE. ROSE as designed may be no more but the principles on which it was built live on in the changes that have overtaken it.

The *consequences* of innovation is such a neglected area in educational change that it can hardly feature as a stage in figure 9.1. Yet it is so important that it needs to be studied. An innovation introduced into a school never leaves that school unscathed. And not all innovations result in achieving some good. PRIMER, for example, sought to raise achievement levels in literacy and numeracy, to foster independence in learning, to reduce educational costs by having teachers function in a different capacity. It did not achieve any of these goals, but it left teachers feeling like guinea pigs and treated like "stone-age obstructionists". It resulted in acrimony between the teachers and the project team. The principals were dismissed as uncooperative. How did all this impact on the students? If the teachers fared so badly, they must have been adversely affected too. Yet the reports on PRIMER are silent on this. There is an issue here of moral responsibility towards students and teachers when the consequences of an innovation are not for the better. Schools are not science laboratories and pupils and teachers are not expendable objects on which one conducts an "experiment" and assume no responsibility for its outcome.

Drivers for Change

Political Support

Government support is critical for innovations to get off the ground and eventually to become institutionalized. Support by itself, however, does not guarantee success. The nature of the support is important. The Sixth Form Geography Project had the blessings of the Ministry of Education in Jamaica, but nothing else; not even an incentive for the teachers who were involved. Jamaica's Basic Education and Early Childhood Education programme sought to support the government's plans to improve the quality of basic education particularly for poor children from birth to twelve years. United Nations Children's Emergency Funds' funding of the BSPS project was in support of that policy. The delegation that visited the Philippines to study project IMPACT was led by the minister of education who represented the government's concern to improve the quality of education in rural Jamaica and to achieve cost reduction in education. PRIMER had the backing of the government and in fact the schools involved were in the constituency of the prime minister's brother (Cummings 1986). That support, however, was short-lived because one year after PRIMER was introduced, the government was ousted from power by the landslide victory of the opposition party at the 1980 elections. All the persons who could have served as advocates for PRIMER were swept from office except for a Ministry of Education official who became the project director of PRIMER. The new government expressed support for the initiative but not in the form of advocacy. PRIMER plummeted to an inevitable end.

The director of NCERD served as the advocate for the use of the Skills Reinforcement Guides. He was able to win over the support of the regional education officers and other field officers in the Ministry of Education who articulated their work programmes with that of NCERD. This, however, did not meet with the approval of senior personnel in the Ministry of Education because "field officers . . . started to feel obliquely threatened by the Ministry's response . . . some officers were pointedly asked by top level administrators in the Ministry whether they worked for the Ministry of Education or NCERD" (Craig 2006/07, 25). NCERD is a part of the Ministry of Education in Guyana. Petty jealousies found expression even in the minister of education commandeering for his personal use of the vehicle which a donor agent had provided for the use of NCERD fieldwork (Craig 2006/07).

CSEC, EduTech 2000 and REAP (see table 9.1) provide examples of the kind of political support needed for innovations to be sustained. CSEC could not have come into being without strong political support; at the outset this took the form of commitment from fourteen CC countries. EduTech 2000 was part of a major sector enhancement programme in Barbados. The Ministry of

Table 9.1. Drivers/Inhibitors of Change in Innovations in School Systems in the Commonwealth Caribbean

Innovation	Country	Political Support	Staff Stability	Tertiary-Level Collaboration	Adequate Finance/ Costing/ Timely Procurement	Research/ Monitoring Evaluation	Adequate Time	Strategic Planning	Multi-Agency Collaboration	Ongoing Training of Users	Timely Provision of Resources
REAP (1975–85)	Belize	√	√	√	√	√	√	√	√	N	√
NCERD (SRG) (1989–91)	Guyana	√#	N	N	N (Yr. 1) √ (Yr. 2)	√	N	√#	N	N	N
CETT (2002–06*)	5 CC countries##	√	√	√	√	√	√	√	N	√	√
Literacy 1-2-3 (2002 to present)	Jamaica	√	√	N	N	#	√	N	N	N	N
BSPS (2002–05)	Jamaica	√	√	√	N	√	N	N	N	N	N
PRIMER (1979–83)	Jamaica	√ (to 1980)	N	N	N	N	N	N	N	N	N
EduTech 2000 (1999–2008)	Barbados	√	#	√	N	√	N	√	#	N	N
ETV (1964 to present)	Jamaica	√	#	N	√	N	#	√	N	#	#
Grade 10–11 (1971–78)	Jamaica	√	N	N	N	N	N	N	N	N	N
CSEC (1979 to present)	14 CC countries**	√	√	√	√	√	√	√	N	N	√

Programme	Jurisdiction									
Sixth Form Geography (1979–81)	Jamaica	N	N	N	N	N	N	N	N	N
ROSE (1993–98)	Jamaica	√	√	√	N	√	√	√	N	N
R&T (1993 to present)	Jamaica	√	√	N	N	√	√	√	N	N
e-Learning project (2006–10)	Jamaica	√	#	√	√	√	√	N	√	N
e-Cal (2010–15)	Trinidad and Tobago	√	#	#	N	#	N	N	N	N
ASTEP (2010–12)	Jamaica	√#	N	N	N	√	N	N	N	N
GUIDE (1995–99)	Guyana	√	√	√	N	√	√	√	√	√
BEdSecDE (2001–11)	Jamaica	√	√	√	√	√	√	N	√	√

Key: √ = Yes; √# = Yes with reservations; N = No; # = No research evidence or insufficient evidence on which to judge. *CETT was extended to 2009. ** Antigua, Barbados, Belize, British Virgin Islands, Cayman Islands, Dominica, Grenada, Jamaica, Guyana, Montserrat, St Kitts/Nevis/Anguilla, St Lucia, St Vincent, Trinidad and Tobago, Turks and Caicos Islands, Cayman Island withdrew in 1977. ##Belize, Guyana, Jamaica, St Lucia, SVG.

Education, Youth Affairs and Culture itself served as a strong advocate.[5] REAP received strong ideological support from the People's United Party (PUP) which formed the government at the time of its initiation. The minister of education was REAP's strongest advocate. He was able to provide leadership in introducing REAP into the urban areas in 1983 when the acronym was changed to mean "Relevant Education for Agriculture and Production". The PUP lost the general election in 1984, but by then REAP had survived for almost a decade and District Councils were already enacting plans for its sustainability.

The Grade 10–11 Programme also had a very strong advocate in the prime minister of Jamaica who was so determined for it to succeed that he made it a project in his own office. However, the innovation was introduced at a time when the country was experiencing severe economic constraints. Within four years of its implementation, the prime minister was ousted from office in the general election of 1980. The new government was opposed to his ideology of democratic socialism and so innovations associated with it suffered due to lack of support. The SIM and the Life Skills programme gradually disappeared. The new secondary schools survived but as "schools for failures". Their intake was students from low-income homes who had failed the primary exit examination. Political support therefore needs to come from the head of government, a minister of education or other high ranking official with the power to influence. It can find expression in various ways, for example: providing incentives for teachers, principals or members of a community for involvement in an innovation and ensuring that the innovation is adequately funded. It can also come in the form of advocacy through articulation of the value and importance of the innovation to achieving not only educational goals but also social and economic goals pursued at the national level. Political support needs to endure the life of the innovation, from invention to institutionalization, even if there is a change of government in between.

Strategic Planning

Fullan (1994, 31) argues that "spending too much time and energy on advance planning, even if it builds in principles of flexibility, is a mistake". The case studies presented in this book, however, underscore the importance of spending much more *time* on planning so that important issues are not overlooked. *Strategic* planning contrasts with tactical planning which is built on the assumption that change is an event. Hall and Hord (2006) describe tactical planning as having a short-term focus, typically involving one formal training session for teachers before school begins and no on-site coaching. This description captures quite well what happened in the development process for the Grade 10–11 Programme. It was so "fast-tracked" that training for the teachers was by "model classes" shown on television (Jennings-Wray 1984). Planning for the

BSPS also appears to have been short term, as insufficient thought was given to the most productive use of donor funds. Rather than try to implement a new curriculum in hurricane-damaged schools with inadequate physical infrastructure it would have been better to use some of the funds to first improve the physical conditions of the schools to make them "ready" for the innovation.

Strategic planning assumes that change is a process and takes time. Its focus is on the long term and on institutionalization and sustainability. It is not piecemeal. Hall and Hord (2006) describe it as involving three to five years for implementation during which the resources needed to support formal training and to provide ongoing support are provided. Furthermore, "data will be collected each year to inform the planners and further assist implementation in subsequent years" (Hall and Hord 2006, 5). This is an apt description of the planning involved in Belize's REAP, except that its time frame was much longer. REAP was conceived in three phases extending over a ten-year period before becoming institutionalized (Jennings 1988). There was a pilot phase (1976–79) in which the REAP curriculum and the LAPs were developed, the teachers were trained and a formative evaluation done. The District Level phase (1979–82) followed in which revisions were done to the curriculum, radio programmes were used to disseminate knowledge about REAP and REAP District Councils (RDC) were set up to plan for the institutionalization of REAP. The final phase began towards the end of 1982 when REAP was expanded nationally to include urban schools and continuing support for REAP was transferred from the international organizations to the RDCs.

An important aspect of strategic planning is how innovation projects are managed. Many governments have chosen to house the management of innovations in project implementation offices which are often set up in Ministries of Education, but sometimes are housed outside. This, however, can be counterproductive to the sustainability of the innovation. Resentment on the part of the Ministry officials can develop towards project officers who are paid higher salaries for work which is eventually foisted onto them when the project ceases. The issue of salary differentials (which must be addressed in the context of public-sector reform) can have a negative impact on attempts to introduce change into school systems. Delisle (2012), for example, described the project coordinating unit of the SEMPCU in Trinidad and Tobago as perceiving its role as that of developing the innovation and then handing it over to the relevant units in the Ministry of Education. "The conflict between the MOE and the SEMPCU over roles resulted in many core implementation functions being neglected" (Delisle 2012, 73).

ROSE 1 abandoned the idea of a Project Implementation Unit and instead had a national coordinator and a secretariat. According to the World Bank

ROSE was guided by a Reform Management Committee (RMC) chaired by the permanent secretary, with the ROSE national coordinator as the deputy, and with participation of some twenty-two other officials from the Ministry of Education and one representative from the JBTE. "The RMC collectively planned, implemented, and monitored the reform" (World Bank 2001, 10). Functioning as an advocate, the national coordinator had the effect of keeping ROSE in the public eye through frequent appearances in the public media and giving updates on ROSE in the ROSE periodical and press. The strategy used by ROSE sought to ensure that project activities were fully integrated into the regular work of the Ministry of Education staff. However, of the two national coordinators who were appointed during the life of ROSE, neither was employed by the Ministry of Education. Once external funding was exhausted the secretariat was closed, the appointment of the national coordinator was terminated and ROSE was absorbed into the work of the Core Curriculum Unit of the Ministry of Education. This is where it should have been from the beginning but, as Riddell (2011) argues, embedded project management is desirable, but it is difficult to achieve.

The importance of the proximity of the project office to the site of the innovation is underscored by the experience of PRIMER. The project office of PRIMER was based in the city of Kingston, some 160 kilometres away from the rural schools involved in the project. This resulted in the project staff "having difficulty in comprehending the rhythm of life and the constraints on education found at the site" (Cummings 1986, 59). This explains why the level of difficulty of the SIM came as such a shock to the project staff. They had little knowledge of the children in rural schools. The amount of time spent travelling between the project office and the site resulted in visits to the schools being much less frequent than desired.

In sum, because change is a process which takes time, planning for change should be strategic in that it is long term and makes provisions for sustainability of the innovation. Ideally, the innovation should be managed in such a way that it ensures that project activities are fully integrated into the regular work of the Ministry of Education staff. It is therefore important that the approach used for managing the innovation does not alienate Ministry staff. Decisions on the selection of innovation site and project office should be part of the planning to ensure that there is easy communication between the two.

Adequate Finance, Costing and Timely Procurement

NCERD's Skills Reinforcement Guides (SRGs) and the Sixth Form Geography Project provide the only examples of innovations introduced without special funding. The attempt to train teachers to implement the SRGs in over four hundred primary schools spread across ten administrative regions of 83,000 square miles of the country and to do this in the first year (1989) by relying on the goodwill of the regional education offices was beyond a leap of faith. The poor quality of the materials and the inability to provide sufficient teachers' guides for the schools were the result of operating on a shoestring budget. Fortunately, financing for the implementation of the SRGs improved in 1990 with the introduction of the PEIP, which was funded by the IDB. One of the goals of PEIP was the production of textbooks and related materials for grades 1–6 in language arts, mathematics, science and social studies. It was envisaged that the "methodologies of the NCERD's Skills Reinforcement Guides would give teachers an essential preparation and orientation towards the use of the IDB-funded textbook and other materials" (Craig 2006/07, 21). Without any source of funding, the Sixth Form Geography Project could not provide the teachers with the training in curriculum development that they needed. As a result, the teachers produced nothing.

In CC countries where education is project driven, the normal pattern is for governments to seek financial assistance from international aid agencies. It is often the case, however, that there is serious cost underestimation in financial proposals. This problem is not new. London (1993), for example, described how the Short-Term School Building Project was implemented when Trinidad and Tobago's economy was booming on account of earnings from its petroleum industry. This pushed up the prices of land for the school sites, labour costs and project management beyond what had originally been budgeted. Nevertheless, the schools were still constructed with the result of huge cost overruns for the project. In ROSE 1 there were plans to build three schools but, in the end, only one was built and funds were not available to hire critical staff (e.g. a building officer for ROSE 1) (World Bank 2001). In the case of EduTech 2000, a total of US$39.4 million was allocated for civil works projects to make the schools IT ready. After seven years, three-quarters of this money had been spent and only one-third of the work completed (Pirog and Kioko 2010). Delays in the civil works projects impacted the central focus of EduTech 2000 – the integration of information technology into teaching and learning. IT was the most expensive component of EduTech 2000, initially budgeted at US$68.9 million. Pirog and Kioko (2010) noted that by the end of the seven-year-loan period only 23.6 per cent of the technology had been installed (although 41 per cent of the funds had been spent). Underestimation of the recurrent cost for e-Cal in Trinidad and Tobago resulted in damaged laptops not being replaced (Mitchell and Harry 2012).

While funds can be inadequate, there are often cases of failure to use up funds allotted with the result of what Riddell (2011, 31) describes as the "all-too-common rush to spend in the last few weeks of the financial year, monies distributed that are not spent otherwise being returned to the consolidated fund". This happened in ROSE 1 where about 10 per cent of the US$32 million loan could not be disbursed mainly due to non-completion of all civil works contracts by some contractors (World Bank 2001). Non-completion of work not only could be caused by inefficiency on the part of contractors but it could also be an issue of procurement.

Procurement is the acquisition of goods and services (e.g. of contractors and consultants) using a process which includes budgeting, advertising and requesting quotations, evaluation of bids and award of contract. The procurement process can have a negative impact on the timely completion of a project because "it can be highly bureaucratic and time consuming" (McKessey 2008, 18). In the BSPS it took much too long for the equipment and resource materials ordered to be delivered to the schools. In fact, they arrived when the project was near its end! Delays in the completion of civil works impacted ROSE 1. The national coordinator for ROSE concluded that "for the ROSE project, the most serious challenge revolved around the purchase of books, equipment and supplies for schools, and the procurement of services for construction work" (Griffith 1997, 9). EduTech 2000 had the additional problem of a limited labour pool to select from. "It took longer than anticipated to award contracts in an environment in which the government had to compete for contractors working in the lucrative tourism and luxury home market" (Pirog and Kioko 2010, 89).

What emerges from the case studies is that innovations that are undertaken with inadequate or no funding at all are unlikely to achieve their goals. There is also a need for accurate costing of innovations to be presented in financial proposals submitted to aid agencies. The policy of procurement on the part of both the aid agency and the Ministry of Education should be considered as early as during deliberations on the design of the innovation and not left to be encountered at the implementation stage when ordering resources or hiring contractors. There is also the suggestion that "the capacity of the private sector's construction industry needs to be assessed and strategies introduced in the project design to improve cost effectiveness and the quality of work" (World Bank 2001, 29).

Timely Provision of Adequate Resources

The BEdSecDE ensured that the courses were prepared for delivery by distance well ahead of time. Both CETT and GUIDE used materials which were already developed and available and thus avoided the issue of timely provision of adequate resources which has bogged so many of the innovations. Delays in the delivery of foundation textbooks "made it difficult to fully evaluate the impact of ROSE on student learning at the end of the project" (The World Bank 2001, 14). The SIM for the Grade 10–11 Programme were late in production "consequently, the teachers' guides accompanying the students' materials usually went out late and would reach the teachers after the students had covered the materials in their booklets" (Jennings-Wray 1984, 48).

Changes in teaching methods require classroom designs which can accommodate the new behaviours desired. Herein lies the challenge particularly in the classrooms of many Caribbean primary schools. They are often not made "ready" for the innovation. The head teachers who participated in the training to implement the Skills Reinforcement Guides in Guyana protested that the introduction of the innovation was untimely because "their buildings and classrooms were dilapidated, poorly furnished and uncomfortable. They were forced to operate without even the most basic of educational materials such as paper, chalk, and other writing materials. There were no books for reading or other activities in their schools" (Craig 2006/07, p18). The single teachers' guide given by NCERD to each school was secured in the head teacher's office, like a rare treasure to be kept under lock and key. Physical resources in the BSPS made the learning environment unconducive to learning. Hurricane damage in some schools had not been repaired and some schools could not use the computer provided as they were without electricity. There were delays in the delivery of equipment and materials to the schools. Literacy 1-2-3 was implemented in classrooms with large unwieldy wooden combination desks and children were seated theatre style facing the chalkboard and separated from the neighbouring class by a piece of ply board. Refurbished classrooms had moveable desks and chairs but in some the space was so cramped that "the children moved around with their chairs on their heads when grouping for activities" (Jennings 2011, p99). These were the classrooms in which teachers were to use a constructivist approach to teaching. Mitchell and Harry (2012, 61) observe that for e-Cal "the traditional classroom was not found suitable to accommodate technology infusion. There was the absence of basic elements such as electrical outlets." In another study which focused on five teachers and implemented e-Cal successfully, the teachers were reported as saying that "resources were available. We had plugs that worked; access to the internet at all times" and "we purchased lots of software to use" (Harry and Mitchell 2015, 1063).

The curriculum for ASTEP was originally designed to include a music programme that would develop the musical talents of the children. The cost of importing the musical instruments proved too challenging for the budget and in any case at the planning stage, little thought was given to the problem of storage in the schools. The few schools that did obtain some instruments had to stand the additional cost of burglar proofing a room to store them. Even so the instruments were such a rare resource in the school that they were shared by all members of the school and the students in ASTEP hardly benefited. Within a two-year period, the Literacy 1-2-3 materials became too worn for use and were taken off the reading list of many schools (Jennings et al. 2012). In the case of R&T in ROSE 1, a shortage of space for teaching home and family management resulted in the practice of rotation in which about one-quarter of the class would do the practical work while the remaining did written work in another room. In the following week one-quarter of these students would have their turn with the practical work. The process became too tedious and repetitive for the teachers. Lack of land space and equipment resulted in the agriculture and the environments component of R&T being taught as theory in classrooms (Jennings 2012).

The experience of the case studies shows that when teachers implementing innovations are described as "stone-age obstructionists" (Doyle and Ponder 1977/78) we need to be mindful of the reality of the contexts in which they teach. In the *BSPS*, for example, some of the teachers had to teach in situations where they had no classroom to speak of because they had to remove all classroom materials out of the church in which the school was located two or three times per week to make way for the church services. Under such conditions teachers could not reasonably be expected to set up learning centres or demonstrate mastery of an integrated approach to teaching. Teachers cannot be expected to use new technologies in old physical environments where there are inappropriate desks and a lack of power outlets. This is like pouring new wine into old skins. Schools are not rebuilt to accommodate new ideas as they are introduced. The environment in which teachers have to function impacts their attitude to change proposals. Policymakers and educational planners expect teachers to teach twenty-first-century skills in classrooms which were built to accommodate the use of an early-twentieth-century transmission model. Under these circumstances, we can hardly be surprised when innovative teaching practices do not take root and teachers revert to their accustomed practices.

Tertiary-Level Collaboration/Support and Involvement of Teacher Educators

Collaboration with teacher training institutions is essential in any attempt to change schools' curricula because such curricula can only become institutionalized if they are built into the teacher training programme. The innovative curriculum of the BSPS was developed by lecturers in the teachers college which has a long history of specialization in EC education. This created the opportunity for the influence of ideas from the BSPS to be spread in the pre-service training of teachers at the EC level. The curriculum for ASTEP was developed by teachers' college and university lecturers, but there was no tertiary-level involvement beyond this.

Collaboration with a teacher's college or with the UWI proved to be important particularly for the institutionalization of innovations. The post of REAP lecturer was established at the Belize College of Education to make training in REAP part of the pre-service training of teachers. ROSE lecturers were appointed in teachers colleges in Jamaica that focused on secondary education to train teachers in the methods and new content of the ROSE programme. The training of teachers at the secondary level whether at college or university level focuses on the methods, skills and content of the subject syllabi that are examined in CSEC. The e-Learning Jamaica programme upgraded fifteen teachers' college lecturers in educational technology through a master's degree from British Columbia University (Miller and Munroe 2014). This has ensured that training teachers to integrate IT into their teaching has become a core part of the pre-service training of teachers. The same has been achieved by the Erdiston Teacher Training College in Barbados which had the main responsibility for training related to IT infusion into the classroom and child-centred and constructivist approaches to teaching in EduTech 2000.

Caribbean Ministers of Education at a meeting of CARICOM's Council of Human and Social Development considered "the integration of the Caribbean CETT reading programme into the regular education system" (Bryan 2019, 144) as a distinct advantage. CETT started in five CC countries and then extended to an additional four countries, including Trinidad and Tobago. A major reason for its facility in dissemination is CETT's linkage with the UWI. The UWI is a regional institution which receives most of its funds from the contributing countries and territories in the region. CETT was coordinated by the JBTE[6] (which is part of the School of Education at the UWI, Jamaica) in conjunction with the JBTE which is similarly located at the campus of the UWI in Barbados. Integrating the CETT methodology into the pre-service training of teachers was readily facilitated because up to 2016 the JBTE in both countries had responsibility for the curriculum, the examinations, the general monitoring of the teachers' colleges and the initial certification of teachers (Bryan 2019).

Cummings (1986) observed that the success of IMPACT could be attributed in part to the link established with a higher educational institution. PRIMER, which was modelled on IMPACT, made no attempt to involve the teachers college which was in the same parish where the schools were located. Nor did it involve the UWI which was close to its project office in Kingston. One of NCERD's major responsibilities is in-service teacher training and the development, implementation and assessment of schools' curricula. At the time of the development of the SRGs Guyana had only one teachers college (the Cyril Potter College of Education (CPCE)) with responsibility for pre-service training. The CPCE was not involved with the SRGs in any way. GUIDE was under the umbrella of NCERD and while the CPCE was one of the stakeholders consulted, the main involvement of the college was at the stage of selecting graduates of GUIDE who were qualified to do the college's pre-service training programme. It so happened that for the Sixth Form Geography Project, Morrissey was himself a teacher educator, but he did not give the A-level geography teachers the training that they needed in curriculum development even though he had skills in this area. This project involved no training at all.

While collaboration with a higher education institution is seen as desirable, teacher educators themselves tend not to be perceived as persons who are part of the change team that need to be trained or even involved. This may be yet another reason why the pre-service training they offer does not adequately prepare the teachers to deal with the real-world classroom life. Teacher educators are experts at articulating theoretical knowledge. If they are to be able to correct the dissonance between the training they offer and the practical knowledge that teachers need to deal with the realities of classroom life (Evans 1997) as well as keep abreast of the changing demands on the teacher (Hordatt-Gentles 2017), they need to position themselves in the vanguard of change. This involves being involved in the process of curriculum change outlined in figure 9.1. Not only should they be among the stakeholders consulted at the initiation stage, but they should also have representation at the design and development stages. Involvement during training for implementation should be as wide as possible, given that it is at this stage that teachers are trained in the new methods and content of the new curriculum. Observation of teachers implementing the new curriculum will give the teacher educators first-hand experience of the contextual realities that teachers face as they seek to master the innovation.

Ongoing Training of Users of Innovation during Implementation

Fullan and Stiegelbauer (1991, 85) observe that "most forms of in-service training are not designed to provide the ongoing, interactive, cumulative learning necessary to develop new conceptions, skills, and behaviour. Failure to realize that there is need for in-service work during implementation is a common problem." In-service or on-the-job training is not just necessary when an innovation is being implemented, it is essential as part of a teacher's ongoing professional development. This is seen as "a process of learning to put knowledge into practice through engagement in practice within a community of practitioners" (Schlager and Fusco 2003, 205). As can be seen in table 9.1, a number of the innovations had problems with training for implementation. NCERD did not directly train teachers for the SRGs. That was left to the head teachers. No plan was in place to train new teachers who entered the system after the initial training for e-Cal with the result that such teachers had limited information about the programme (Onuoha, Ferdinand and Onuoha 2015). Jennings-Craig et al. (2012) reported observing teachers who had not received any formal training to implement Literacy 1-2-3 and had to rely on what they could "pick up" from teachers who were among those originally trained. The problem with the Grade 10–11 Programme was finding teachers who could teach at those levels at the time the programme was introduced. Teachers had to be selected from lower grade levels and some of these had been trained to teach at the primary level. The time between development and implementation was so short that there wasn't even time for using the cascade approach to training. Teachers were trained by looking at "model classes" on television. CETT's approach to training was exemplary. It involved in-service training at the cluster and school levels based on the expressed needs of the teachers. The training was ongoing with reading specialists visiting teachers at least every two weeks and providing support as they implemented the new teaching strategies.

While it is recognized that teachers need to be trained to implement an innovation, similar training is not accorded to principals of schools. Yet the training of the leadership within schools is important because it is these leaders who have to provide the support that teachers need as they struggle to implement the innovation. Harry and Mitchell (2015, 1063) report a teacher from a school who implemented e-Cal successfully saying, "initially, I was resistant to using the technology, but the principal motivated and encouraged me to use it. . . . The principal was also very supportive and accommodating in providing resources that were needed." PRIMER's experience underscored the need for principals to be trained in the management of change which sensitizes them to the importance of cultivating harmonious relationships with and between staff members and to the need for support for teachers as they grapple with pressures and feelings of incompetence and fear of failure during the implementation process.

Lack of understanding of the innovation on the part of principals can lead to actions that compound the difficulties of the teachers implementing the innovation. Some principals failed to give teachers of R&T time in school to get together to plan a thematic approach to teaching the subject (Jennings 2012), and this resulted in the integrative holistic approach desired for the delivery of R&T not being achieved. Jennings (2009) cites the example of teachers involved in the piloting of the Literacy 1-2-3 materials expressing their concern about the unsupportiveness of their principals. One principal insisted on literacy lessons being planned in a way that was contrary to the new methodology of the Literacy 1-2-3. Furthermore, when education officers who were supposed to be guiding the teachers visited the schools, they had no idea what the new methodology was about. What this suggests is that there is need for a more holistic approach to training to implement change. It is not only teachers who need to be trained. Principals, education officers and senior teachers in the school who are expected to offer guidance especially to newly trained teachers also need training.

While one would expect that a project management team would comprise persons who have the knowledge and skills for managing change, the PRIMER experience shows that this is not necessarily the case. There was a lack of clarity in the minds of PRIMER's project team resulting in conflicting advice being given to the teachers in different workshops. They were unable to articulate to the teachers the new role they were expected to adopt, and they failed to win over the teachers' confidence. Pirog and Kioko (2010) refer to variability in training across centres in EduTech 2000, particularly training related to IT infusion into the classroom. Concerns about school-based assessment in CSEC subjects stem from a lack of clarity about the nature of these assessments as seen for example in the problems that teachers have in differentiating between their role as guide to the student and that of an assessor of the student's achievement (Griffith 2015).

Staff Stability

The case studies also underscore the importance of stability of staff who have lead roles in an innovation as well as those who have been trained to implement the innovation. Marsh and Huberman (1984), in fact, contend that instability of programme staff is a threat to an innovation becoming institutionalized. This is evident in table 9.1 where it can be seen that those innovations that were sustained did not have issues related to staff instability. Evaluations of REAP (Massey 1982) did not mention staff instability as an issue. The same applies to CETT. Jennings-Craig et al. (2012) found that primary school teachers in Jamaica were very stable. In all, 75 per cent reported being in their present post for six years or more and 28 per cent had served for more than twenty years. Literacy 1-2-3 (L1-2-3) benefited from such stability, but there was no guarantee that the "master trainers" who were trained using the cascade approach would reach all the teachers. As noted earlier, Jennings-Craig et al. (2012) observed teachers who reported having to "pick up" what they could about the L1-2-3 from other teachers.

Innovations that were not successful experienced staff instability. The evaluator of PRIMER who was appointed at the beginning of the project resigned soon after and was never replaced. During the second year of the project half of the team of writers resigned, and during the life of PRIMER one-third of the original cohort of staff who received training left the project (Jennings 1993). All the teachers who were specially trained to teach in ASTEP found employment elsewhere with the result that the students who were low achievers from disadvantaged communities were taught by teachers unprepared to teach them. The director of NCERD who was the key advocate for the Skills Reinforcement Guides (SRG) left for another job in 1991. Most of the writers who developed the SRGs left NCERD in 1992 and "by the beginning of the 1993/94 school year only one of the original team remained" (Craig 2006/07, 27).

The training of teachers for the implementation of an innovation needs to be ongoing, interactive and ideally supported by a coach or mentor who can help to address the needs and concerns of the teachers as they try to develop new concepts, skills and behaviours. Teachers also need the support of principals not only to provide needed resources and facilitate training but also to make organizational changes that may be needed to accommodate the innovation. Staff instability can prove detrimental to the institutionalization of an innovation. The same can be said about leaders of innovation projects who lack knowledge about the management of change and are unable to develop a harmonious relationship with the schools in which the innovation is implemented.

Research, Monitoring and Evaluation to Inform Change

Figure 9.1 indicates some key areas that should be the subject of research that informs the initiation and design of an innovation. ROSE 1 in Jamaica was informed by nine research studies including studies of the levels of achievement in mathematics and language arts of the students who would be entering grades 7–9 targeted by ROSE 1 as well as studies of the school types (Ministry of Education and Culture, Jamaica 1993). Research should be timely as the experience of PRIMER shows. PRIMER encountered problems with the SIM prepared for the children because the materials were written above the level of attainment of the students. The actual reading levels of the students were not obtained until *after* the materials had been developed. The same applied in ASTEP.

In the case of Jamaica's BEdSecDE, the Ministry of Education's requirement for three thousand teachers to be trained in this programme was clearly not based on research into the number of teachers who would satisfy the entry requirements. Only eight hundred teachers were trained in the programme.

Part of the problem was that primary trained teachers were employed to teach in secondary schools and the programme required that the teacher should be trained to teach at the secondary level and be actually teaching in a secondary school.

EduTech 2000 was such a massive educational reform that the research that informed its design should have surpassed that of ROSE 1. Yet the Ministry of Education, Youth Affairs and Culture (1998) makes no reference to research that informed EduTech 2000. Pirog and Kioko (2010, 75) note that "delays occurred because the physical decay of many schools exceeded what had been anticipated, and consequently the scope of the work required was greater than what had been planned". This could have been avoided had substantive research into the condition of schools been done.

Not only research which informs programme initiation and design needs to be done, provision should also be made for the evaluation of the innovation in the proposal submitted for funding. Summative evaluations were done for a number of the innovations studied: for example, CETT (Chesterfield and Abreu-Combs 2011), the BSPS (Jennings 2005a), ASTEP (Ministry of Education Jamaica Programme and Evaluation Unit 2012), GUIDE (Jennings 1997) and the BEdSecDE (Doreen Faulkner Consultancy 2010). There is a tendency not to treat formative evaluation in a systematic way, with few exceptions. For example, a six-year formative evaluation of REAP was done by Massey (1982). NCERD put in place a system for evaluating the SRGs which involved reports from the heads of schools at the end of each term, the evaluations of the workshops and samples of independent writing of the children. The purpose of this requirement "was to provide a cumulative record of the possible influence of the programme over a period of years, since it could be that writing in any given grade level before the programme started might possibly be both quantitatively and qualitatively different from what it might be after the programme had influenced both teachers and children" (Craig 2006/07, 15). The data were collected and analysed except for the children's writing.[7]

Provision was made for the formative evaluation of PRIMER and five control schools were identified for comparison with the experimental schools. Formative evaluation did not materialize as the evaluator resigned early in the project and was not replaced (Jennings 1993). From the perspective of the project director, the absence of an evaluator and the use of the control schools are informative:

> There is such an interaction of inputs in the experimental schools, that it is difficult to determine which are the ones causing or influencing the change process to the greatest degree. Informal observations made at the control schools certainly do not reveal this. (McKinley 1982, 4)

Had formative evaluation been done for PRIMER, feedback received could have informed intervention strategies which were clearly needed to address the needs and concerns of the teachers and may well also have forced the PRIMER team to take an objective look at their own behaviour and attitudes. This in turn may have prevented the deterioration in relationships with the schools. In the absence of summative evaluation of PRIMER, three studies were commissioned on aspects of PRIMER: programmed teaching, tutoring and use of SIM (Jennings 1993). PRIMER's experience is not exceptional. Delisle (2012, 73) points to the fact that although an initial monitoring and evaluation programme was set up at the start of the Secondary Education Modernization Programme in Trinidad and Tobago "posts were never filled despite more than 200 applications".

Funds from the World Bank were used to strengthen the capacity of the Ministry of Education, Youth and Culture in Jamaica to manage and evaluate the impact of ROSE (World Bank 2001). A Programme and Evaluation Unit (PEU) was established in the Ministry of Education and evaluators were appointed. ROSE Press (1997) refers to a meeting of evaluators from the Caribbean Applied Technology Centre along with other specialists in the field of education to review the evaluators' findings on the ROSE curriculum. The evaluators' terms of reference included determining the level of articulation between the ROSE curriculum and the CXC syllabus, assessing the teachers' guides and the teachers' use of the curriculum guides. The World Bank (2001, 10) noted that "the Evaluation Unit has generated a lot of studies to monitor the impact of the ROSE Project. However, the unit is seriously understaffed for the kind of work it does." The question is whether there is a need for more staff in the unit or the need for better allocation of staff in the Ministry of Education. The PEU and the Student Assessment Unit (SAU) are separate entities in the Ministry of Education and yet to assess the impact of a curriculum, the PEU would need to assess student achievement. An amalgamation of the PEU and the SAU is a possible solution to understaffing. However, the alignment of the work programmes of both units has proven problematic. With reference to the PEU, the World Bank (2001, 17) also pointed out that "while many studies have been carried out, some aspects of evaluation design, instrument and data analysis remained technically weak". Some innovations were not evaluated at all: for example, e-Learning Jamaica and the Grade 10–11 Programme. In fact, it appears that the monitoring and evaluation of e-Learning Jamaica depended on what the board of the entity learned from the annual reports submitted (Henry 2020). In other words, no thought was given to a carefully designed evaluation, collecting and analysing data on the contexts in which the innovation is implemented, the inputs, the process of implementation, the outcome/product and the cost effectiveness of the innovation (see figure 9.1).

CETT provides a novel way of evaluating an innovation using technology. Each participating school was provided with a web-based management information system, a PSM that principals could use to manage their schools but, most importantly, the project could use to "track and monitor the progress of each student, each class, and each grade of every school" (Warrican, Spencer-Ernandez and Miller 2013, 10). A central version of the PSM was installed at the JBTE[8] at the UWI in Jamaica. Members of the Project Implementation Unit could use this to monitor student performance in all schools in the project. ICT technicians supported the schools in implementing and operating the PSM and ensured that data was transferred from the PSM in the schools to the central PSM at the JBTE.

Adequate Time to Achieve Innovation Goals

"Change is a process, not an event", says Hall and Hord (2006, 4). This implies that change takes place *over time*. Innovations that are politically motivated tend to abuse this principle. The Grade 10–11 Programme is an example. A commitment to address youth unemployment was a central feature of the manifesto of one of the political parties contesting the general election in Jamaica in 1972. Following victory at the polls, the new government determined that the solution to the problem was to introduce two new grade levels (grade 10 and 11) in a new type of school in Jamaica (new secondary). When by 1974 the development of curricula for the new schools by officers at the Ministry of Education had not proceeded at the pace expected, the Grade 10–11 Programme was made a special project in the office of the prime minister. From May throughout the summer of 1974, curriculum development and dissemination proceeded at a miraculous pace. What should have taken one year was squashed into less than six months (Jennings-Wray 1984). It was imperative that the Grade 10 programme should be implemented at the beginning of the 1974–75 school year, so that it would be possible for the government to declare success by the time of the 1976 elections. Treating change in this way as an *event* exacerbates the difficulties that participants in the process of change will experience because there was insufficient planning to forestall these difficulties.

Time is important for other reasons. As pointed out in an earlier chapter, innovations do not comprise a single new idea. Innovations come in *bundles* and comprise several new ideas, each of which the teacher has to master. Adopting a constructivist approach to teaching is not easy for teachers who have been accustomed to using "chalk and talk". Constructivism itself involves several ideas which were "new" to the teachers, for example: learners constructing knowledge for themselves, learning which is meaningful and related to real life, active learning, the use of higher-order thinking skills, student-initiated questions and the use of authentic assessments. It is therefore not just the specific strategy for Literacy 1-2-3 and integration that the teachers were expected to implement but all these other new ideas. It is like juggling with many balls simultaneously. Only an expert juggler who has had years of practice will be able to balance all the balls in the air. Such new learning on the part of teachers takes *time*: a fact that is not considered in the cascade approach to training for implementation which is normally used by Ministries of Education. Time was recognized as important by CETT because the teachers were trained on an ongoing continuous basis over two years and supported by reading specialists who could address their concerns at a more individual level.

It is not only teachers who are expected to achieve so much in so little time. The time frame set for an innovation to achieve its goals and objectives is invariably unrealistic. For example, ASTEP (originally conceived as ASEP) was expected to raise the level of achievement in literacy from grade 4 to grade 7 in *two* years; and this was with children who had failed a literacy test at the grade 4 level on four consecutive occasions! Some innovations, like EduTech 2000, were able to secure additional time by seeking an extension of funding from the external aid agency, while others, like PRIMER, had to terminate without achieving its goals.

Educational planners tend to set a time frame of five years within which to achieve set goals, but even this seems unrealistic. The initiators of REAP seemed to recognize this because they planned for at least a decade from initiation supported by external funding to institutionalization supported with resources identified by REAP District Councils (Jennings 1988). Time for achieving innovation goals must be determined with reference to the context in which the innovation is implemented. This includes the children themselves, their home backgrounds and cognitive achievement, and the environment and resources of the schools that these children attend. CETT sought to "have approximately 90% of the grade 3 students mastering the fundamentals of reading and 60% reading at or above the level prescribed for grade 3 in their country by *the end of five years*" (Warrican, Spencer-Ernandez and Miller 2013, 1). At the end of three years, it was found that "nine schools had already met the goal of having 60 per cent of the students exiting grade 3 at or above grade level. . . . Eight schools had already met the goal of having 90 per cent of the students exiting grade 3 at a functional level" (Warrican, Spencer-Ernandez and Miller 2013, 1). The number of schools involved was sixty-eight "mostly deemed as failing", according to the authors, and the children were from disadvantaged backgrounds. Two years for fifty-nine "failing" schools to achieve the goals seems optimistic. That the importance of *time* cannot be overemphasized for the measurement of the outcome of a reform is underscored by Pirog and Kioko (2010) who acknowledged that additional years of data would have permitted a better assessment of the outcome of EduTech 2000.

Multi-Agency Collaboration

Curriculum change is not a purely educational undertaking. In none of the case studies was this better understood than in REAP. This innovation was initiated by a group comprised of representatives from the Ministries of Education and Sports, Social Welfare and Natural Resources (agriculture), the CARE, Heifer Project International and the United States Peace Corp. This group later formed the REAP Advisory Committee. The Heifer Project International supplied at cost feeders, wire, chicks, baby rabbits and some feed. Peace Corps volunteers served both as technical support/coordinators of the pilot schools and as the first lecturers in the REAP programme at the Belize College of Education. The Cooperative American Relief Everywhere supplied tools, equipment, some agricultural supplies and financial assistance in the construction of Outdoor Education Centres which contained all that was needed for the practical application of learning in an agricultural setting (e.g. school garden, crops and rabbit hutches). The Ministry of Education assigned an education officer to manage REAP (Jennings 1988). e-Learning Jamaica is a collaboration between the Ministry of Science Technology energy and Mining and the Ministry of Education.

Other case studies have shown that to achieve the desired outcome of a change requires attention to be paid to the factors that will enable the children to attend school to benefit from the change being introduced. School attendance (or absenteeism) was identified as the main cause for the failure of ROSE 1 to improve academic achievement as an outcome measure (World Bank 2001). Subsequent research into the causes of absenteeism in secondary schools in Jamaica revealed that these spanned parental, school, student and community factors (Jennings and Cook 2015). These include the financial constraints experienced by parents, which make it difficult for them to provide their children with breakfast, lunch money and other resources needed for school. Poor sanitary convenience and lack of canteen facilities in schools, lack of electricity and poor water supply, bad roads and poor transportation in certain communities served as inhibitors to school attendance. If innovations ultimately seek to impact student learning and achievement, attention has to be given to the factors that inhibit school attendance. Much of these are outside the control of the Ministry of Education and fall under the purview of Ministries of Health, Labour, Transportation and Social Security. The experience of the Grade 10–11 Programme underscored the importance of private- and public-sector employers to its outcome.

An integral part of the Grade 10–11 Programme was the work experience programme (WEP) which involved grade 11 students spending twenty-one days in workplaces or agencies in both the public and private sectors to get experience in the world of work. It was felt that this programme would give the students an advantage in finding jobs on graduation. However, this was not the case, not only on account of the acuteness of the unemployment problems among the youth, but many workplaces considered that the technical/vocational preparation of the students had not given them the necessary preparation to use equipment and machines in the workplace. This indicates that public- and private-sector employers should have been among the stakeholders consulted and their involvement and support sought when the programme was being designed.

Figure 9.1 indicates the need for research into the communities in which the innovation is to be implemented to ascertain their attitudes, resources available and so on. This is particularly important for innovations that include community support in their design. An issue that was discussed at the NCERD SRG workshops was the possibility of mobilizing community support to help address the poor physical conditions of the schools. "But this topic did not prove popular since too much of the teacher's time would have to be spent 'mobilizing' community assistance rather than teaching children" (Craig 2006/07, 20). One can appreciate this position if one bears in mind the fact that in the rural and hinterland schools in Guyana the head teacher also teaches. In PRIMER members of the community were expected to volunteer assistance as teachers' aides, but this did not materialize. Initially, the members of the community appeared enthusiastic as they helped to clean up and paint the school buildings, but their interest waned after they saw no effort on the part of the government to refurbish the schools or construct new buildings, as promised (Minott 1988). It is not only teachers who need incentives for the work they put into innovations. As the World Bank (2001, 18) observed, "community members were not used to the idea of contribution without remuneration or stipend."

Conclusion

If future attempts at curriculum innovation are informed by these ten drivers, would this guarantee successful change? If they give due thought to them, policymakers and educational planners should at least have "greater sensitivity to their plans for change and as a result improve the probability for success in their programmes" (London 2002). The important word here is "probability" because as Fullan (1994, 19) says the change process is uncontrollably complex and "unplanned factors are inevitable-government policy changes, or gets constantly redefined, key leaders leave, important contact people are shifted to another role, new technology is invented . . . recession reduces available resources, a bitter conflict erupts, and so on".

There is no blueprint for curriculum change. It is like setting out on a journey. We can plan in the finest detail how to reach our destination, but there is no guarantee that we will get there, because we cannot control the unpredictable. Nothing made this clearer than the sudden impact of the Covid-19 pandemic in 2020, particularly on education with the closure of schools and the launch almost overnight into online teaching and learning. For years we had struggled to use technology to make teaching student-centred but found what Cuban (2008, 128) also discovered in the United States "a seemingly stubborn continuity in the character of instruction despite intense reform efforts to move classroom practices toward instruction that was more student-centred". It took a pandemic to force us to take the radical step of freeing learning from the boundaries of the school walls and opening it up to homes and other places in the wider society with the necessary technology to give students access to learning. It was a form of *liberation*, but it was also a step that threatened not only to widen the social divide between children with parents who could afford to buy them laptops and those with parents who could not but also to jeopardize goals of equity, social justice and quality of education that our societies prize. How do we sustain the values that we prize beset as we are with dwindling resources? A key lesson that the pandemic has taught us is that we cannot return to the status quo. We have to do things differently. What do we need to do differently in introducing change into our schools? It is to this question that we turn in the final chapter.

10.

"Doing Change" Differently

In the last chapter I proposed a model of the innovation/change process based on the experiences of curriculum innovations in CC education systems. The process is by no means linear, and the complexity of the process was clear in the interconnected and dynamic relationship among the various stages. Evidence from the case studies shows that at the point of implementation, innovation developers had to revisit earlier stages such as the design and development of curricula, as in the case of PRIMER and ASTEP. In both cases the research that informed earlier stages had not been done. Institutionalization and sustainability are presented as final stages in the change process, but factors on which they are dependent are considered as early as the design stage. The proposed model listed several factors that needed to be considered at each stage of the process. Timely progression through the stages is facilitated by what I called "drivers for change". I suggested ten of these based on the experiences of the case studies presented. These drivers are (1) political support, (2) strategic planning, (3) adequate finance, costing and timely procurement, (4) timely provision of adequate resources, (5) tertiary-level collaboration/ support and involvement of teacher educators, (6) ongoing training of users of innovation during implementation, (7) staff stability, (8) research, monitoring and evaluation to inform change, (9) adequate time to achieve innovation goals and (10) multi-agency collaboration. The drivers are not presented in order of importance. Individually they will not impact innovation outcomes but the extent to which they are considered in totality will determine whether innovation goals are realized.

The innovations studied span fifty years (1971 to present day; see table 9.1). Of the innovations, the CSEC has survived the longest – from 1979 when it was first offered to present day. When the Covid-19 pandemic struck in 2020, the CXC realized that the mode of examination for the CSEC had to change. Having offered paper-based examinations for over forty years, in 2020 the CSEC had to shift to electronic tests. It was not just CSEC that was affected. The entire school system in the CC – and indeed the rest of the world – was affected. e-learning became the "new normal" that children had to adjust to. But is this "new normal" just for the time of Covid-19? Will we return to "business as usual" when the pandemic is over? Hardly likely, because what the pandemic has underscored for small island states like those in the CC is that we in the developing world cannot take for granted what we have relied on in the past. Using the drivers of change is not "doing business as usual" because it involves making decisions and taking actions which are informed by knowledge gleaned from past experience. In a real sense it is establishing a "new normal".

I want to go even further in this final chapter by issuing eight challenges to policymakers and educational planners as they move forward in charting a "new normal" in introducing change into our school systems.

Free Our Minds from Dependency on External Funding for Education

Small island developing states in the CC are vulnerable to economic shocks, natural disasters and pandemics, as Covid-19 has shown. In early 2021 CC countries had to watch in disbelief as the developed countries bought up in advance most of the Covid-19 vaccines available. Some countries even bought twice the number of vaccines that their populations needed. CC countries appeared paralysed by their economic stringencies and indebtedness. The persistence of their indebtedness is underscored in a recent publication by the IDB:

> The history of public debt in Caribbean countries is striking. Several countries in the region have been among the most indebted in the world since gaining independence beginning in the 1960s. . . . While economic and debt crises have been common throughout Latin America and the Caribbean over the past century – particularly when compared to other regions – the frequency, depth, and duration of such episodes for Caribbean countries makes it an outlier relative to the rest of the world. (Mooney, Prats and Rosenblatt 2021, 153)

Unquestionably, the pandemic has thrown countries worldwide into economic recession, including those on which CC countries have relied for external funding. The amount of aid which those countries can allocate to the developing world will be compromised by the impact of Covid-19 on their economic growth. Another important reason for not relying on foreign aid is that education is no longer high on the agenda of priorities of the broad international community. Of seventeen sustainable development goals, only one pertains to education. Aid agencies are more likely to give aid to countries to address issues pertaining to health, sustainable development and climate change than to education, even though education has a role to play in addressing these issues.

The case studies presented in this book include examples where external funds have been wasted or have had to be returned. Developing countries cannot afford either of these situations. We need to free our minds from the dependency on external funding for our attempts to introduce change into our education system because, as Riddell (2011, 36) points out, "in practice it would appear that each donor continues to be driven particularly by its own agenda, which largely influences how it wishes to intervene, reducing the effectiveness of joint work. And the dominance of the donors provides little room for government education sector leadership in shaping future directions". Pirog and Kioko (2010, 90) aptly state that "international financial aid coupled with best practices gained in industrialized countries are not always a panacea for the problems facing developing countries". What Keith Lewin says is also insightful: "After five decades of development new approaches are needed which are designed to end dependence on aid and generate a political economy of education that depends on the development of fiscal states able to finance their own public goods. This is long overdue" (Lewin 2020, 1).

How do we become able to finance innovations in our education systems? To begin with our governments could become more efficient in the collection of taxes. As Lewin (2020) argues, tax, not aid, is now the dominant source of public finance in most countries and "tax avoidance, transfer pricing, money laundering, fraud and illicit trading result in the loss of many times the revenue generated by aid" (Lewin 2020, 13). Reflecting on the experience of NCERD in Guyana, Craig (2006/07, 28) contends that "even the poorest of countries can, without special financing embark on educational improvements, through adequate planning, the abandonment of ineffective operations, and the re-alignment of resources to achieve desired goals".

If CC countries were able to finance their education systems, many of the barriers to introducing change would be overcome. Educational innovations would cease to be treated as fleeting projects which die when external funding ends. CC countries would no longer have to contend with donor-driven ideas which are incompatible with their local contexts, or agendas from the North for research in a contrasting context in the developing world. They would be able to design innovations which are relevant to their contexts and consistent with their national policies and education goals. Moreover, they would ensure "readiness" in so far as they have the capacity, the staffing, and the skills to implement the innovation. Ownership and issues of responsibility and accountability would also be more readily addressed as the management of the change process would be embedded in the normal operations of the Ministry of Education from the outset.

Make Better Use of Resources and Reduce Costs

Inadequate provision of resources (human, physical, material) inhibited the effective implementation of several innovations including those in rural and hinterland primary schools in Guyana, in basic and primary schools in rural Jamaica and in schools in Barbados. This is not new, as Bacchus (2005, 85) notes: "The legacy of poor and inadequate school accommodation that existed in the region prior to 1945, continued to be felt, even four decades later." And it persists today. However, these are changing times. If blended learning (combining online teaching/learning with face-to-face instruction) becomes an integral part of education at the school level (and it should), there should be less need for expenditure on capital works. Overcrowded classrooms should become a thing of the past. Fewer school places will be needed at any one time as some students would work from other venues (e.g. homes, libraries, internet cafes). This in fact would be a blessing in disguise because when attempting change or reform of the education system, Ministries of Education could put much less emphasis on civil works and give more attention to the curriculum and student learning.[1]

Cost reduction in education which was an objective of PRIMER needs to be revisited and pursued this time with earnest. Teachers' salaries are still the biggest expenditure from the annual budget of Ministries of Education. Where the use of self-instructional materials failed, the use of modern technology can help to reduce cost. A master online teacher can deliver high-quality instruction to much larger numbers of students than can be reached by a teacher in a classroom. A small pool of such teachers could achieve far more than a large pool of poorly trained, uncommitted and ineffective teachers. Students could obtain ongoing support from teachers' aides such as parents, community members and tutors like the "programmed teachers"[2] used in PRIMER. These aides should be adequately trained and appropriately remunerated.

This is in no way to diminish the importance of teachers. Rather it is to caution against past decisions which have resulted in limited financial resources not being put to the best use. The BEdSecDE is a case in point. The Ministry of Education allotted millions of dollars which trained just over eight hundred out of three thousand teachers targeted. A sound feasibility study to determine if the teachers targeted were in the system would have led to a differently designed and more cost-effective training programme. Some of the funds could have been redirected to other levels of the education system that were in dire need of financial resources.

In sum, we need to make better use of the resources available. The BSPS case study illustrates this. Should available resources have been put into educational innovation or the alleviation of rural poverty? Ideally into both. The seeds of underachievement are sown in early childhood education and rooted in poverty. Children like those in the BSPS case study are led along a path where they are always trying to "catch up". Given insufficient help in "catching up", these children end up learning little and achieving two or more years below their nominal grade level. The government then must find resources to mount programmes like ASTEP. Underachievement cannot be addressed solely by education. Resources also need to be put into addressing poverty alleviation.

Avoid Overreach

Sometimes resources appear inadequate because of a failure on the part of educational planners "to cut the suit according to the cloth". NCERD's case appears to be one of "overreach" in planning. Given the "lack of resources" and "scarcity of personnel" (Craig 2006/07, 14), a pilot of the SRGs in selected schools in fewer regions would have been more manageable. Overreaching, however, is not uncommon in educational planning. The aspirations of educational planners tend to outreach the reality of what can be achieved. As Eisner (2000, 343) maintains, "by definition, educators seek more than they can accomplish". The ROSE 1 curriculum was originally designed "to improve the quality and equity of Grades 7 through 9, with emphasis on schools serving the poorest students" (World Bank 2001, 2). It was also intended to be implemented in seventy-two rural all age and urban new secondary schools (World Bank 2001). It was not originally intended to be used in the traditional high schools. Because school types in Jamaica are differentiated by social class, offering ROSE 1 to all age and new secondary school students alone would have been tantamount to designating it as a curriculum for low achievers which by common perception could not be one of quality. The consequence of overreach is evident in the weaknesses in the implementation of R&T. This is only one of the subjects in the lower-secondary curriculum.

Literacy 1-2-3 is another example of overreach. Although a limited amount of funds was identified in Jamaica's Primary Education Support Programme (PESP) for a "Literacy Pilot to introduce a four-year literacy programme in eighty low performing urban schools"[3] the decision was taken to "stretch" the funds to address literacy at the national level. Literacy 1-2-3 was developed. It is interesting that although it came about as an amendment or variation from the original proposal for the PESP, it was the success in training over 70 per cent of eight thousand teachers that the minister of education chose to highlight in his message on the completion of the PESP (Holness 2008). The permanent secretary in the Ministry of Education declared that in the PESP "one of the signature achievements is the development of the Literacy 1-2-3 Programme" (Sewell 2008, 3). Because of "stretching" limited funds to cover more than was intended, the Ministry of Education did not have the resources to replenish stocks of the L1-2-3 materials. This resulted in the teachers having to use other materials that were readily available. "Stretching" limited funds also runs the risk of backfiring because those limited funds may even be further reduced, given the fact that while Ministries of Education make policies, it is the Ministry of Finance which controls the funds that bring those policies into fruition.

Give Change Agents Specialized Training

If CC countries are to seek to introduce change into their education systems without external funding, it is imperative that they develop capacity in planning and managing change. Riddell (2011) makes the point that "despite years of capacity development and millions of dollars of investment in the education sector, a significant proportion of which has been directed specifically at capacity development in educational planning and management, there is clearly a dearth of capacity within the Ministry of Education, even if skilled capacity still exists within the country" (Riddell 2011, 37). Riddell's focus here was on Guyana, but there are several instances in the case studies presented in this book where capacity building was clearly necessary.

The inability to replace the evaluator of PRIMER, and the fact that the director of PRIMER had to double as an editor point to a dearth in capacity. Although one of the goals of ROSE 1 was to "strengthen the MOEYC's capacity to manage and evaluate the impact of such a reform" (The World Bank 2001, 2) aspects of the impact evaluation carried out by the Program Evaluation Unit were described as "technically weak" (The World Bank 2001, 17). This together with the fact that evaluation was either absent or weak in several of the case studies suggests the need for capacity building in programme evaluation. It is also important that persons appointed to do specialized tasks should have received specialized training. Charles (2011) noted that teachers in CETT in Trinidad and Tobago did not consider that the reading specialists appointed to mentor them were able to help them as their qualification was not any better than theirs. A similar situation was observed in PRIMER where "the teachers resented the fact that the writers were teachers like themselves" (Minott 1988, 179). In fact, this is a problem which applies to the cascade approach to training. Those identified as "master trainers" are in many instances no more qualified than the teachers they have to train. The case studies have shown that the training they receive in the one-week workshops is in most instances inadequate. When the grade 11 curriculum was implemented in 1975, seven implementation officers were selected from among classroom teachers who were judged to have achieved success in the grade 10 curriculum (Jennings-Wray 1984). Their task was to serve as models for the grade 11 teachers. The training of teachers to implement a new curriculum should be done by trainers who have received specialized training to do the job. Project directors should also have received specialized training, as the case of PRIMER clearly shows.

Pay More Attention to Changing Beliefs and Attitudes

In introducing change into our school systems, we have concentrated most of our effort on the change or innovation, and less on the users of the innovation, namely, the teachers and students. We have not given much attention to what they think about the innovation, their concerns, how they feel and what they believe. In their study of five teachers in schools in which e-Cal had been implemented successfully, Harry and Mitchell (2015, 1062) observed that "the teachers' belief in the importance of the initiative propelled them to address the obstacles encountered and to make great effort to achieve the perceived goals of the initiative".

When grades 10–11 students who specialized in agriculture chose to seek jobs in other sectors, even though jobs were available in agriculture (Jennings-Wray and Teape 1982), we found this surprising. This is despite our knowledge of a persistent negative attitude towards agricultural work in our societies, because "the incomes, job security, and social status of farm labourers and skilled craftsmen were much lower than for those with white-collar jobs" (Bacchus 2005, 302). REAP was successful in Belize because the Belizeans did not have such negative attitudes towards agriculture.

Some PRIMER teachers believed that students could not be trusted to work independently and so the self-instructional modules were a waste of time (Minott 1988). Teachers have to believe in the value of self-instruction if it is to work. ROSE sought to achieve equity through a common curriculum for all students in grades 7–9, regardless of school type. However, the teachers in the traditional high schools "believed that their social status and prestige as a grammar school were eroded when a common curriculum made them appear to be equal to all age and new secondary schools, attended by students of a different social class" (Evans 1997, 10). ROSE did not include any intervention to change this belief and it has persisted, despite the espousal of goals of equity and social justice in the policies of our education systems. In the BSPS project, boxes of toys and other learning aids were unopened and packed away. Perhaps this was to appease parents. Play-based learning is supported in the National Play Policy of Jamaica's Ministry of Education (Tortello and Minott 2015), but parents insist that they do not send their children to school to play. They want to see children reading, writing, spelling words and counting. Ideally the BSPS should have included an intervention to address the parents' beliefs about learning through play.

Put More Emphasis on the Adaptation of Innovations

The fidelity perspective of implementation assumes that because teachers have a low level of understanding and skills to implement the innovation, "the planned curriculum must be highly structured, and teachers must be given explicit instructions about how to teach it" (Marsh and Willis 2003, 242). The teachers are expected to implement the innovation just as the developers intended it to be. The problem is that how the innovation is to be implemented is not clearly communicated to the teachers. As Hall and Hord (2006, 115) point out, "The situation in which teachers are not sure about what they are to do occurs in part because innovation developers have a hard time imagining the extent to which their innovation can be adapted." Simms (2010, 70) did not observe any instance of a teacher using the recommended strategy for teaching Literacy 1-2-3 and attributed this to "a lack of clarity in using the literacy design. Teachers showed a general confusion." Teachers selected from L1-2-3 what suited their particular purpose in the lesson (Jennings-Craig et al. (2012)). A teacher who shares classroom space with a church service is hardly likely to implement the new curriculum for the BSPS in the same way as one whose classroom is a fixed space, albeit separated from the next classroom by a chalkboard. When there was adequate supply of self-instructional materials, the grade 10–11 students were allowed to use them independently. However, as copies dwindled, the teachers used the few that remained as their own text and taught the students using it. The context in which action occurs can define, inform and transform that action and give it a unique appearance. This is because the context functions actively to transform the curriculum in ways that are peculiar to each educational situation (McLeod 1987). Innovation developers do not think in terms of it being implemented in a specific situation. They have an ideal or a "generalized idea" in mind. Teachers do not deal with the ideal. They function in specific situations. Therefore, when mandated to implement an innovation, whatever is in the mind of the innovation developer, the teachers will adapt to suit their particular situations. This suggests that in future rather than emphasizing fidelity implementation, it would be more realistic for innovation developers to think in terms of multiple contexts in which the innovation will be implemented and configure how the innovation can be adapted in these situations without jeopardizing the integrity of the innovation. Hall and Hord

(2006) provide a good starting point. They have developed a process and a tool for use in visualizing and assessing the different configurations that are likely to be found for any innovation.[4]

Focus Innovations More Directly on Learners and Learning

Although the ultimate aim of curriculum innovations is to enhance student learning, innovation developers have sought to reach the students through the teachers who are traditionally viewed as the "knowledge givers". Writing on the "learning crisis", the World Bank (2018, 4) notes that "individuals already disadvantaged in society – whether because of poverty, location – learn the least". The children who attended basic schools in the BSPS innovation are good illustrations of this. They were from impoverished backgrounds and despite their exposure to innovations designed to prepare them for a smooth transition to primary school, they were far from "ready" as was evident from their performance. Their test scores were far below the national average. The BSPS focused on resource materials, new furniture, a new curriculum, teacher training and the acquisition of a computer which had to be kept at the head teacher's home. Had the focus been primarily on what students needed to learn within the constraints of their particular environment, the outcome of the BSPS may well have been different.

The same could be said of ROSE 1. The World Bank (2001, 8), from an analysis of test results to measure the effects of factors associated with ROSE implementation, concluded that "raising the overall academic achievement and reducing the variability of learning outcomes remain the most important challenge".

Since ROSE and the BSPS, education has taken a dramatic turn with the emphasis on online learning. Putting a laptop in the hands of each child is symbolic of handing power to the children – the power to discover knowledge for themselves. They are now at the centre and the teacher has to function as a facilitator of learning, not a knowledge-giver. Technology may well in the future force innovation developers to focus more directly on the children, on helping them to use this new power to initiate or invent, create new ideas for solving problems. Jamaica's ROSE programme tried to do this through R&T. R&T sought to develop problem-solving, creativity, critical thinking skills by using a more student-centred approach. Essentially what students were supposed to learn from R&T is that "technology" is not the television, the computer or cell phone (which are the products of technology), but "the thinking, the rational and creative capacity that man uses to initiate and develop such products" (Jennings-Wray and Wellington 1985, 182). Because R&T incorporated career education, the expectation was that the students would learn the need to become entrepreneurs who could create their own employment. R&T also gave the students experience in designing mini enterprises through which they could make products that would generate income. Unfortunately, R&T had more barriers than drivers of change. But the goals of R&T are worth pursuing using modern technology because creating their own employment at some point in their working life is the reality that our young people today must face. That reality summons up their rational and creative capacity and resilience. The bottom line is that innovations of the future must focus more directly on the students and their learning and the contextual environment in which that learning takes place.

Re-imagine How We Measure Change

The outcome or impact of an innovation is measured in terms of student achievement usually in primary or secondary school exit examinations. Performance in the Belize National Primary School Examination was taken as the measure of the impact of REAP (Jennings 1988). In CETT, the mean change in student achievement tests was correlated with indicators of teacher performance (Chesterfield and Abreu-Combs 2011). Measures of student achievement are what the international aid agencies consider acceptable criteria for determining the impact of an innovation. The World Bank, for example, considered students' achievement in the Junior High School Certificate taken at the end of grade 9 as a more reliable measure of the impact of ROSE 1 than formative evaluations of improvement in students self-image or similar measures (World Bank 2001). However, given that ROSE targeted disadvantaged schools that took in children from low-income homes who had also failed the primary exit examination, improvement in their self-image seems a valid measure of the impact of the innovation. Moving forward, we need to reimagine how we measure change. Student achievement is important, but it can be measured in different ways. Given the segregation of our school system, the extent to which innovations narrow the social divide, impact self-concept, develop positive values, build critical and creative thinking, encourage greater community involvement in the school should also become measures of change. Valid and reliable means for measuring these should be developed.

Summary

The Covid-19 pandemic has taught us many things, one being that we cannot expect a going back to the way things were before the pandemic. We must establish a "new normal" by doing things differently. Ten drivers for change were suggested in the previous chapter to spur innovation developers in this direction. This chapter went further and exhorted the need for those with responsibility for managing change in education systems in the CC to do eight things differently: free our minds from dependency on external funding, make better use of resources and reduce costs, avoid "overreach", give change agents specialized training, pay more attention to changing beliefs and attitudes, put more emphasis on adaptation of innovations, focus innovations more directly on learners, and learning and re-imagine how we measure change.

Conclusion

Will we do things differently in the future when we introduce change into our school systems? This is a question that only future research can answer. This book has attempted to fill a gap in research on curriculum innovations in the CC, but there is a wider gap that still needs to be bridged. Most of the innovations in this book had their origins in Jamaica because the writer had first-hand experience of these as well as those in Guyana. There is a wealth of innovations in education in the Organization of Eastern Caribbean States waiting to be explored by interested researchers, because there is much more that small island states in other parts of the developing world can learn from the CC. The use of qualitative methods could illuminate unique aspects of our experiences with change which are not captured in this book. Delisle (2012, 69), for example, refers to a "lack of flow of information between personnel" in a particular Ministry of Education and the "highly personalized atmosphere" which can prevent the development of collective capacity needed in managing change. Jules (2008, 211) argues that "many good innovations are being made in the curriculum in different countries in different curriculum areas". The Caribbean Community Health and Family Life curriculum is singled out for special mention as well as reading strategies in Anguilla. My hope is that this book will inspire others to research innovations like these and others. Furthermore, with Guyana soon to become one of the largest oil exporters globally, I am hopeful that its government will take the lead in freeing the country of the postcolonial inheritance that afflicts all CC countries – the begging bowl for foreign aid for education. That is where meaningful change in education begins.

Notes

Introduction

1. Project for the Improved Management of Educational Resources. See chapter 5.
2. London (2002, 69).

Chapter 1. Context, Change and the Curriculum: Background to the Case Studies

1. These are: Anguilla*, Antigua and Barbuda, Bahamas, Barbados, Belize, British Virgin Islands*, Cayman Island*, Dominica, Grenada, Guyana, Jamaica, St Kitts/Nevis, St Lucia, Montserrat*, St Vincent and the Grenadines, Trinidad and Tobago, Turks and Caicos Island*. *These remain British dependencies. These countries do not possess full political independence or sovereignty as a state, but they have a certain amount of autonomy represented by local government. Under the United Nations Charter, Article 73, the United Kingdom is obligated to ensure the economic, social, educational and even political advancement of these countries. When known as "British dependent territories citizens", the nationals of these countries did not have automatic right to live and work in the United Kingdom, but they automatically became British citizens in 2002.
2. Source by country – The Statistics Portal. https://www.statista.com/statistics /527076/gross-domestic-product-gdp-per-capita-in-jamaica/.
3. See note 2.
4. See note 2.
5. The Amerindians are the descendants of the indigenous people of Guyana. The tribes that live in the coastal areas are the Caribs, Arawaks and the Warao. Those who live in the interior of Guyana are the Arecuna, Akawaio, Macusi, Patamona, Waiwai and Wapisiana.
6. Manley (1982).
7. See Sustainable Development Goal 4 https://www.globalgoals.org/4-quality -education.
8. PRIMER: The delivery of mass primary education, Jamaica. Description and objectives of the proposal and Programme Director's Evaluation. Personal communication sent to vice dean of School of Education, the University of the West Indies, Kingston, Jamaica, 6 June 1979.
9. See note 8.

10. See note 8.

11. From "Online Learning Heartache" by Kimberley Hibbert. *The Jamaica Observer*, Sunday, 18 October 2020.

Chapter 2. How Do We Introduce Change into Our School Systems? Contrasting Models of Change

1. Participating countries are Antigua and Barbuda, Barbados, Belize, British Virgin Islands, Cayman Islands, Dominica, Grenada, Guyana, St Kitts/ Nevis–Anguilla, St Lucia, Montserrat, St Vincent and the Grenadines, Turks and Caicos Island. Jamaica and Trinidad and Tobago joined in 1973 (Griffith 2015). Political difficulties with the associated state of St Kitts-Nevis–Anguilla led to the withdrawal of Anguilla, but Anguilla rejoined the CXC in 1987 (Griffith 2015). The Cayman Islands withdrew in 1977 because of concerns with Jamaica's dominance and close relation with Cuba at the time but rejoined in 1993. The CXC has two external territories: St Maarten joined in 1985 and Saba in 1995 (Bray 1998).

2. The JBTE is part of the School of Education at the UWI, Kingston, Jamaica. Since its inception in 1965, it has been engaged in quality assurance in teachers colleges and the initial certification of teachers mainly in Jamaica, Bahamas and Belize. For further information on the work of the JBTE, see Bryan (2019).

Chapter 3. Implementing Curriculum Change at the Secondary Level: What Measure of Success?

1. Principals of primary schools in Guyana are referred to as "head teachers". The term "principal" is reserved for the heads of secondary schools. Head teachers are the most qualified academically in schools where several teachers are untrained.

2. After the BP level was discontinued, the Caribbean Certificate of Secondary Level Competence was developed and first offered in 2007. For further details, see http://www.cxc.org/examinations/ccslc/.

3. The Reform of Secondary Education Secretariat (1975) proposed that ROSE 11 focus on grades 10 and 11. The Ministry of Education's preferred model was for access to grades 7–9 institutions be determined by performance in the primary exit examination. Access to grades 10–11 institutions would be determined by performance in the Junior High School Certificate Examination. At the end of grade 11 all students would sit the CSEC, the number of subjects being determined by their ability. The World Bank (2001) emphasized that ROSE 11 should focus on improving reading achievement, raising the overall level of academic achievement and aligning the ROSE curriculum with the CXC syllabuses. The Bank advised that this should be a school-based and demand-driven approach.

4. This was for a Social Policy Analysis (SPA) which was viewed as a subcomponent of ROSE. The Bank was the administrator of the Dutch Grant on

behalf of the minister for development cooperation of the Netherlands. SPA was implemented by the Planning Institute of Jamaica and operated as a free-standing project (World Bank 2001).

5. For further information, see https://ncel.gov.jm/content/jamaica-cutting-edge-curriculum-design-national-standards-curriculum.

Chapter 4. Implementing Innovations in Literacy in Caribbean Primary Schools

1. The GSAT was replaced by the Primary Exit Profile in 2019. For further information, see https://www.moey.gov.jm/sites/default/files/FAQs%20Updated.pdf.

2. See note 2 in chapter 2.

Chapter 5. Innovations in ICT: Can Technology Revolutionize Teaching and Learning?

1. Jamaica, for example, supplied laptops to children on the Programme of Advancement through Health and Education (PATH). This is a conditional cash transfer programme funded by the GOJ and the World Bank and is aimed at delivering benefits by way of cash grants to the most needy and vulnerable in the society. PATH was introduced island wide in 2002.

Chapter 8. When Fidelity Implementation Fails: A Case Study in Early Childhood Education

1. This is the Pre-Primary to Primary Transition Pilot Project which was initiated in 2002 as part of United Nations Children's Emergency Fund's support for Jamaica's Basic Education and Early Childhood Education programme. It sought to support the government's plans to improve the quality of basic education particularly for poor children from birth to twelve years.

2. The other institutions are *infant schools* and *infant departments in primary schools* which are owned and funded by government. *Kindergartens* in privately owned preparatory schools (operated by or affiliated with churches) cater largely to the middle- and upper-social classes. As basic, infant and preparatory schools prepare children for entry to primary schools; they are also referred to as "preschools".

Chapter 9. Lessons Learned: Drivers for Change

1. The curriculum was not part of the funds for EduTech 2000. It was funded as part of Barbados' larger education modernization programme of which EduTech was a part. Curriculum reform took place concurrently with EduTech project implementation.

2. This also applies to the Organization of Eastern Caribbean States (OECS) which comprises full members (Antigua and Barbuda, Commonwealth of Dominica, Grenada, Montserrat, St Kitts/Nevis, St Lucia, St Vincent and the Grenadines. The British Virgin Islands, Martinique and Guadeloupe are associate members) that collaborate and align their national education strategies and plans. The Education Development Management Unit (EDMU) has responsibility for regional coordination and oversight of the implementation of the strategies and plans. For further details, see https://drive.google.com/file/d/1SYg5EIX8FTvlAC RKylw9Mlo9sCUx_mN0/view. Downloaded, 29 October 2020.

3. For more in-depth discussion of institutionalization, see Jennings (1993).

4. The National Standards Curriculum (NSC) provides the framework for this. The NSC was introduced on a phased basis beginning in 2016. See https://ncel.gov.jm/content/jamaica-cutting-edge-curriculum-design-national -standardscurriculum#:~:text=The%20Ministry%20now%20has%20in,level%20as %20per%20subject%20area downloaded, 29 October 2020.

5. In 1996–97 the editor of the *Journal of Education and Development in the Caribbean* invited the Ministries of Education in all of the Commonwealth Caribbean countries to write about major new developments in their education sector for a "Country Focus" segment of the journal. Barbados was one of only two countries that responded.

6. The JBTE was established in 1971. It is responsible for the curriculum, the examinations and the general monitoring of the teachers' colleges in Jamaica, Bahamas and Belize. It is responsible for the certification of teachers trained at teachers colleges in these countries. It is located on the campus of the UWI in Kingston, Jamaica. Its membership is made up of representatives from the Ministry of Education, teachers colleges, teachers' unions and the UWI. There is a similar JBTE on the Cave Hill campus of the UWI in Barbados which has similar responsibilities to the one in Jamaica, but with teachers colleges in the Eastern Caribbean. For further details, see Bryan (2019).

7. The analysis of the children's writing would have required the skills of a linguist, a function that the director of NCERD could have performed, but he left NCERD in 1992 to take up the position of vice chancellor at the University of Guyana. The new director switched the focus to cross-curriculum integration, thereby moving emphasis away from the SRGs.

8. See note 6.

Chapter 10. "Doing Change" Differently

1. During the 1980s I was hired along with another consultant by a British aid agency that was funding reform at the lower secondary level in one of the small islands. The emphasis was on schools that had children from disadvantaged backgrounds. The aid agency was concerned that while the civil works component had moved ahead, the curriculum and student learning were not being addressed. The consultants were to advise what needs to be done to improve student learning

at the lower secondary level. Having completed our investigation, on the final day we were kept waiting for over two hours to present our exit report to a small group of top officials in the Ministry of Education. When we were finally given audience, we were basically told by the chief planner that they were not interested in what we had to say as they already had what they wanted out of the project – the school buildings. This was not a unique experience.

2. These are students from the upper grades who had been trained to tutor those in the lower grades in literacy and mathematics. Wood (1983) identified positive outcomes of tutoring such as building confidence and self-esteem, providing opportunities for modelling, helping the low achiever and the student with behavioural problems, and providing a career tryout for teacher.

3. Primary Education Support Project End of Project Evaluation, pages 5–4. Ministry of Education, 5 December 2008.

4. See chapter 6: Clarifying the Change in (Hall and Hord 2006).

References

Abbott, M.E. 1980. *Education for Development: A Case Study of Curriculum Change, Jamaica. West Indies.* Unpublished EdD thesis, New York: Columbia University, Teachers College.

Abdul-Majied, Sabeera, and Margaret Chin. 2013. "Teachers' Views of Quality Teaching and Learning at the Infancy Level in a New Primary School". *Caribbean Curriculum* 20: 161–85.

Allsopp, Jeannette, and Zellynne Jennings. 2014. *Language Education in the Caribbean: Selected Articles by Dennis Craig.* Kingston, Jamaica: The University of the West Indies Press.

Apple, Michael. 2003. "Is the New Technology Part of the Solution or Part of the Problem in Education?" In *The Critical Pedagogy Reader*, by Antonia Dardar, Marta Baltodao, and Rodolfo D. Torres, 440–58. New York: Routledge Falmer.

Ashby, Pauline, Hyacinth Evans, and Molly Thorburn. 2004. *Report on the Pre-primary to Primary Transition Pilot Project.* Kingston, Jamaica: School of Education, The University of the West Indies.

Bacchus, Kazim. 2005. *Education for Economic, Social and Political Development in the British Caribbean Colonies from 1896 to 1945.* Ontario, Canada: The Althouse Press.

Bailey, Arlene, Maurice McNaughton, Nadine Muschette, and Sameer Verna. 2015. "The Role of Information and Communication Technologies (ICTs) in Early Childhood Education in Jamaica: Early Observations from a One-Laptop-Per Child Pilot Project". *Caribbean Journal of Education* 37 (1&2): 102–26.

Bailey, Barbara. 2000. "School Failure and Success: A Gender Analysis of the 1997 General Proficiency Caribbean Examinations Council Examination for Jamaica". *Journal of Education and Development in the Caribbean* 4 (2): 1–18.

Bailey, Barbara, and Lois Parkes. 1995. "Gender: The Not-So-Hidden Issue in Language Arts Materials in Jamaica". *Caribbean Journal of Education* 17 (2): 265–78.

Bailey, Barbara, and Monica Brown. 1997. "Re-engineering the Primary Curriculum in Jamaica: Improved Effectiveness". *Caribbean Journal of Education* 19 (2): 147–61.

Beane, James. 1997. *Curriculum Integration: Designing the Core of Democratic Education.* New York: Teachers College Press.

Bearden, David L. 2014. "St. Kitts and Nevis: An Overview". In *Education in the Commonwealth Caribbean and the Netherland Antilles*, edited by Emel Thomas, 308–22. London: Bloomsbury.

Beastall, Liz. 2006. "Enchanting a Disenchanted Child: Revolutionising the Means of Education by using Information and Communication Technology and e-Learning". *British Journal of Sociology of Education* 27 (1): 97–110.

Becher, Tony, and Stuart Maclure. 1978. *The Politics of Curriculum Change.* London: Hutchinson.

Bennis, Warren G., Kenneth D. Benne, and Robert Chin. 1969. *The Planning of Change*, 2nd ed. New York: Holt, Rinehart and Winston.

Ben-Peretz, Miriam. 1980. "Teachers' Role in Curriculum Development: An Alternative Approach". *Canadian Journal of Education* 5 (2): 52–62.

Bernstein, Basil. 1971. "On the Classification and Framing of Educational Knowledge". In *Knowledge and Control: New Directions for the Sociology of Education*, edited by Michael F.D. Young, 47–69. London: Collier-Macmillan.

Bray, Mark. 1998. "Regional Examinations Councils and Geopolitical Change: Commonality, Diversity, and Lessons from Experience". *International Journal of Educational Development* 18 (6): 473–86.

Bray, Mark, and Steve Packer. 1993. *Education in Small States: Concepts, Challenges and Strategies*. Oxford: Pergamon Press.

Brown, Adele, and Loveda Jones. 1994. "Training: Reform of Secondary Education (ROSE)". *ROSEGRAM*, November: 5.

Brown, Janet, and Barry Chevannes. 1995. "Gender Socialization Project". *Caribbean Journal of Education* 17 (2): 336–9.

Bruns, Barbara, and Javier Luque. 2014. *Great Teachers: How to Raise Student Learning in Latin America and the Caribbean*. Washington, DC: The World Bank.

Bryan, Beverley. 2010. *Between Two Grammars: Research and Practice for Language Learning and Teaching in a Creole-Speaking Environment*. Kingston, Jamaica: Ian Randle Publishers.

Bryan, Patrick, E. 2019. *The History of the Joint Board of Teacher Education, Mona: The Evolution of Teacher Education in Jamaica and the Western Caribbean, 1956–2016*. Kingston, Jamaica: The Joint Board of Teacher Education, Mona.

Butler, Kareisha. 2012. *The Impact of Gender, Age, Subject Matter and School Type on Teachers' Perceptions of the e-Learning Jamaica Project*. Unpublished M.Ed project, Kingston, Jamaica: The University of the West Indies.

Caribbean Examinations Council (CXC). 1982. *Capsule-the First Decade-CXC 10th Anniversary*. St. Michael, Barbados: CXC.

Caribbean Examinations Council. 1991. *Secondary Education Certificate Regulations*. St. Michael, Barbados: CXC.

CARICOM. 2005. *A Harmonized Policy Framework for Teacher Education in the Caribbean*. Georgetown, Guyana: The Caribbean Community Secretariat.

Carroll, Christopher, Malcolm Patterson, Stephen Wood, Andrew Booth, Jo Rick, and Shashi Balain. 2007. "A Conceptual Framework for Fidelity Implementation". *Implementation Science* 2 (Art. 40): 1–9. Accessed 7 October 2020. https://implementationscience.biomedcentral.com/articles/10.1186/1748-5908-2-40.

Carter, D.S.G., and R.G. Hacker. 1988. "A Study of the Efficacy of a Centre-Periphery Curriculum Implementation Strategy". *Journal of Curriculum Studies* 20 (6): 549–52.

Charles, Janice. 2011. *An Investigation into Two Reading Specialists Connected to CETT in Enhancing Student Reading Achievement in Underperforming Primary Schools in Trinidad*. Unpublished M.Ed Research Project, St. Augustine, Trinidad and Tobago: The University of the West Indies.

Chesterfield, Ray, and Adriana Abreu-Combs. 2011. *Centers for Excellence in Teacher Training (CETT): Two Year Impact Study Report (2008-2009)*. Prepared for review by USAID Bureau for Latin America and the Caribbean, Office of Regional Sustainability, Education and Human Resources Team, Aguirre Division of JBS International, Inc.

Chin, Robert, and Kenneth Benne. 1969. "General Strategies for Effecting Changes in Human Systems". In *The Planning of Change*, edited by W. Bennis, K. Benne, and R. Chin, 4th Edition, 22–43. New York: Holt.

Christie, Jason, and Henry Mooney. 2020. "Country Summary: Jamaica". *The Caribbean Quarterly Bulletin: The Pandemic Saga Continues* 91, no. 2 (July): 42–6.

Clark, David L., and Guba, Egon G. 1965. *An Examination of Potential Change Roles in Education*. Washington, DC: National Education Association, Centre for the Study of Instruction.

Clarke, Christopher. 2007. "Boys' Gender Identity, School Work and Teachers' and Parents' Gender Beliefs". *Caribbean Journal of Education* 29 (1): 126–60.

Cook, Loraine, and Austin Ezenne. 2010. "Factors Influencing Students' Absenteeism in Primary Schools in Jamaica: Perspectives of Community Members". *Caribbean Curriculum* 17: 33–57.

Cousins, Jackie. 1995. "Why have We used Jamaica Creole in the SSTP-MOEYC Foundation Textbooks?" *ROSEGRAM*, May: 15–16.

Craig, Dennis R. 1994. "Language Education Revisited in the Commonwealth Caribbean". Paper presentation at 10th Biennial Conference of the Society for Caribbean Linguistics August 24–27, Georgetown, Guyana.

———. 1998. "The Commonwealth Caribbean Performance of Countries in the Caribbean Examinations Council Secondary Education Certificate Examinations". *Journal of Education and Development in the Caribbean* 2 (1): 49–63.

———. 2006. *From Vernacular to Standard English: Teaching Language and Literacy to Caribbean students*. Kingston, Jamaica: Ian Randle Publishers.

———. 2006/7. "Constraints on Educational Development: A Guyanese Case Study". *Journal of Education and Development in the Caribbean* 9 (1&2): 1–30.

———. 2014a. "Reading and the Creole Speaker". In *Language Education in the Caribbean: Selected Articles by Dennis Craig*, by Jeannette Allsopp and Zellynne Jennings, 81–7. Kingston, Jamaica: The University of the West Indies Press.

———. 2014b. "English Language Teaching: Problems and Prospects in the West Indies". In *Language Education in the Caribbean: Selected Articles by Dennis Craig*, by Allsopp Jeannette Jennings Zellynne, 123–32. Kingston, Jamaica: The University of the West Indies Press.

CRC Sogema, Canada. 2008. *Primary Education Support Project(PESP): End of Project Evaluation*. Report to Ministry of Education, Jamaica, Montreal Canada: CRC Sogema.

Crossley, Michael, and Sprague Terra. 2012. "Learning from Small States for Post-2015 Educational and International Development". *Current Issues in Comparative Education*, Teachers College, Columbia University, 15 (1): 26–40.

Cuban, Larry. 1998. "How Schools Change Reforms: Redefining Reform, Success and Failure". *Teachers College Record* 99 (3): 453–77.

———. 2001. *Oversold and Underused: Computers in the Classroom*. Cambridge, MA: Harvard University Press.

———. 2008. *Frogs into Princes: Writings on School Reform*. New York: Teachers College Press.

Cummings, William K. 1986. *Low-Cost Primary Education: Implementing an Innovation in Six Nations*. Ottawa: International Development Research Centre.

———. 2010. "How Educational Systems Form and Reform". In *The Politics of Education Reforms*, edited by Joseph Zajda and Macleans A. Geo-JaJa, 19–40. London and New York: Springer.

Dadds, M. 2014. "Continuing Professional Development: Nurturing the Expert Within". *Professional Development in Education* 40: 9–16.

Daley, Myrtle, and Joyce Thompson. 2004. *The Early Childhood Movement in Jamaica: Building Blocks for the Future*. Kingston, Jamaica: Chalkboard Press.

Dalgety, Florine, William Kellman, and D. Thomas. 1999. *GUIDE: The Baseline Study: Providing a Basis for Monitoring and Evaluating the Project's Performance*. Georgetown: Unpublished Report.

Dalin, Per. 1983. "Strategies of Innovation". In *Challenge and Change in the Curriculum*, edited by T. Horton and P. Raggatt, 2nd ed., 131–6. Open University: Hodder and Stoughton.

Davies, Rose. 1998. "Striving for Quality in Early Childhood Development Programmes: The Caribbean Experience". *Institute of Education Annual* 1: 61–77.

———. 2015. "Advancing the Early Childhood Development Agenda in the Caribbean in the New Millennium: Achievements, Challenges and Prospects". *Caribbean Journal of Education* 37 (1&2): 1–20.

Davis, Ray A. 1994. "ROSE... A Brief History". *ROSEGRAM*, November: 1, 10.

———. 1995. "Reflections and Update". *ROSEGRAM*, May: 2, 8.

Dawson, Karl, and David Smawfield. 2014. "The British Virgin Islands: An Overview". In *Education in the Commonwealth Caribbean and Netherland Antilles*, edited by Emel Thomas, 152–65. London: Bloomsbury.

Delisle, Jerome. 2012. "Explaining Whole System Reform in Small States: The Case of the Trinidad and Tobago Secondary Education Modernization Program". *Current Issues in Comparative Education*, Teachers College, Columbia University, 15 (1): 64–82.

Devonish, Hubert S., and Karen Carpenter. 2007. *Full Bilingual Education in a Creole Language Situation: The Jamaican Bilingual Primary Education Project*. Occasional paper No.35, Trinidad and Tobago: Society for Caribbean Linguistics, The University of the West Indies.

Doreen Faulkner Consultancy. 2010. *Evaluation of the B.Ed. Secondary (Distance) Project*. Kingston, Jamaica: The University of the West Indies, and the Ministry of Education, Youth and Culture, Jamaica.

Doyle, Walter, and Gerald A. Ponder. 1977. "The Practicality Ethic in Teacher Decision-Making". *Interchange* 8 (3): 1–12.

Earle, Joseph. 1977. "Jose Marti Secondary School: An Experiment in the Work/Study Concept". *CARSEA* 2 (2): 6–10.

Edmond, Daniel. 1985. *The Influence of Belize's REAP Programme on Attitudes to Agriculture and Rural Employment*. Unpublished B. Ed study, Kingston, Jamaica: The University of the West Indies.

Eisner, Elliot W. 2000. "Those Who Ignore the Past... 12 'easy' Lessons for the Next Millennium". *Journal of Curriculum Studies* 32 (2): 343–57.

Eisner, Elliot W., and Elizabeth Vallance. 1974. *Conflicting Conceptions of Curriculum*. Berkeley: McCutchan Publishing Corporation.

Evans, Hyacinth. 1997. "Transforming Policy into Action: Facilitating Teacher Change in a Jamaican Innovation". *Journal of Education and Development in the Caribbean* 1 (1): 1–20.

Fabian, Hilary, and Aline-Wendy Dunlop. 2002. *Transition in the Early Years: Debating Continuity and Progression for Children in Early Education*. London: Routledge Falmer.

Fanfare, Myrtle, and R. van Dongen. 2003. *Report of the Stakeholder Workshop on Teacher Education in the Hinterland*. Georgetown: Ministry of Education, Guyana.

Feraria, Paulette. 2000. "Preparing the Teacher as a Reflective Practitioner: Some Emerging Trends in a Professional Training Programme at the University of the West Indies, Jamaica". *Journal of Education and Development in the Caribbean* 4 (2): 107–22.

Feraria, Paulette J. 2018. "Radio Waves and Curriculum Pathways: Jamaican 'At-Risk' Learners Construct Media". *Journal of Media Literacy Education* 10 (1): 42–58.

Figueroa, Mark. 2004. "Male Privileging and Male Underachievement in Jamaica". In *Interrogating Caribbean Masculinities: Theoretical and Empirical Analyses*, edited by R.E. Reddock. Kingston, Jamaica: University of the West Indies Press.

Forrest, Winston. 2008. "The Curriculum Implementation Team-Success or Failure for Sustainability?" *Primary News* 4, no. 4 (December): 15.

Fraser, Kirsten. 1997. "ROSE Curriculum under Review". *ROSE PRESS*, August: 1.

Fullan, Michael. 1994. *Change Forces: Probing the Depths of Educational Reform*. London: The Falmer Press.

Fullan, Michael, and Alan Pomfret. 1977. "Research on Curriculum and Instruction Implementation". *Review of Educational Research* 17 (1): 335–97.

Fullan, Michael, and Suzanne Stiegelbauer. 1991. *The New Meaning of Educational Change*. London: Cassell.

Fuller, Francis. 1969. "Concerns of Teachers: A Developmental Conceptualization". *American Educational Research Journal* 6 (2): 207–26.

Gaible, Edmond. 2008. *Survey of ICT and Education in the Caribbean: A Summary Report, Based on 16 Country Survey*. Washington, DC: infoDev / World Bank. Available at http: // www. infodev.org/en/Publication.441.html.

Ganesh, Latchman. 1992. *An Evaluation of the Use of the Skills Reinforcement Level 5 Mathematics Guide in a Sample of Schools in Regions 3 and 4*. Unpublished M.Ed thesis, Georgetown: The University of Guyana.

Glewwe, Paul, Eric A. Hanushek, Sarah Humpage, and Renato Ravina. 2013. "School Resources and Educational Outcomes in Developing Countries: A Review of the Literature from 1990 to 2010". In *Educational Policy in Developing Countries*, edited by Glewwe Paul, 13–64. Chicago and London: The University of Chicago Press.

Government of Guyana. 2002. *Education for All-Fast Track Initiative Country Proposal.* Georgetown: Government of Guyana.

———. 2003. *Ministry of Education Strategic Plan 2003–2007.* Georgetown: Government of Guyana.

Granston, Carol N., and Donald Clayton. 2009. "ICT in Jamaica's Primary Schools: A Review of the Instructional Technology Subcomponent of PESP". *Institute of Education Publication Series* 6: 10–21.

Greenberg, Brian. 2020. "This Is Going to be the Hardest Fall We've had Maybe in the History of Modern Education". *Education Next* 20 (4). Accessed 12 October 2020. https://www.educationnext.org/journal/vol-20-no-4.

Greene, Cloreth. 1994. "The Trelawny Encounter". *ROSEGRAM*, November: 6–7.

———. 1996. "Developing New Perspectives, Skills and Insights". *ROSEGRAM*, May: 6, 11.

Griffith, Stafford. 1981. "Report on the CXC/USAID Secondary Curriculum Development Project". *Caribbean Journal of Education* 8 (3): 322–31.

———. 1997. "Reflections on Aspects of Project Implementation". *ROSEGRAM*, July: 5, 9.

———. 2015. *School-Based Assessment in a Caribbean Public Examination.* Kingston, Jamaica: The University of the West Indies Press.

Gyamfi, Stephen Adu. 2017. "Pre-service Teachers' Attitude towards Information and Communication Technology Usage: A Ghanaian Survey". *International Journal of Education and Development using Information and Communication Technology* 13 (1): 52–69.

Hall, Gene E., and Shirley M. Hord. 2006. *Implementing Change: Patterns, Principles and Potholes.* Boston: Pearson Education Inc.

Hamilton, Evelyn. 1999. *The Institutional Future of Distance Education in Guyana.* Final Report, Georgetown, Guyana: Ministry of Education.

Hanuchek, Eric A., and Ludger Woessmann. 2020. *The Economic Impacts of Learning Losses.* EDU/WKP (2020)13, Paris, France: OECD Education Working Papers.

Hargreaves, Andy, and Dennis Shirley. 2009. "The Fourth Way of Change". In *The Challenge of Change: Start School Improvement Now!*, edited by Michael Fullan, 29–40. Thousand Oaks: Corwin.

Hargreaves, Andy. 2012. "Singapore: The Fourth Way in Action?" *Educational Research for Policy and Practice* 11 (1): 7–17.

Harry, Sharmila, and Beular Mitchell. 2015. "An Investigation into Teachers' Perspectives of the Factors that Facilitate the Implementation of the e-Cal Curriculum Change Initiative in Trinidad and Tobago". *International Journal of Digital Society* 6 (3): 1058–65.

Havelock, Ronald G. 1971. "The Utilization of Educational Research and Development". *British Journal of Educational Technology* 2: 84–98.

Heeks, Richard. 2010. "Do Information and Communication Technologies (ICTs) contribute to Development?" *Journal of International Development* 22: 625–40.

Henry, Balford. 2020. "E-Learning Upgrading, Monitoring and Evaluation of Services, Says Chair". *Jamaica Observer*, November 17 Tuesday. http://www.jamaicaobserver .com/news/e-learning-upgrading-monitoring-and-evaluation-of-services-says-chair _153985?profile=1373#disqus_thread.

Heyneman, Stephen P., and D.T. Jamison. 1984. "Textbooks in the Philippines: Evaluation of the Pedagogical Impact of a Nationwide Investment". *Educational Evaluation and Policy Analysis* 6 (2): 139–50.

Hibbert, Kimberley. 2020. *Online Learning Heartache*. Kingston: Jamaica Observer Sunday.

Hickling-Hudson, Anne. 2002. "Revisioning from the Inside: Getting under the Skin of the World Bank's Education Sector Strategy". *International Journal of Educational Development* 22: 565–77.

Holness, Andrew. 2008. "Message from the Minister, Ministry of Education". *Primary News* 4, no. 4 (December): 2.

Hoover-Dempsey, Kathleen V., Joan T. Walker, Howard M. Sandler, Darlene Whetsel, Christa Green, Andrew Wilkins, and Kristen Clossan. 2005. "Why do Parents become Involved?: Research Findings and Implications". *The Elementary School Journal* 106 (2): 105–30.

Hordatt-Gentles, Carol. 2017. "Issues in Teacher Education in the Commonwealth Caribbean". In *Re-Imagining Education in the Commonwealth Caribbean*, edited by Zellynne Jennings and Deon Edwards-Kerr, 77–92. Kingston, Jamaica: Ian Randle Publishers.

House, Ernest R. 1979. "Technology versus Craft: A Ten-Year Perspective on Innovation". In *New Directions in Curriculum Studies*, by Philip Taylor, 137–52. Lewes, Sussex: The Falmer Press.

Isaacs, Ian. 1984. *Project Primer Research Study 3: Achievement in Grade 3*. Final Report, Kingston, Jamaica: School of Education, The University of the West Indies.

James, Joan, S. 2018. "A Model of Professional Development and Best Practice for Primary Science Teachers". *Journal of Education and Development in the Caribbean* 17 (1): 37–64.

Jennings, Zellynne. 1988. "Belize's REAP Programme". *Prospects* XVIII (1): 115–25.

———. 1993. "The Non-institutionalization of the Use of Self-instructional Materials in Primary Schools in Jamaica: The Case of Project PRIMER". *Journal of Curriculum Studies* 25 (6): 527–42.

———. 1994. "Innovations in Caribbean School Systems: Why Some have Become Institutionalised, and Others have Not". *Curriculum Studies* 2 (3): 309–31.

———. 1996. *Evaluation of the Hinterland Teacher Training Programme (June 1994– June 1995)*. Georgetown, Guyana: Education and Development Services Inc.

———. 1997. *Assessment of the Impact of the Guyana In-Service Distance Education (GUIDE) Project*. Georgetown, Guyana: Education and Development Service Inc.

———. 1998. "Basic Skills in Guyana". In *Basic Skills and Further Education: Communities Confront Linguistic Elitism and Social Exclusion*, edited by Frankel Anna, Liz Millman, and Frank Reeves, 132–42. Bilston: Bilston College Publication in association with Education Now.

———. 1999. "Innovation with Hesitation: Distance Education in Commonwealth Caribbean Universities". *Journal of Education and Development in the Caribbean* 3 (2): 115–44.

———. 2001. "Teacher Education in Selected Countries in the Commonwealth Caribbean: The Ideal of Policy versus the Reality of Practice". *Comparative Education* 37 (1): 107–34.

———. 2002. "Perspectives on Curriculum Change in the Caribbean". *Journal of Education and Development in the Caribbean* 6 (1&2): 105–35.

———. 2005. *Evaluation of the Pre-primary to Primary Transition Pilot Project in South-west Clarendon, Jamaica*. Report to UNICEF, Kingston, Jamaica: University of the West Indies.

———. 2009. "Implementing the Constructivist Approach to Teaching: The Challenge for Teachers in Jamaica's Primary Schools". In *Voices from the Field*, edited by Carol Gentles and Nadine Scott, 90–113. Kingston, Jamaica: Institute of Education, The University of the West Indies.

———. 2011a. "From the Pomeroon to Portland: Relevance and Responsiveness to Teacher Training Needs in Contrasting Contexts in the Commonwealth Caribbean". In *Higher Education in the Caribbean: Research, Challenges and Prospects*, edited by Austin Ezenne, 292–334. Charlotte, NC: Information Age Publishing.

———. 2011b. "A Review of Studies on the Implementation of Literacy 1-2-3 in Jamaican Primary Schools". *Journal of Education and Development in the Caribbean* 13 (1 &2): 84–109.

———. 2012a. "Alternative Secondary Transition Education Programme (ASTEP): Report on Workshop Held on April 3, 2012 at the Mona Visitors' Lodge and Conference Centre". Unpublished report to the Ministry of Education, Jamaica, Kingston.

———. 2012b. "Resource and Technology: A Beacon for Change in the Reform of Jamaica's Secondary Education System – or a 'pipedream'?" *International Review of Education* 58 (2): 247–69.

Jennings, Zellynne, and Lorraine D. Cook. 2015. "Causes of Absenteeism at the Secondary Level in Jamaica: Parents' Perspectives". *Development in Practice* 25 (1): 99–112.

Jennings, Zellynne, William Kellman, Carol Clarke, and Valerie Joseph. 1995. *Functional Literacy Survey of Out-of-School Youth in Guyana*. Georgetown: University of Guyana.

Jennings-Craig, Zellynne. 2007a. *Primary Education Support Project (PESP) Literacy 1-2-3: Curriculum Specialist Report for January-May 2007*. Kingston, Jamaica: The University of the West Indies.

———. 2007b. *Primary Education Support Project: Literacy 1-2-3: Piloting of the Materials 2006–2007: Report of the Curriculum Specialist*. Kingston, Jamaica: The University of the West Indies.

———. 2011a. *ASTEP: Report on Workshop Held on June 21 2011 at the Mona Visitors Lodge and Conference Centre, UWI, Mona*. Kingston, Jamaica: The University of the West Indies.

———. 2011b. *Alternative Secondary Transition Education Programme (ASTEP): Report on Workshop Held on October 14, 2011*. Report to Ministry of Education, Jamaica, Kingston, Jamaica: School of Education, The University of the West Indies.

———. 2011c. *Proposal for Alternative Secondary Transition Education Programme*. Kingston, Jamaica: School of Education, The University of the West Indies.

Jennings-Craig, Zellynne, Deon Edwards-Kerr, Clement Lambert, Peter Joong, Camella Buddoo, Michelle Stewart, Schontal Moore, and Dejon Lingo. 2012. *Evaluation of the National Curriculum Strategies in Mathematics, English and Modern Languages*. Kingston, Jamaica: The University of the West Indies Consulting Inc.

Jennings-Wray, Zellynne. 1984. "Teacher Involvement in Curriculum Change in Jamaica: Advocacy and Reality". *Compare* 14 (1): 41–58.

———. 1985. "Towards an Appropriate Strategy for Curriculum Change in the Third World: Experiences from Jamaica". *Perspectives in Education, a Journal of the Society for Educational Research and Development, Baroda, India* 1 (3): 175–94.

Jennings-Wray, Zellynne, and Veronica Teape. 1982. "Jamaica's Work Experience Programme". *Prospects* XII (4): 499–509.

Jennings-Wray, Zellynne, and P.I. Wellington. 1985. "Educational Technology Utilization in Jamaica's Secondary School System: Present Problems and Future Prospects". *British Journal of Educational Technology* 16 (3): 169–83.

Johnson, Janet. 1995. "Curriculum Development". *ROSEGRAM*, May: 4, 6.

Joint Board of Teacher Education. 1996. "JBTE Bulletin Board". *ROSEGRAM*, May: 4.

Jules, Didacus. 2008. "Rethinking Education for the Caribbean: A Radical Approach". *Comparative Education* 44 (2): 2003–214.

Jules, Didacus, Errol Miller, and L. Thomas. 2000. *Pillars for Partnership and Progress*. St. Lucia: OERU.

Kay, Stafford. 1975. "Curriculum Innovations and Traditional Culture: A Case History of Kenya". *Comparative Education* 11 (3): 183–91.

King, Ruby. 1998. "Educational Inequality in Jamaica: The Need for Reform". *Institute of Education Annual* 1: 61–77.

Kinkead-Clark, Zoyah. 2018. "Teacher's Tensions and Children's Readiness: Taking a Discursive Approach to Understanding Children's Readiness for Primary School". *Early Years* 1–13. DOI:10.1080/09575146.2018.1481826.

Koul, Badri N. 1999. "Distance Education as an Agent of Change and Development". *Journal of Education and Development in the Caribbean* 3 (2): 105–14.

Leo-Rhynie, Elsa. 1995. "Girls' Toys, Boys' Toys: Forming Gender Identity". *Caribbean Journal of Education* 17 (2): 248–64.

Lewin, Keith M. 2020. "Beyond Business as Usual: Aid and Financing Education in Sub Saharan Africa". *International Journal of Educational Development* 78: 1–14.

Lewin, Keith M., and Janet S. Stuart. 1991. *Educational Innovation in Developing Countries: Case Studies of Changemakers*. London: The Macmillan Press Ltd.

Lewis-Fokum, Yewande. 2011. "Examining the 'discourse' Behind the Grade Four Literacy Test: Evidence from Two Primary Schools in Jamaica". *Journal of Education and Development in the Caribbean* 13 (1&2): 110–32.

Little, Angela. 1996. "Globalisation and Educational Research: Whose Context Counts?" *International Journal of Educational Development* 16 (4): 427–38.

London, Norrel A. 1993. "When Education Projects in Developing Countries Fail: A Case Study". *International Journal of Educational Development* 13 (3): 265–75.

———. 2002. "Curriculum Convergence: An Ethno-Historical Investigation into Schooling in Trinidad and Tobago". *Comparative Education* 38 (1): 53–72.

Manley, Michael. 1974. *The Politics of Change: A Jamaican Testament*. London: Andre Deutsch.

———. 1982. *Jamaica: Struggle in the Periphery*. London: Third World Media Ltd in association with Writers and Readers Publishing Cooperative Society Ltd.

Margetts, Kay. 2007. "Understanding and Supporting Children: Shaping Transition Practice". In *Informing Transitions in the Early Years: Research, Policy and Practice*, edited by A.-W. Dunlop and H. Fabian, 143–53. Maidenhead: Open University Press.

Mark, Paula, Raymonde Joseph, and Cheryl Remy. 2005. *A Harmonized Policy Framework for Teacher Education in the Caribbean: Responses to the Challenge of Improving the Quality of Recruitment and Selection, Initial Formation, Professional Development and Evaluation of Teachers in Countries of the Hemisphere*. Port of Spain: Ministry of Education Trinidad and Tobago.

Marsh, Colin, and Michael Huberman. 1984. "Disseminating Curricula: A Look from the Top Down". *Journal of Curriculum Studies* 16 (1): 53–66.

Marsh, Colin, and George Willis. 2003. *Curriculum: Alternative Approaches, Ongoing Issues*, 3rd ed. Upper Saddle River: Merrill/Prentice Hall.

Marshall, Phylicia. 2002/2007. "Teaching Strategies used by Teacher Educators and their Influence on Beginning Teachers' Practices". *Journal of Education and Development in the Caribbean* 9 (1&2): 70–96.

Mascoe-Johnson, Nadine. 2012. *Comparing the Implementation of Literacy 1-2-3 in Multigrade and Single Grade Schools in West Rural St. Andrew*. Unpublished M.Ed project, Kingston, Jamaica: The University of the West Indies.

Massanari, K. 1981. *Report of Mid-Project External Evaluation of the CXC/USAID Secondary Curriculum Development Project*. Unpublished Report to CXC.

Massey Ronald, M. 1982. "A Six-year Formative Evaluation Report (July 1, 1976 to June 30, 1982) of the Rural Education and Agriculture Program (REAP)". Report to CARE and the Rural Education and Agriculture Program Advisory Committee, Belize City.

McEwan, Patrick J. 1998. "The Effectiveness of Multigrade Schools in Colombia". *International Journal of Educational Development* 18 (6): 4325–452.

McKessey, Marlene. 2008. "The Procurement Process". *Primary News* 4, no. 4 (December): 18.

McKinley, Lola. 1982. *Project for Reshaping and Improving the Management of Educational Resources (PRIMER): A Summary Report on the Progress of the Project*. Kingston, Jamaica: Ministry of Education.

McKoy, Audrey. 2007. *Strategies Used for Child-Centred Approach to Teaching in a Sample of Jamaican Primary Schools*. Unpublished M.Ed Project, Kingston, Jamaica: The University of the West Indies Mona.

McLeod, John. 1987. "Curriculum as Anthropology". *Curriculum Perspectives* 7 (1): 17–21.

Miles, Matthew B. 1964. *Innovation in Education*. New York: Teacher's College, Columbia University.

Miller, Errol. 1981. "From Research to Action: Language Policy in Jamaica". *Prospects* 11 (3): 372–80.

———. 1999. "Educational Reform in Independent Jamaica". In *Educational Reform in the Commonwealth Caribbean*, by Errol Miller, 199–253. OAS: Interamer 54 Educational Series.

Miller, Errol, and Grace-Camille Munroe. 2014. "Education in Jamaica: Transformation and Reformation". In *Education in the Commonwealth Caribbean and Netherlands Antilles*, edited by Emel Thomas, 221–47. London: Bloomsbury.

Ministry of Commerce, Science and Technology. 2005. *E-Learning Project*. Kingston, Jamaica: Ministry of Commerce, Science and Technology. Accessed 15 October 2020. https://www.elearningja.gov.jm/wp-content/uploads/2019/03/ministry_paper _for_e-learning_project_may_2005_rb1.pdf.

Ministry of Education and Culture, Jamaica. 1993. *Reform of Secondary Education: A Summary Document*. Kingston, Jamaica: Ministry of Education and Culture.

———. 2003. *Jamaica Education Statistics 2000–2001: Annual Review of the Education Sector*. Kingston, Jamaica: Ministry of Education and Culture.

Ministry of Education, Jamaica. 1977a. *The Jamaica Five-Year Development Plan*. Kingston: Ministry of Education.

———. 1977b. *Five Year Education Plan 1978–1983*. Kingston, Jamaica: Ministry of Education.

———. 1979. *Project for Reshaping and Improving the Management of Educational Resources (PRIMER): An Experimental Research Project in Primary Education*. Kingston, Jamaica: Ministry of Education.

———. August 1982. *Annual Statistical Review of the Education Sector, 1980/1981*. Kingston, Jamaica: Ministry of Education.

———. 2008. *Primary Education Support Project (PESP): End of Project Evaluation*. Kingston, Jamaica: Ministry of Education.

———. 2010. *Alternative Secondary Education Programme (ASEP): Conceptual Framework*. Kingston, Jamaica: Ministry of Education.

———. 2012. *National Education Strategic Plan 2011–2020*. Kingston, Jamaica: Ministry of Education.

———. 2013. *Alternative Pathways to Secondary Education-A Response to the Alternative Secondary Transitional Education Programme (ASTEP)*. Ministry Paper, Kingston, Jamaica: Ministry of Education.

Ministry of Education, Jamaica, Programme Monitoring and Evaluation Unit. 2012. *Evaluation of the Alternative Secondary Education Programme (ASTEP): Executive Summary*. Kingston, Jamaica: Ministry of Education.

Ministry of Education, Trinidad and Tobago. 2010. *The e-Connect and Learn Programme Policy*. Port of Spain: Ministry of Education, Trinidad and Tobago.

Ministry of Education and Youth. 2005. *Literacy 1-2-3: The Literacy Intervention Model for the Language Arts Window*. Kingston, Jamaica: Ministry of Education and Youth, Primary Education Support Project.

Ministry of Education, Youth Affairs and Culture, Barbados. 1998. "Education and Technology in Barbados: The Challenge for the Twenty-First Century". *Journal of Education and Development in the Caribbean* 2 (2): 135–44.

Ministry of Education, Youth and Culture. 2001a. "Language Education Policy". Unpublished Report, Kingston, Jamaica.

———. 2001b. *Contract for the Development and Implementation of a Distance Degree Programme for Teachers in Secondary Schools*. Kingston, Jamaica: Ministry of Education, Youth and Culture.

Minott, Beverly. 1988. *A Study of the Institutionalization of an Innovation: The Use of Self-instructional Materials in Project PRIMER*. Unpublished M.A (Educ.), Kingston, Jamaica: The University of the West Indies.

Mitchell, Beular, and Sharmila Harry. 2012. "The e-Connect and Learn Curriculum Change in Trinidad and Tobago: The Voice of the Teacher". *Journal of Education and Development in the Caribbean* 14 (2): 48–71.

Mooney, Henry, and David Rosenblatt. 2020. "Regional Overview". *The Caribbean Quarterly Bulletin: The Pandemic Saga Continues* 91, no. 2 (July): 1–19.

Mooney, Henry, Joan Prats, and David Rosenblatt. 2021. "Debt Management and Institutions in the Caribbean: Best Practices and Priorities for Reform". In *Economic Institutions for a Resilient Caribbean*, by Moises J. Schwarts and Diether W. Beuermann, 153–86. Washington: Inter-American Development Bank.

Morris, Ruth, B. Allen, and Salomie Evering. 2008. *Competence-based Transition from the Primary to the Secondary Level*. Kingston, Jamaica: Ministry of Education.

Morrissey, Michael. 1981. *The Sixth Form Geography Project, Jamaica*. Unpublished M.A. (Education) thesis, Kingston, Jamaica: The University of the West Indies.

———. 1984. "Teacher Participation in Curriculum Development in a Third World Country". *Caribbean Journal of Education* 11: 143–57.

Newhouse, C. Paul. 2014. "Learning with Portable Devices in Australian Schools: 20 Years On!" *The Australian Association for Research in Education* 41: 471–83. DOI:10.1007/s13384-013-0139-3.

Ngoungouo, Abass. 2017. "The Use of ICTs in the Cameroonian School System: A Case Study of Some Primary and Secondary Schools in Yaoundé". *International Journal of Education and Development using Information and Communication Technology* 13 (1): 153–9.

Nyarigoti, N.M. 2013. "Continuing Professional Development Needs for English Language Teachers in Kenya". *International Journal of Research in Social Sciences* 3: 138–49.

Onuoha, Chinyere, D., Ferdinand, and Philip Onuoha. 2015. "Evaluation of a Government ICT programme for Secondary Schools: A Case Study of Teachers' Perceptions of Caribbean Boys' High School". *Journal of Educational Research and Behavioral Sciences* 4 (1): 005–19.

Parry, Odette. 2000. *Male Underachievement in High School Education in Jamaica, Barbados and St. Vincent and the Grenadines*. Kingston, Jamaica: Canoe Press, The University of the West Indies.

Pirog, Maureen A., and Sharon N. Kioko. 2010. "Evaluation of the Education Sector Enhancement Program in Barbados". *International Public Management Journal* 13 (1): 72–99.

Priestley, Mark, Richard Edwards, Andrea Priestley, and Kate Miller. 2012. "Teacher Agency in Curriculum Making: Agents of Change and Space for Manoeuvre". *Curriculum Inquiry* 42 (2): 191–214.

Programme Monitoring and Evaluation Unit. 2012. *Evaluation of the Alternative Secondary Education Programme (ASTEP): Executive Summary.* Kingston, Jamaica: Ministry of Education.

Ramani, Srinivasan. 2010. "The Internet and Education in the Developing World-Hopes and Reality". *Smart Learning Environments* 2 (8): 1–16. DOI: 10.1186/s40561-015-0015-x.

Raymond, Dorothy. 2006. *The Perceptions of Principals, Teachers and Students about the Impact of the Reform of Secondary Education on Access, Quality and Equity in Secondary Education in Jamaica.* Unpublished PhD thesis, Kingston, Jamaica: The University of the West Indies.

Reform of Secondary Education Secretariat. 1994. "Resource and Technology". *ROSEGRAM*, November: 4.

———. 1995. *Planning and Building Together: Options for Upper Secondary Education in Jamaica.* A Discussion Paper, Kingston: The Ministry of Education, Youth and Culture.

———. 1996. "Tribute to a Son of ROSE". *ROSEGRAM*, May: 3, 11.

———. 1997. "What Are Students Saying about the SSTP Foundation Textbooks?" *ROSEGRAM*, July: 6, 7.

Rickards, S. 1995. "The Language of Patois". *ROSEGRAM*, May: 3, 11.

Riddell, Abby. 2011. *Donors and Capacity Development in Guyana and Bangladesh.* Paris: International Institute for Educational Planning.

Rogers, Everett M. 2003. *Diffusion of Innovations Fifth Edition.* New York: Free Press.

Rogers, Everett M., and F. Floyd Shoemaker. 1971. *Communication of Innovations: A Cross-Cultural Approach,* 2nd ed. London: Collier Macmillan.

Rose Press. 1997. *ROSE Curriculum under Review.* Kingston, Jamaica: Ministry of Education, Youth and Culture.

Rowntree, Derek. 1988. *Educational Technology in Curriculum Development.* London: Paul Chapman Publishing Ltd.

Samms-Vaughan, Maureen. 2004. *Report of the Profiles Project.* Kingston, Jamaica: Planning Institute of Jamaica.

Sarason, Seymour. 1971. *The Culture of the School and the Problem of Change.* Boston and London: Allyn and Bacon Inc.

Schlager, M.S., and J. Fusco. 2003. "Teacher Professional Development, Technology and Communities of Practice: Are We Putting the Cart before the Horse?" *The Information Society* 19: 203–20.

Schon, Donald A. 1971. *Beyond the Stable State.* London: Temple Smith.

School of Education UWI. 2011. *MOE-ASTEP Training Evaluation /July-August 2011.* Kingston, Jamaica: The University of the West Indies.

Sewell, Audrey. 2008. "Message from the Permanent Secretary, Ministry of Education". *Primary News* 4, no. 4 (December): 3.

Shaughnessy, Michael. 2015. "An Interview with Amy Azano: Fidelity of Implementation". *World Journal of Educational Research* 2 (1): 1–5.

Simmons-McDonald, Hazel. 2014. "Revisiting Notions of 'Deficiency' and 'Inadequacy' in Creoles from an Applied Linguistics Perspective". In *Education Issues in Creole and Creole-Influenced Vernacular Contexts*, edited by Robertson Ian and Hazel Simmons-McDonald, 43–62. Kingston, Jamaica: The University of the West Indies Press.

Simms, Michelle. 2010. *An Investigation into Teachers' Use of the Literacy 1-2-3 Model in Teaching the Language Arts in Grade One of Three Rural Primary Schools.* Unpublished M. Ed Study, Kingston, Jamaica: The University of the West Indies Mona.

Spencer-Ernandez, Joan. 2011. "Transitioning from GSAT to CSEC: A Longitudinal Study of the Impact of Literacy Development of Students in Jamaican Primary School on their Performance in CSEC English A". *Journal of Education and Development in the Caribbean* 13 (1&2): 133–61.

Spencer-Ernandez, Joan, and Deon Edwards-Kerr. 2014. *Interim Report on the Testing of Grade 6 Students for Placement in the Alternative Secondary Transitional Education Programme.* Report to Ministry of Education, Jamaica, Kingston, Jamaica: The UWI School of Education Centre for the Assessment and Treatment of Exceptionalities.

Stephens, C., and M. Jones. 2011. "Teacher Participation in Realising January Sitting of English B in 2011". *The Caribbean Examiner* 9 (1): 54–6.

Stills, Helen. 1996. "From the JTA". *ROSEGRAM*, May: 2, 9.

Stromquist, Nellie. 1982, 19–21 May. "A Review of Educational Innovations to Reduce Costs". *Financing Educational Development: Proceedings of an International Seminar Held in Mont Sainte Marie, Canada.* Ottawa: International Development Research Centre.

Stufflebeam, Daniel, and Arthur J. Shinkfield. 2007. *Evaluation Theory, Models and Applications.* San Francisco: Jossey-Bass.

Task Force on Educational Reform. 2005. *Early Childhood Education, Care and Development Sector Report.* Kingston: Ministry of Education, Youth and Culture.

Tecsult International Limited. 2004. *Primary Education Support Project (PESP): Mid-Term Summative Evaluation Report.* Report to Ministry of Education, Jamaica, Montreal, Canada: Tecsult International Limited.

The Reform of Secondary Education Secretariat. 1995. *Planning and Building Together: Options for Upper Secondary Education in Jamaica.* A discussion paper, Kingston: Ministry of Education, Youth and Culture.

Thompson, Claudette T. 1982. *A Study of the Preparedness of Belizean Primary School Teachers for the Introduction of an Integrated Curriculum.* Unpublished B.Ed Study, Kingston, Jamaica: The University of the West Indies.

Thwaites, Ronald. 2013. *Alternative Pathways to Secondary Education: A Response to the Alternative Secondary Transitional Education Programme (ASTEP).* Kingston: Ministry of Education, Jamaica.

Tortello, Rebecca, and C. Minott. 2015. "Make Time to Play". *Caribbean Journal of Education* 37 (1&2): 77–101.

UNESCO. 1983. *Jamaica: Development of Secondary Education.* Paris: UNESCO.

———. 1990. *World Declaration on Education for All*. Paris: UNESCO.

———. 2004. *Education for All: The Quality Imperative: EFA Global Monitoring Report 2005*. Paris: UNESCO.

———. 2012. *EFA Global Report: Youth and Skills: Putting Education to Work*. Paris: UNESCO.

———. 2014. *Position Paper on Education Post-2015*. Paris: UNESCO.

United Nations. 2020. *Policy Brief: The Impact of Covid-19 on Children*. New York: United Nations.

United Nations Development Programme. 2004. *Human Development Report 2004 : Cultural Liberty in Today's Diverse World*. New York: UNDP Human Development Report Office.

———. 2010. *The Real Wealth of Nations: Pathways to Human Development*. New York: UNDP Human Development Report Office.

———. 2013. *Human Development Report: The Rise of the South: Human Progress in a Diverse World*. New York: UNDP Human Development Report Office.

Walker, Decker. 1971. "A Naturalistic Model for Curriculum Development". *School Review* 80 (1): 51–65.

Warrican, Joel S., Joan Spencer-Ernandez, and Errol Miller. 2013. *Monitoring Reading Progress in the Caribbean Centre of Excellence for Teacher Training: Measuring the Impact of the First Phase of Implementation in Schools*. Kingston, Jamaica: School of Education, The University of the West Indies, Mona.

Warschauer, Mark, and Morgan Ames. 2010. "Can One Laptop Per Child Save the World's Poor?" *Journal of International Affairs* 64 (1): 33–51.

Warwick, Donald P., Fernando M. Reimers, and Noel F. McGinn. 1991. *The Implementation of Educational Innovations in Pakistan: Cases and Concepts*. Development Discussion Paper No. 365ES, Cambridge, MA: Harvard Institute for International Development.

Welch, Pedro. 2014. "Barbados: Modelling the Educational System-A Socioeconomic and Historical Investigation". In *Education in the Commonwealth Caribbean and Netherlands Antilles*, edited by Emel Thomas, 63–85. London: Bloomsbury.

Whinnon, Keith. 1971. "Linguistic Hybridization and the 'Special Case' of Pidgins and Creoles". In *Pidginization and Creolization of Languages*, by Dell Hymes, 91–117. Cambridge: Cambridge University Press.

Whiteman, Burchell. 1992. *The Next Steps in the Reform*. Extract from a speech at a Forum for Educators, Kingston, Jamaica: Government of Jamaica.

Williams-McBean, Claudia. 2018. "Implementing the School-Based Assessment in English in Jamaica: Teachers' Perceptions, Preparedness and Challenges". *Journal of Education and Development in the Caribbean* 17 (2): 67–101.

Wintz, Peter, and Godryne Wintz. 2015. "Old Technology-New Experience: Teachers' and Pupils' Reactions to Interactive Radio Instruction (IRI) in Grade Two Mathematics Classrooms in Guyana". *Caribbean Journal of Education* 37 (1&2): 127–51.

Wood, Robert. 1983. *Summing Up and Conclusions. Study 2. Evaluation of Tutoring System*. Kingston, Jamaica: School of Education, The University of the West Indies.

World Bank. 1993. *Caribbean Region: Access, Quality and Efficiency in Education*. Washington, DC: The World Bank.

———. 2001. *Implementation Completion Report: Jamaica Reform of Secondary Education*. Report No.22460, Washington, DC: The World Bank.

———. 2018. *World Development Report 2018: Learning to Realize Education's Promise*. Washington, DC: World Bank. Doi:10.1596/978-1-4648-1096-1. License: Creative Commons Attribution CC BY 3.0 IGO.

Xeureb, Kay, and A. Peart. 2006. *Evaluation of the Bachelor of Education Secondary Programme at the University of the West Indies*. Kingston, Jamaica: Unpublished Report, Department of Educational Studies, The University of the West Indies, Mona.

Yeboah, D. 2001. "Transition from Early Childhood Education to Primary School: What Works". *Journal of Education and Development in the Caribbean* 5 (1): 1–21.

Index

Note: page numbers followed with "n" refer to endnotes

CPSIA information can be obtained
at www.ICGtesting.com
Printed in the USA
LVHW020503080922
727808LV00002B/297